Fundamentals of Fast Swimming

How to Improve Your Swimming Technique

Gary W. Hall, M.D.

Devin Murphy

Dedicated to my coach and mentor, James 'Doc' Counsilman, who inspired and taught many people about the sport of swimming. And to my wife, Mary, and my son, Richard, who have devoted so much time, talent and effort to The Race Club.

Doc with his sidekick, Hobie Billingsley, former head diving coach at Indiana University.

Acknowledgments

Many great people have contributed to my knowledge of swimming along my long career in the sport. Starting from my beginning as a competitive swimmer at the age of seven, I'd like to thank all of the coaches I have been honored to work with and that shaped my path. Some of these coaches also shaped my children's path in the sport of swimming. The following list reads like a Hall of Fame of swimming coaches: Rick Rowland Sr, Lee Arth, Jon Urbanchek, Flip Darr, Don Gambril, Peter Daland, George Haines, Doc Counsilman, Charlie Hickcox, Pierre LaFontaine and Mike Bottom.

I'd like to thank my son, Gary Jr, who co-founded The Race Club, for providing me with an opportunity to start a second career as a swimming technique coach. Not everyone has a chance to do that, but I did. I am grateful. Coaching swimmers has breathed new life into my older body.

Special thanks to Nunzio Lanotte, who developed the technology that helped further our understanding of swimming technique.

I'd like to thank my friends and fellow Masters swimmers, Alan Bernard and Bob Colyer, for editing and correcting my many grammatical and organizational errors, leading to the final edit of this first version of the book.

I thank my son, Richard, and Eric Brandt, who have the ability to take dry, boring science and turn it into entertaining videos for The Race Club. Their production quality is what makes The Race Club special.

And, of course, I thank my wife Mary, who is the real boss and driving force behind The Race Club. She encouraged me to write this book, which helped keep me from going crazy during a pandemic.

Many of the coaches I mention above are no longer with us, but thank you all for helping to make swimming the best sport in the world.

Gary Sr.

Foreward

Nestled in the coconut-palm landscaped beauty of the Florida Keys and the charming Coronado Island near San Diego are two locations for the most technologically advanced swimming company in the world, The Race Club. Once a training ground for over 50 Olympic swimmers, The Race Club has evolved into a premier teaching institution, using cutting-edge technology. Their expert team of coaches are razor-focused on improving the techniques of swimmers from six years and older, of all ability levels, and from all around the world.

Co-founded in 2003 by 10-time Olympic medalist, Gary Hall Jr, The Race Club has since expanded to two beautiful locations, Islamorada, Florida Keys and Coronado, California. In both locations, swimming technique camps and private or semi-private instruction are offered year-round. In addition, swimmers can subscribe to and receive some of the highest quality videos and articles produced and written in the sport of swimming.

In *Fundamentals of Fast Swimming*, Race Club Technical Director Gary Hall Sr. and Head Coach Devin Murphy guide you to a better understanding of the science and nuances of what makes great swimmers so fast. In each chapter, every swimming stroke is broken down into its most important and basic components, explained in great detail with photos, including helpful drills at the end.

After reading *Fundamentals of Fast Swimming*, you will become more knowledgeable about the sport of swimming. If you are a swimmer, you will become more efficient and faster. If you are a coach or parent, you will develop a much better appreciation for and understanding of swimming technique.

To get all of the links in the e-book, you must sign in on http://www.theraceclub.com/, under any Lane. Lane 1 is free, but you must register first to join.

We hope that *Fundamentals of Fast Swimming* will increase your passion for the sport of swimming.

Gary Jr. and Gary Sr. at the 2004 Olympic Games in Athens.

Table of Contents

Fundamentals of Fast Swimming

Introduction

Swimming is a sport that takes place, for the most part, at the interface between water and air. When it comes to making mistakes, water is not very forgiving. Because of that, one could easily consider that swimming is the most technique-sensitive sport in the world. Yet, relative to other sports or businesses, and with our current state of knowledge and technology, the swimming world is a relatively low-tech world. I hope to see that change.

My son, Gary Hall, Jr and his training partner, Anthony Ervin, have each won 2 Olympic gold medals in the 50-meter sprint by a combined total of .02 seconds in three events. The two swimmers tied for one gold medal in 2000 and each won another individual gold medal by .01 seconds in another, Gary in 2004 and Anthony in 2016. One little mistake made by either swimmer in any of those three races and the gold would have turned to silver, bronze or perhaps no medal at all. In a sport that often results in differences between winning or not winning being measured in hundredths of seconds, we would be negligent to think that technique does not matter in the sport of swimming. The old philosophy of working your way to an Olympic gold medal just doesn't float any longer. It takes more. Much more.

Thus, in 2008, when my son, Gary Jr., retired from competition, we transitioned The Race Club from a training environment for elite swimmers into a learning environment for anyone who dared to get better. That year, The Race Club, as a teaching organization, was born.

Having spent 25 years of my life as a physician, and having always done a lot of clinical research, science and technology are at the front of my mind for The Race Club. I am particularly dedicated to teaching based on good data, research and intelligent analysis, not just tradition, history, observation or theory. I was determined to get and utilize more technology in swimming and focus our evidence-based teaching on technique, as opposed to training. That quest began in 2015 when we acquired our first technology, the Velocity Meter, and has continued with our subsequent purchase of the Pressure Meter and finally, the Propulsion/Drag Meter. I am particularly indebted to the developers of all three of these technologies, Nunzio Lanotte (APLab Italy) and Paolo Villanis (BioMovie), as they have helped me understand more about the sport of swimming than through any other methods. More great technology is entering the sport of swimming every year. It is an exciting time. However, having the technology is one thing. Knowing how to use it, interpret it and apply it is another. As far as I am concerned, all of the best technology in the world doesn't matter if it doesn't help swimmers get faster.

In the past five years of learning how to use and interpret this technology, I have already come to several conclusions. First, all swimmers, including Olympians, are making mistakes. The poor swimmers just make more of them. Second, the data from this technology is very good (not perfect) and reproducible. Third, analyzing the data and images simultaneously is essential (synchronizing video to the technology) and, if done carefully, can lead to accurate conclusions. Fourth, swimmers can learn from the knowledge. In other words, they can apply the technical changes that they have been taught, some better than others, and swim faster. Some swim much faster.

Although purely subjective, great swimming technique is equally important as great swimming training. To swim fast, one needs both, and even more. For the future of our sport, I hope to push the envelope of swimming technology. In the process, a new breed of swimming coach is arising, the *swimming technique* coach. I am proud and excited to be one of those new breeds of coaches. We can make a difference with swimmers, if we use and interpret the technology properly.

For years, I have written articles, or what I call *Aquanotes*, about much of what I have learned. Most of those articles are focused on swimming technique, based on our technology and testing, with some anecdotal stories thrown in. There has been no particular order or reason to what I have written, just whatever was on my mind or what we had recently learned or tested. At the suggestion of my wife, Mary, I have decided to compile my thoughts into this book in an organized fashion, where you can learn more about swimming technique in a logical progression or order. In that manner, it should be easier for you to learn.

The focus of this book is on swimming technique, with a few training tips thrown in. In my opinion, technique is half of the equation toward fast swimming. The other half is conditioning. For the most part, swimming coaches do an excellent job of training swimmers. However, we can all get better at understanding and teaching swimming technique.

This book will be continuously updated, as I learn new information about swimming almost every day. It is a work in constant progress. Much of the information in this book, and much more, is also presented, or will be presented, through our outstanding video content on line at The Race Club. We have hundreds of extremely well-produced videos in our Race Club library. My son, Richard, who was a great swimmer in his day, does all of our video production. In fact, since a picture is worth a thousand words, the videos he produces for our subscribers are far more valuable than this book.

I also want to thank our Race Club Head Coach, Devin Murphy. His valuable insight into the sport of swimming has helped shape the content of this book.

I hope that this book will become one of your favorite swimming resources and will help you understand this complex and amazing sport. It is intended to help coaches and swimmers of all types, including beginners, competitive swimmers, recreational swimmers and triathletes. If you find the first chapters on science and technology too complex, skip to the technique chapters. I hope it will also inspire you to become a member of The Race Club and, better yet, to come to Coronado, California, or Islamorada, Florida and see us at one of our camps or for private instruction.

Yours in swimming,

Gary Sr.

Chapter 1

The Basic Sciences of Swimming

Physics

To understand the complexities of fast swimming starts with understanding the major sciences that govern it. There are really four basic sciences that intersect and converge on the sport of swimming: physiology, physics, kinesiology (biomechanics) and the neural, cognitive and behavioral sciences. All have a profound impact on how fast one swims and, in some ways, they are interrelated.

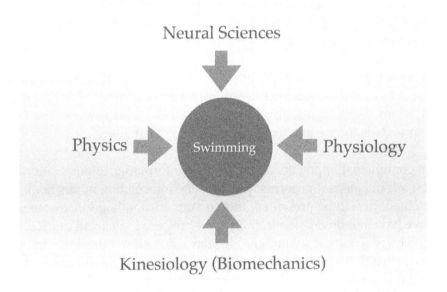

The following is a simplistic description of the four sciences:

Physics provides the laws that govern bodies in motion. In swimming, physics relates mostly to Newtonian and Fluid Mechanics, pertaining to forces of drag, propulsion, lift and the law of inertia. Our ability to quantitate frontal drag in both active (while swimming) and passive (fixed positions) forms, and to understand how the fluid dynamics and flow (vortices) of a swimmer affect the ability to generate propulsion largely influence the swimming techniques we should teach. Of the four basic sciences, the application of physics is perhaps the least understood or studied in the sport of swimming.

Physiology is important because it is largely improved by training methods and with breathing techniques. In swimming, physiology relates to our ability to provide sufficient energy, and from the right systems, to enable the muscles involved in the ideal biomechanical swimming motions to generate propulsion. The muscle contractions must sustain the propulsion for the duration of the competitive event. Physiology also relates to our ability to improve the muscle composition and mass to maximize and sustain the propulsion. Physiology involves a large number of human organs and systems, most of which can be improved with training. Some cannot. The best swimming coaches in the most advanced swimming nations of the world have done an incredibly good job at improving the physiology of swimmers through conditioning and training.

Kinesiology is important because it defines the body movements required to swim fast. Kinesiology relates to our ability to understand the ideal motions that maximize a swimmer's velocity for the duration of the event. Kinesiology includes more than biomechanical motions, however. It also considers how the physiology, anatomy, and psychology influence the ideal motions of an athlete. Ideal biomechanics of swimmers are also inextricably tied to physics.

Neural, Cognitive, and Behavioral Sciences are critical in understanding how the mind controls athletic performances in training and in competition. In swimming, these sciences relate to the power or ability of the mind to enable the body to perform at the highest possible level. Virtually every cognitive function we perform is controlled by our minds. Swimming is no exception. Neuromuscular adaptation and responses are two of the most important aspects of training and competing. Mental training in the sport of swimming is still in its infancy, compared to what is known about improving the physiology and biomechanics of swimmers. I believe that there is a great opportunity for improvement in these sciences.

There are other sciences that influence the speed of a swimmer, but these are the basic sciences in the sport of swimming. Of the four major sciences, I would say that swimming coaches around the world have done a very good job of improving the physiology, or the development of robust energy systems and power, in swimmers. They also have a pretty good handle on the biomechanics of swimming, understanding the muscles, flexibility and motions required to swim fast. Where we have not done such a good job is with the understanding of the physics of swimming and the neural sciences that control the mind's ability to enable a swimmer to swim faster—the neuromotor response. I think we have much to learn in understanding these two sciences with respect to applying them to the sport of swimming.

One could argue that the neural, behavioral and cognitive sciences that control our mental toughness are the most important science, particularly on race day. In Championship meets, all of the swimmers are physically well-trained. The difference in mental toughness often determines the winner of the race. We will discuss what we believe are the five most important steps toward increasing mental toughness in Chapter 37, as one of the five disciplines of fast swimming.

Because of the sensitive relationship between drag and propulsion forces in swimming, the ideal body movements of a swimmer to generate speed are not necessarily obvious. One might assume, for example, that the ideal biomechanics of a swimmer will generate the maximum amount of propulsion, but that is not true. In water, consideration of frontal drag forces is of paramount importance. In swimming, the biomechanics that generate the most propulsion are often the ones that cause excessive amounts of frontal drag. Therefore, to reach a maximum sustainable velocity, the ideal biomechanics of a swimmer's technique involves compromise between these two forces of propulsion and drag. Achieving the ideal biomechanics of any swimmer is also often constrained by anatomical limitations, such as joint flexibility, strength or injury.

The human body was not designed or engineered very well to move fast through water. To become more proficient swimmers, humans need to have or develop certain extraordinary tools, such as extreme plantar flexion of the ankles, hyperextension of the knees, extreme extension of the shoulders and lower back, internal rotation of the hip (breaststroke), among others. Then, to perform the ideal biomechanical motions of fast swimming, humans need to become strong in muscles that are not normally very strong for purposes on land, such as the four primary muscles of the scapula and other muscles involved in high-elbow pulling motion, hip and knee extensors and hip flexors.

A book or more could easily be written on all of the four basic sciences as they relate to swimming. I am not an expert in any of these sciences, but at least I know where to look for help. To that end, I have relied on Dr. David Costill, a respected expert in exercise physiology, and Anton Zajac, one of the smartest physicists I know, to offer their assistance on the information presented. Since the physics involved in swimming partly determines the ideal biomechanics, that is a good place to start.

Introduction to Physics in swimming

While there are many laws in physics that have some influence on the speed of a swimmer, the most significant are those pertaining to Newtonian and Fluid mechanics. Sir Isaac Newton, a brilliant mathematician from the UK, defined the three laws of motion back in the 17th century, and they are as important to a swimmer today as they were then. The physical laws of Fluid mechanics, made more complex by the liquid medium, are derived from Newtonian mechanics.

Physics tends to get complicated and confusing very fast, so we will try to keep this subject as simple as we can. Newton's laws applied to swimmers tell us that when a swimmer is at rest (not moving) or when the swimmer is moving at a constant speed, then the forces applied to him are balanced. If the swimmer is speeding up or slowing down, they are not balanced. The objective is to get the swimmer moving down the pool (and back) as fast as possible. What are the forces that act on a swimmer?

Since the weight of a swimmer in water ranges from zero (with lungs inflated with air) to about 8 pounds (full exhale), gravitational forces are not very significant, though they do come into play some, particularly on the arm recovery and breath (when arms and head are out of the water). The most important forces for a swimmer are those that move us forward in our line of motion (propulsion) and those that slow us down (frontal drag). Because a swimmer is moving between air and water while swimming, and because there is a huge difference in density between air and water (784 times greater in water), lift forces that elevate the swimmer's body position are also important. Like a boat, and assuming that we don't tilt our bodies, the more of a swimmer's body that is in air rather than water, the less frontal drag he or she will encounter.

This last statement is complicated by the fact that when a swimmer's body is in a relatively streamlined position, he or she can move slightly faster underwater than he or she can on the surface, similar to a submarine. By being underwater, a swimmer reduces or eliminates one of the three types of frontal drag, called *surface or wave drag*, that accounts for about 20-25% of the total drag forces of a freestyle swimmer at race speed. An elite swimmer in a streamlined position will always kick faster underwater than he or she can kick on the surface. Some swimmers that have really fast kicks are faster underwater kicking in a streamline than they are swimming on the surface. While swimming, there are certain times in the stroke cycle when the swimmer is relatively streamlined. At those moments, the swimmer is better off being under water than on the surface. Swimming breaststroke is the most notable example of this. There are other times, when the swimmer's body is not as streamlined, when he or she is better off as elevated at the surface as possible, with more of the body in air than in water.

The acceleration or deceleration of a swimmer at any given moment in a race is determined by the sum of the propulsion forces (+) minus the frontal drag forces (-). If the swimmer's propulsion is greater than the drag forces, then he or she is accelerating, or speeding up. If the drag forces are greater than the propulsion, then the swimmer is decelerating, or slowing down. If the swimmer's speed is constant, then the forces of frontal drag and propulsion are equal.

At The Race Club, we use a technology called the Velocity Meter (VM) to test swimmers. With it, we can measure the velocity, acceleration and deceleration of the swimmer at each .02 seconds in the stroke cycle. These measurements are synchronized to the swimmer's video. While knowing the swimmer's velocity is important, knowing the acceleration and deceleration at any given moment is even more important. At the peak of acceleration, the propulsion is greatest and the amount of the peak acceleration is correlated with the amount of propulsion that was generated at that moment. That helps us determine roughly how much propulsion is coming from the kick or pull or both. At the peak of deceleration, the drag forces are greatest and the amount of deceleration is correlated with the amount of frontal drag that occurred at that moment. That helps us identify and quantify the mistakes in technique that were made that caused that frontal drag.

Lift forces are perpendicular to our swimming motion and help reduce frontal drag by elevating us higher in the water. Lift is derived from the Bernoulli effect (planing lift) and Newtonian forces downward. Since the forces we create are not just down or backward, motions of our kicking and pulling that generate propulsion also generate lift. In fact, most of the time while swimming, both lift forces and propulsion forces are occurring simultaneously.

Next, we will discuss what we have learned from Newton's laws of motion—how to reduce frontal drag, how to increase propulsion, and how to use the law of inertia to our advantage. Finally, we will discuss how the law of conservation of energy can help us with our turns.

Reducing Frontal Drag

Most sports take place in air, where drag forces apply but are not nearly as detrimental to performance as they are in swimming. With the density of water being 784 times greater than air, significant drag forces occur at much slower speed than they do on land. Any errors swimmers make in their body positions or stroke mechanics are compounded at almost any speed, but even more so at higher speeds. The faster the swimmer, the bigger price paid for mistakes. Frontal drag is enemy #1 of swimmers. There is no mercy in the water.

There are four factors that determine how much frontal drag will slow a swimmer down. The first is position. Is the swimmer underwater or on the surface? The second is the cross-sectional surface area of the swimmer moving forward, or the shape of the swimmer. How large is the swimmer? How flat or round is the swimmer? What is the body angle? Are the legs and arms protruding out too far? Is the head too high? The third is the surface characteristic of the swimmer, including the suit, cap and goggles. How slippery is the swimmer? The fourth, and most important, is the swimmer's speed. How fast is he or she moving in the water?

There are three different types of frontal drag forces that can slow a swimmer down, and they are all important. The first and most profound is *pressure drag* which occurs as a result of two important facts we see in good swimmers. First, swimmers are non-streamlined objects, even in the best position they can achieve. Second, good swimmers are in water and travel at top speeds approximating 2 meters/second or higher. The physical shape of a swimmer (surface area and shape moving forward), the medium of water, and the speed of the swimmer in the water are factors that determine what is called the Reynold's number. This determines the flow characteristics around the moving swimmer. At the Reynold's number of a good swimmer wearing a tech suit, the nature of the boundary layer (the layer of water adjacent to the swimmer) will change from laminar (smooth, at the head and shoulders) to transitional (a foot or so behind the head and shoulders) to turbulent (somewhere near the waist). As the boundary layer separates from the swimmer's body, it forms a low pressure area (wake or slipstream) behind the swimmer.

The difference between the higher pressure at the head of the swimmer and the lower pressure behind the swimmer in the slipstream determines the *pressure drag*.

The second drag force is caused by *friction. Friction* occurs as a result of molecules rubbing against each other as an object moves through a medium—in this case, water. In general, the rougher the object (swimmer), the more *friction*. The smoother or slicker the object (swimmer), the less *friction*. Thus, the *friction* of a swimmer is largely determined by the surface characteristics of the swimmer: the cap, the skin, the goggles and the suit.

The third type of drag force is called *surface or wave drag.* It occurs as a result of the swimmer being partly in the water (submerged) and partly out of the water. Virtually all of the wave drag of a swimmer occurs from the front end of the swimmer's body (head and shoulders), and most of it from the head.

In a study done in 2004, Mollendorf et al determined the contribution of all three types of frontal drag forces on swimmers while being towed at various speeds in a fixed, streamlined position (passive drag forces).[1] When low friction (high tech) suits were worn, and at approximately race speed for elite swimmers, they found that *pressure drag* forces accounted for about 50% of the total drag force, while *wave drag* forces and *friction* each accounted for about 25% of the total drag force. The total frontal drag forces were about three times greater at 2 m/sec (race speed)

---

[1] Mollendorf, J.C., Termin A.C., Oppenheim E., and Pendergast D.R., Effect of Swim Suit Design on Passive Drag, MEDICINE & SCIENCE IN SPORTS & EXERCISE 0195-9131/04/3606-1029

than they were at 1 m/sec. At lower speeds (less than 1 m/sec) and while underwater, *friction* was a greater contributor to total drag than *pressure drag*.

At The Race Club we utilize a technology, called the Propulsion/Drag Meter (PDM), that measures the passive drag forces with a swimmer in a fixed position at a constant speed across a 50 meter pool. The speed can be adjusted and so can the position or the gear of the swimmer. With this technology, we have tested the drag forces of several swimmers by changing variables, such as the hand position, head position, type of bathing suit, type of cap, releasing air bubbles, streamline technique and feet position. Here are just some of the results of those studies which we tested at race speed (2.3 m/sec).

1. *Hyperstreamline* (arms behind the head) reduced drag compared to biceps over the ears streamline by 11%. We call it *hyperstreamline* because with the arms placed behind the head, the arms can be *hyper*extended from the shoulder joints more easily.
2. The fingers spread wide apart on the streamline increased drag by 18%.
3. Shoulders hunched on a breaststroke pullout compared to relaxed shoulders reduced drag by 4%.
4. Bubbles released under the chest in the streamline position compared to holding the breath reduced drag by 9.1%.
5. Lifting the core (3-5 degrees of hip flexion) with hands at side compared to straight body position reduced drag by 10%.

The reason that the swimmer's speed is the most important factor in determining frontal drag is that all three types of drag forces are exponentially related to the swimmer's speed. Both *pressure drag* and *friction* are proportional to the square of the swimmer's speed, while *wave drag* is proportional to the fourth power of the swimmer's speed. From this observation, we can conclude the following:

1. All three types of frontal drag are important and need to be reduced as much as possible.
2. Small changes in a swimmer's shape or position, cap and suit can have profound impacts on frontal drag at race speed.
3. Getting under water is desirable (eliminating wave drag) whenever possible while in a relative streamline position at race speed.
4. The stronger and faster a swimmer becomes, the more important technique becomes (the frontal drag forces at 2 m/sec are about three times greater than at 1 m/sec).

The real challenge in correcting poor, drag-producing swimming techniques is that a swimmer does not really feel the major drag forces occurring while he or she is swimming. Swimmers may be aware of the pressure on their hands or feet as they kick or pull, or perhaps they may be somewhat aware of the water passing over their heads or backs, but that is about it. There are simply too many complex movements happening at once and the human brain cannot contemplate all of them. Swimming is like riding a bicycle, struggling to gain ground into a 20 mile per hour head wind, yet not being able to feel the wind in your face. Swimmers can be working really hard and still not understand why they are not moving faster.

How can swimmers correct poor technique if they can't even feel the problems the poor technique is causing? For the most part, they can't. That is why coaching and testing are so important in the sport of swimming.

Increasing Propulsion

Outside of the starts and turns, the propulsive forces of a swimmer are derived purely from the kick and the pull. More specifically, except for the up kick, where the entire lower leg and sole of the foot can generate propulsion, nearly all of the other propulsive forces (down kick and pull) occur at the feet and hands. Some might be surprised to know that the hand generates the vast majority of propulsion from the pull. There is a widely held belief that the forearm contributes a considerable amount of propulsion from the pulling arm, but it does not. The forearm has a rounder shape than the flatter-shaped hand, so the flow around it is smoother, and the forearm does not move backward as fast in the water as the hand.

In addition, the propulsion from the kick and pull can be influenced by other motions of a swimmer's body that produce no propulsion at all. These are called coupling motions. Two examples of coupling motions in freestyle are the rotation of the body and the recovery of the arm over the water. Neither motion generates any propulsion by itself, but when timed or coupled with a propulsive pull or kick, either motion can make either force greater. High energy coupling motions can significantly increase the propulsion of a swimmer in all four strokes, as well as on the start.

The propulsion of a swimmer derived from the hands differs from that derived from the feet by the fluid dynamics surrounding the swimmer. The hands are moving through water that is essentially still (static fluid), while the feet are moving through water that is flowing (dynamic fluid). Some understanding of fluid mechanics is therefore necessary to understand how propulsion is generated within these two different environments.

Since water is liquid, not solid, to generate propulsion, the hand or foot needs to be moving backward relative to the water. In shoulder-driven freestyle technique, with a relatively higher stroke rate, if one were to map the pathway of the pulling hand from the side, relative to a fixed point in the pool, one would find that the hand moves in nearly a perfect circle of around 2-2.5 feet in diameter.

If we consider the circle as a clock face, with the swimmer moving from left to right, the hand would enter the water at 12 o'clock. Since the swimmer's body is moving forward, as the hand enters the water, the hand will move forward also. The swimmer begins the pulling motion by pushing the hand downward to reverse its direction and then by pushing it backward. The result is that the hand follows the clock to the 3 o'clock position, moving both downward and forward. We call this the *lift phase*, since most of the forces are downward, creating lift.

From 3 o'clock, when the hand is just in front of the swimmer's shoulder, it begins moving backward, generating propulsion. The hand continues going deeper in the water as it follows the clock from 3 o'clock to 6 o'clock on its way backward. In an effort to continue pushing the hand backward past 6 o'clock with the maximum hand surface area, the arm needs to elevate and the wrist dorsiflex, resulting in the hand cutting a part of the clock off in moving from 6 o'clock to 9 o'clock in nearly a straight line. The backward hand motion from 3 to 9 o'clock is called the *propulsion phase*.

Once the hand reaches 9 o'clock, the arm runs out of length, so the hand cannot move backward any farther. Instead, it turns the little finger up and quickly slides forward with the least resistance possible. The hand then leaves the water nearly exactly where it began the circuitous route, at 12 o'clock. This last phase is called the *release phase*. The net distance that the hand travels from entry to exit is close to zero. We describe the four phases of the underwater freestyle pulling motion and the two recovery phases in Chapter 7 on the freestyle pulling cycle.

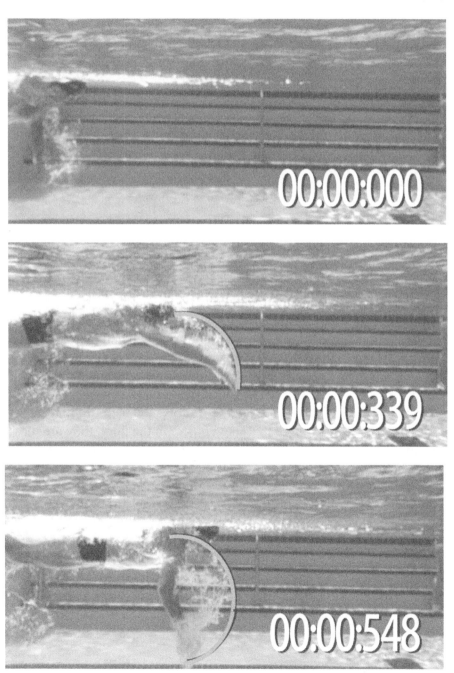

The hand moving in nearly a perfect circular motion underwater with Shoulder-driven freestyle technique.

Unlike the hand in generating propulsion, the feet rely on the vortices caused by both the swimmer's body and the motion of the foot and leg itself. In both freestyle and dolphin kick, the motion of the kicking foot is nearly straight up and straight down and then forward, relative to a fixed object in the pool. However, the water is not still in the path of the foot. Because the human body is a non-streamlined shape, there is a forward flow of water following the swimmer caused by the body's vortex or wake (slipstream). There is also a second vortex caused by the motion of the feet and legs, which creates a smaller stream that follows the path of the feet. Even though the feet are not moving backward relative to a fixed object in the pool, they are moving backward relative to the water, which is moving forward. Therefore, the feet can generate propulsion without actually moving backward.

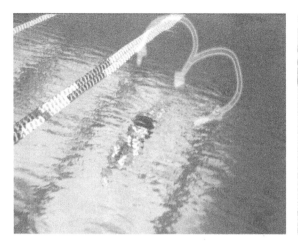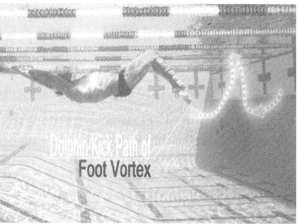

Both the moving feet and the swimmer's body moving forward result in vortices formed behind the swimmer. The pink lines represent the path of the body's vortex and the yellow line represents the path of the feet. The feet use these two vortices to generate propulsion.

In dolphin kick, for example, there are four potential places where the feet can generate propulsion. The first is at the beginning of the down kick. The propulsion here is achieved by quickly reversing the direction of the feet and pushing down against the vortex that was created by drawing the feet and leg upward and forward. The second is achieved as the feet traverse the body's vortex (slipstream) on the way down. The third is achieved at the initiation of the up kick, as the feet and leg quickly reverse direction and push upward against the vortex they created on the way down. The fourth is achieved as the feet and legs move upward and traverse the body's vortex (slipstream) on the way up. Only the fastest dolphin kickers will achieve propulsion in all four of these locations. Most swimmers derive propulsion in only one or two of them. In Chapter 22, we describe the mechanics of the dolphin kick in much greater detail.

In freestyle kick, there are two potential points of propulsion. Since the down kick and up kick occur simultaneously, one point is at the initiation of each, utilizing the vortices of the feet and legs. The second and primary one occurs as both feet pass through the slipstream on the way up or down. You can read more about the freestyle kick and how to improve it in Chapter 8.

With breaststroke kick, nearly all of the propulsion occurs from the instep of the feet and the ankle pushing backward. The peak force occurs when the feet are about 1/2 to 2/3 of the way back toward complete extension of the legs. The narrower the kick, the more advantage the breaststroke kicker will derive from the body's slipstream and large vortex resulting from drawing the legs and feet forward. With a wide breaststroke kick, the feet may be pushing backward in relatively still water, rather than against a stream of water. That can significantly affect propulsion. A small amount of propulsion is also possible from the up kick that occurs at the end of the breaststroke kick. Not every breaststroker will get that second propulsion. You will find more information about the breaststroke kick in Chapter 19.

In summary, the propulsion of the pull is determined mostly by the surface area of the hand pushing backward and the rate at which that effective hand surface area accelerates through the propulsion phase. The propulsion from the kick is determined by the surface area of the feet (and legs), the rate at which the feet accelerate through the vortices and the strength of the vortices (slipstream) that the feet move through. Further, the propulsive forces of either the pull or kick can be augmented by the amount of kinetic energy within the properly-timed coupling motions, such as the body rotating, the head snapping down, or the arms recovering.

Inertia

Newton's first law of inertia, which was originally defined by Galileo, is also important for swimmers to understand. Basically, inertia simply means that objects (swimmers) that are at rest tend to stay at rest and objects (swimmers) that are moving tend to stay moving, unless they are acted on by external forces. Newton's third law of motion states that when we apply a force with our hands or feet in the water or against the wall on a push off, the water or wall applies the same force back against the hand or foot.

For a swimmer to go from the rest state (taking your mark on the starting block or getting ready to push off the wall) to the moving state (gliding or swimming down the pool), external forces must be applied. Whether that force comes from our legs (feet) pushing us off the starting block or wall or our hands and feet propelling us down the pool, once a swimmer starts moving, unless he or she is in a vacuum or outer space, frontal drag forces will start to slow him or her down. That means to keep moving, swimmers must continue applying propulsion.

If the propulsion and drag forces are equal, the swimmer's speed will remain constant. If the propulsion is greater than the drag forces, the swimmer will accelerate. If the drag forces are greater than the propulsion, the swimmer will decelerate. As difficult as it is for swimmers to maintain a constant speed in swimming, it requires more work or energy for them to maintain a given average speed if their speed varies a lot compared to maintaining a more constant speed at the same given average. Consider when a swimmer completely misses the wall on a flip turn in a race and comes to a dead stop. The amount of energy required to get that swimmer back up to race speed is overwhelming. The race is probably over. Similar to the difference in gas mileage people get in their cars while driving in town (stop and go) compared to driving on the freeway (constant speed), the swimmer will use less energy maintaining a more constant speed than he or she will by repeatedly slowing down or stopping and then speeding up again. Swimming at a more constant speed is simply a more mechanically efficient way to swim.

The challenge of swimmers taking advantage of the law of inertia is that with the nature of the propulsion, coming mostly from the hands and feet and at certain intervals of time, swimmers cannot provide a constant propulsion. Only two of the four strokes, freestyle and backstroke, allow swimmers to come close to maintaining constant speed. Breaststroke and butterfly, due to the longer down time (time between propulsion efforts) and the higher drag coefficients that are created at specific times in the stroke cycle, are fraught with a considerable variation in speed. Therefore, these two strokes are either slower (breaststroke) or require more energy to sustain a higher average speed (butterfly). Both strokes are mechanically inefficient.

How do swimmers take more advantage of the law of inertia while swimming and maintain a more constant speed? There are only three ways that we know of, regardless of the stroke. First, swimmers can sustain a more constant kicking speed. Since the kick provides potentially more propulsive moments than the pull, using a six-beat kick or a tighter, faster dolphin kick (creating a shorter kicking cycle time), and emphasizing both the down and up kicks will help.

Second, swimmers can increase their pulling stroke rate or tempo. In freestyle, fly and backstroke, each hand spends about .35 seconds during the propulsion phase of the pull (backstroke is slightly longer than in freestyle). If the stroke rate is 60/minute (cycle rate of 30/minute and cycle time 2.0 seconds), then, in freestyle and backstroke, 35% of the cycle time is spent in propulsion (.70/2.0). The remaining time of the pull is spent in lift, release or recovery, which is so-called *down time.* In fly, at a 2.0 second cycle time (cycle rate of 30/minute), only 18% of that time would be spent in propulsion. The propulsion is greater, however, since swimmers are pulling with both hands simultaneously. In freestyle, with a stroke rate of 120/minute (cycle rate of 60/minute or 1.0 second cycle time), 70% of the cycle time would be spent in propulsion. In fly, at that cycle rate, 35% of the time is spent in propulsion. The higher the stroke rate, the more percentage of time is spent in propulsion. The less down time there is in the pull, the less time there is for the swimmer's speed to drop. However, if the stroke rate becomes too fast, other factors may change, such as lower propulsion achieved with the pulling arm, increased frontal drag, or diminished coupling motions, any of which can lead to lower velocity of the swimmer. Using a faster stroke rate is not always better.

Third, swimmers should avoid any of the technical errors that lead to dramatically increased drag coefficients. The frontal drag of the human body at race speed is extremely sensitive to small changes in a swimmer's shape. Even the smallest mistakes can lead to significant drops in speed. For examples, lifting the head too high, pulling too deep, overbending the knees on the kick or leaving a thumb out on the streamline off the wall can all lead to precipitous drops in speed.

In summary, by paying attention to the techniques that enable a swimmer's speed to remain more constant, a swimmer can become more efficient in all four strokes. He or she will take greater advantage of the law of inertia.

Swimming Efficiency

Swimming efficiently is important, and without it, a swimmer probably won't win a race. Many coaches tend to equate swimming efficiency with speed. They are not the same. Efficiency doesn't become the most important factor in a swimming race. Speed does. Being able to sustain the speed, however, depends on having efficiency, as well as fitness. Sustained speed and efficiency are interrelated.

There are two different ways of measuring efficiency in swimming, which are also related but not equal. Mechanical efficiency has to do with how well the velocity of the swimmer is maintained. The more fluctuation in the swimmer's velocity, the less efficient they are. Mechanical efficiency is governed by the law of inertia. The more the changes in velocity, the more energy it will cost to reach the average velocity.

Physiological efficiency is measured in meters per calorie. Similar to measuring the efficiency of a car in miles per gallon (fuel efficiency), the physiological efficiency simply measures how much energy is expended by a swimmer to swim a certain distance. The less the energy required to swim that distance, the more efficient a swimmer is. A car is more fuel-efficient on the freeway moving at a steady speed than it is in stop-and-go traffic downtown. The same principle can be applied to swimming.

There is no simple way to measure the precise number of calories a swimmer expends or burns to reach a given distance, so using physiological efficiency in swimming is not practical. With Velocity Meter technology, however, we can measure the speed of a swimmer and the variation of that speed accurately. Measuring the mechanical efficiency of a swimmer is relatively easy to do.

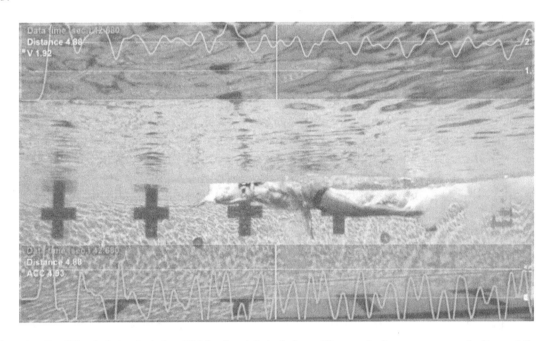

Olympian Brad Tandy being tested on VM for freestyle technique. The graph above measures velocity, and the graph below measures acceleration and deceleration.

A swimmer's efficiency is not necessarily related to his speed. In fact, at higher speeds, swimmers are generally less efficient than they are swimming at slower speeds. Using VM technology, we have noted that the differences between peak (fastest) and trough (slowest) speeds for freestyle sprinting technique are nearly always greater than while using the slower, distance technique. To become an elite swimmer, one cannot be inefficient. Great sprinters swim fast by generating a lot of propulsion (power), while still managing to limit the increase in frontal drag. They also burn a lot of calories. Butterfliers and breaststrokers are far less efficient than freestylers. Backstroke, if swum correctly, is the most efficient stroke of all.

As coaches, it is not our goal to reach maximum efficiency for a swimmer. We are more concerned about achieving and maintaining a swimmer's highest possible speed for the duration of the race. To help achieve that goal, efficiency is just part of the equation. By using a poor technique, such as overbending the knee, pulling too deep, holding a poor body or head position, for example, a swimmer will lose both efficiency and speed.

Don't get us wrong. Fast swimmers must be efficient at all distances. When correcting a swimmer's poor technique, however, not only will his or her efficiency usually improve. More importantly, he or she will swim faster.

Chapter 2

The Basic Sciences of Swimming

Physiology

To swim fast, swimmers need energy, lots of it. Whether awake or asleep, a swimmer's body depends on a constant production of energy for all its functions, such as vision, heart beating, eating, thinking, breathing, digesting, or any physical movements we make. When the swimmer steps up on the blocks for a swimming race, he or she is about to increase the energy demands to a very different and high level and, if the swimmer expects to swim fast, the body needs to be capable of producing it.

The energy used for our body functions, including muscular contraction, is mostly in the form of adenosine triphosphate (ATP). ATP is to our muscles what gasoline is to our cars. A swimmer can't function without it any better than our cars can run without gas. Swimmers have three sources of providing energy for their muscles: *stored energy*, the *anaerobic system* and the *aerobic system.*

The first source is *stored energy*, which comes in the form of ATP or Creatine Phosphate (CP). Stored ATP and CP are the most readily available energy sources in the muscle, but are in very limited supply. Swimmers run out of stored energy after about 10 seconds or less of maximal exertion.

The second source of energy comes from the *anaerobic system* (without oxygen). This system is primordial, presumably developed before we had oxygen in our environment. To produce two molecules of ATP, the anaerobic system requires a molecule of glucose, but no oxygen. It also produces a byproduct called lactate, which frees up a hydrogen ion, making the body more acidic. Once the swim race begins, the anaerobic system is activated quickly, within tenths of seconds, and begins to produce ATP almost immediately.

The third source of energy, the *aerobic system*, requires a molecule of glucose and a molecule of oxygen to work. For each molecule of glucose, the aerobic system will produce 36 molecules of ATP. Once the swim race begins, and with it the demand for increased energy, the aerobic system gets activated, so long as it gets oxygen. Yet it takes longer for this system to actually produce ATP for the muscle contractions, about 20 seconds or so.

Unless the swimmer is demanding a lot of energy for his body, like when he or she is racing, enough energy can be produced from the aerobic system to provide for most of the daily bodily functions. When a swimmer races, however, and it becomes *all-hands-on-deck*, as much ATP needs to be produced as possible. From the first strong exertional effort, the swimmer quickly begins to use up available stored energy. Both aerobic and anaerobic systems immediately get activated and start to work at full capacity to produce energy.

Energy Systems

The rate and technique of breathing in swimming affects the ability of the aerobic energy system to function. To reduce frontal drag in swimming freestyle and butterfly, and to maximize the efficient use of our energy systems, it is vital that swimmers learn how to breathe properly. Breathing properly means using the correct breathing technique and the right frequency of breaths (respiratory rate). The aerobic system depends on getting oxygen to the muscles. Breathing not only starts that process. It also rids the body of carbon dioxide, helping to keep the body less acidic.

While it may sound as if the aerobic system is more efficient than the anaerobic system, producing 18 times more ATP for each molecule of glucose (36 vs 2), it really isn't. The anaerobic system works 200 times faster than the aerobic system. In other words, in the same amount of time it took the aerobic system to produce 36 molecules of ATP, the anaerobic system churned out 400 molecules of ATP, eleven times more energy. However, it also used 200 times the amount of glucose to produce that energy. In some endurance racing, like a 25k open water swim, we simply run out of available glucose, which is called *bonking*.

The problem with the anaerobic system isn't its efficiency, it's the byproduct which lowers the pH of the body, lactate. Along with the production of lactate, a hydrogen ion gets freed up which lowers the body's acidity (pH). All human organs and systems, including muscular contraction, perform well within a very narrow range of pH and temperature. If the body's pH or temperature goes too low or too high, the muscular contractions (and other bodily functions) begin to fail. Those athletes that have competed in any sport know this feeling all too well.

To simplify this science, picture a little men or women sitting on a chair inside the body somewhere. Their job is to keep the swimmer alive. To do so, they watch two meters that are in front of them—one for pH and the other for temperature. When either meter indicator goes too high or low, but before it gets to a red line on the meter, they stand up and pull a big red lever down on the wall, which starts to shut down all non-essential systems, like muscle contraction. By shutting down the muscle's ability to contract, they may keep the swimmer alive, but they wreak havoc on his or her ability to swim fast. While racing, swimmers want to keep those guys in that chair. That means keeping a more neutral pH.

One way to keep the little man or woman sitting down when a swimmer is racing is by developing a more robust aerobic system. That is what swimmers do when they train aerobically. Swimmers increase their ability to deliver oxygen to the muscles (heart, lungs, blood, transport systems, respiratory rate) and to produce ATP at the cellular level (mitochondria).

Another way of keeping that little man or woman seated is by pushing the swimmer even harder in practice, above the heart rate that is called the anaerobic threshold (around 20 beats/min less than maximal heart rate). This type of training is called lactate training, when the swimmer begins to produce more lactate from the increased energy demands. In so doing, the body becomes better at buffering or neutralizing the pH. If a swimmer can get increased ATP production from the more efficient anaerobic system, yet buffer the pH, then he or she will be able to sustain speed better, utilizing all of the muscle fibers, so long as the swimmer doesn't run out of glucose.

By training a swimmer for short, 5-10 second maximum bursts of speed, called *alactic training,* a swimmer may be able to increase the quantity of stored energy available for sprinting.

Therefore, swimmers have the ability to improve their aerobic energy systems, increase their ability to buffer the acidity from the anaerobic system and increase their stored energy. Yet, to do that well for all three systems requires substantially different types of training. And lots of training.

The way in which swimmers train is complicated by having these three different sources of energy that produce or deliver ATP or CP at different rates and at different levels of efficiency. For example, in 50-meter sprints, which involve 20-30 seconds of all out exertion, around 95% of the energy will come from the stored energy and the anaerobic system. Consequently, there is no good rationale for breathing much in 50-meter freestyle or fly sprints for mature swimmers, which only slows the athlete down. Oxygen intake will barely come into play, and only at the end of the race.

In the 200 meters or longer events, requiring about 2 minutes or more of exertion, the majority of energy will come from the aerobic system. The longer the event, the greater contribution of energy comes from the aerobic system, so long as we breathe sufficiently. In these events, oxygen needs to be delivered at the most efficient rate possible. In land sports, over this same duration, the respiratory rate is in the range of 50-60 breaths per minute for maximally sustained exertion. The respiratory rate should be similar while swimming these longer events with the same effort.

The 100 is an interesting race, as it takes place over approximately one minute of exertion. About half (mostly the first half) of the energy needed for the race will come from the anaerobic and stored systems while the other half of the energy (mostly the second half) will come from the aerobic system. However, since the aerobic system gets activated from the start of the race, swimmers need to breath fairly often on the first half of the race, even though they may not feel as if they need the oxygen. If they don't breathe often enough early in the race, they will build up a huge oxygen debt, the pH goes down and the little man or woman will get off the chair at some time during the second half of the race, shutting down the skeletal muscular systems.

At the elite level of swimming, the respiratory rates of females are typically less than of males in the 100-meter freestyle and butterfly events. In freestyle, many elite women swimmers take two breaths every cycle for four strokes, then hold their breath for four strokes. In butterfly, most elite women swimmers breathe every other cycle. Elite male swimmers typically breathe every cycle in the100 fly and the100 freestyle, until the very end of the race.

While there are theories about why the breathing pattern is different between elite men and women, we are not certain we know all of the reasons. Men that have larger muscle mass and a higher percentage of fast-twitch muscle fibers that depend on the anaerobic energy will produce lactate at a higher rate. Women often train more aerobically and develop better aerobic energy systems. Even the diaphragms of men and women are different, which may contribute to the rate of delivering oxygen or ridding the body of carbon dioxide.

In summary, how swimmers train and how often they breathe determines, to a large extent, how much energy they can produce for their muscles and from which systems they will get that energy.

Muscle Composition

Whether a swimmer turns out to be a better sprinter or endurance athlete is largely determined by the composition of the muscle fibers. There are three types of fibers: slow twitch (type I) and two types of fast-twitch (types IIa and IIb). Slow twitch fibers are more suitable for endurance events and fast twitch fibers are better suited for short bursts of power and speed. Slow twitch fibers contract with less force, but recover much quicker than fast twitch fibers. Type IIa fibers, which comprise about 10% of the total muscle fibers, have the ability to convert more toward an endurance function (similar to type I) or toward a power function (similar to type IIb), depending on how they are trained. Type II muscle fibers have no mitochondria. They depend solely on the anaerobic energy system for their contraction.

While the composition of a swimmer's muscle fibers is largely genetically determined, swimmers do have the ability to increase the size (hypertrophy), the numbers of muscle fibers (muscle mass) and, to a smaller degree, to alter the function of the type IIa fibers through appropriate training and nutrition. Larger and/or more type II muscle fibers will increase the contractile strength of the muscle. More type I fibers increase the ability to sustain contractions over a longer time.

The paradox of building too much muscle mass, particularly in the wrong places, is that it can begin to affect the shape (morphology) of a swimmer. In the sport of swimming, bigger and stronger is not necessarily better, if it significantly increases the drag coefficient. In most sports, getting bigger and stronger will make the athlete better. In swimming, that is not always the case. At some point, if swimmers continue getting bigger, they will get slower. The additional power of the swimmer will not overcome the additional drag force caused from their bigger size.

In summary, a simplified understanding of the physiology for swimmers, coaches and parents includes the following:

1. Identify the anatomical composition of the swimmer's muscles (this can be estimated by experience in racing or training or by doing a vertical jump).
2. Build the energy systems according to the duration of the events to be swum (most of the swimming events require a robust aerobic system, while sprinting requires more attention to the anaerobic system and stored energy).
3. Teach swimmers to use an appropriate respiratory rate to properly utilize the aerobic system (when required).
4. Design appropriate training in and outside of the pool to improve the composition and size of swim-specific muscle fibers and improve the coordination and movements for the targeted events.

Chapter 3

Race Club Technology

Velocity Meter

It is an exciting time in the sport of swimming with respect to technology advancement. Many new companies providing hardware (devices) and software have emerged to help coaches and swimmers improve. Companies or products like APLab, CoachCam, Swim Hero, Firebelly, SwimSense, SmartPaddle, TritonWear, SwimTraxx and Form Goggles, just to name a few, are developing really great tools that provide more information and important data than ever before, delivered right to our mobile devices. BMW worked with USA Swimming in Colorado Springs to develop new video/analytical software. That is all good news.

The bad news is it can be very time-consuming to compile all of the new data, analyze it and, perhaps most challenging, interpret how this information should potentially improve a swimmer's technique or performance. Unless there is a full time IT person on the staff that also understands swimming, most coaches simply don't have the time to coach, administer and do all of that analysis for every swimmer's races in each meet. That is a huge burden.

For this reason, we believe there will be an increasing demand for technical coaches or assistants, those that make it a point to analyze and understand data and in turn, provide meaningful and helpful recommendations for a swimmer's improvement. That is what we do at The Race Club, particularly when it comes to technique.

Ever since I did my first rabbit research study as a Resident in Ophthalmology at Indiana University, I have never trusted another rabbit study. They don't cooperate very well and there are too many variables. I have also been very suspicious of any scientist offering advice to a good coach or swimmer. If given the choice between practical experience and pure science, I would always pick practical experience, but it would be nice to have both. To develop swimmers to a higher level, we need both.

The challenge with science is that for it to be meaningful, three things need to happen:

1. The technology and the way the technology is utilized must be capable of producing reasonably accurate and reproducible data.
2. The data from the technology must be analyzed/interpreted correctly and the right conclusions drawn from it.
3. The swimmer must be capable of applying the information derived from the technology to help him or her swim faster or more efficiently.

None of those three requirements are necessarily easily accomplished. If they are not, the science and/or technology can do more harm than good. However, after three years of using Velocity Meter (VM) technology on hundreds of swimmers, extracting as much data as we think will be useful, I am convinced we can meet the three requirements in nearly everyone—even Olympians.

Velocity Meter

At The Race Club, we go well beyond simply analyzing a swimmer's races, including stroke rates, distance per stroke, breakout times, breathing patterns, splits, turn times and so on. We have invested in some new and exciting technology and software from Italy (APLab), called Velocity Meter, that measures a swimmer's velocity, acceleration, and deceleration at each .02 seconds during the stroke cycle. When this data is synchronized to a swimmer's video, we can then determine peak (fastest) and trough (slowest) velocities, differences between peak and trough velocities for both arms (ΔPT) or for the pull and kick, and the peak (highest) accelerations and peak (also highest) decelerations. Peak acceleration points occur when maximal propulsion happens, and peak deceleration occurs when maximal drag occurs.

Identifying the techniques that lead to either maximal propulsion or drag is very important. For the first time, VM technology identifies and quantifies the mistakes in technique that are being made. We also measure the percentage of velocity loss in dolphin kick caused from the knee bend, hip flexion or feet dropping down. We measure the percentage of velocity loss after the kick in breaststroke, which tells us how well the swimmer is streamlining his or her position at both ends of the body.

Velocity Meter device manufactured by APLab (Italy). It is connected to the computer to monitor the data and video.

Since most of these data from the VM is new to our sport, it has taken us a few years to understand what is normal or expected for a given swimmer, depending on gender, age, stroke, and technique. More important than a visual interpretation of what we believe is right or wrong through video analysis, the VM quantitates the severity of mistakes (frontal drag) with the greatest deceleration points, and gives us an idea of the magnitude of propulsion forces with peak acceleration levels.

Glide Into Dolphin
Time to 5M   2.78 Sec
Time to First Peak   1.38 Sec

Dolphin Right Away
Time to 5M   2.66
Time to First Peak   .44 Sec

Dolphin Kick

Time	DT	Time	DP	Difference	Time	UT	Time	UP	Difference
22.53	0.81	22.58	2.57	1.76	22.72	1.38	22.78	1.84	0.46
22.92	0.78	23.00	2.46	1.68	23.16	1.48	23.26	1.81	0.33
23.36	0.84	23.44	2.39	1.55	23.58	1.44	23.64	1.81	0.37
23.78	1.13	23.94	2.42	1.29	24.02	1.27	24.10	1.86	0.59
24.24	1.04	24.32	2.38	1.34	24.46	1.36	24.56	1.85	0.49
24.70	0.98	24.84	2.36	1.38	24.94	1.31	25.04	2.02	0.71
25.14	0.73	25.34	2.28	1.55	25.42	1.29	25.48	1.66	0.37
25.64	1.00	25.82	2.29	1.29	25.92	1.18	26.00	1.74	0.56
AVG	0.91		2.39	1.48	AVG	1.34		1.82	0.49

Dolphin Kick II

Time	DP	Time	UT	Difference	Time	UP	Time	DT	Difference
22.58	2.57	22.72	1.38	-1.19	22.78	1.84	22.92	0.78	-1.06
23.00	2.46	23.16	1.48	-0.98	23.26	1.81	23.36	0.84	-0.97
23.44	2.39	23.58	1.44	-0.95	23.64	1.81	23.78	1.13	-0.68
23.94	2.42	24.02	1.27	-1.15	24.10	1.86	24.24	1.04	-0.82
24.32	2.38	24.46	1.36	-1.02	24.56	1.85	24.70	0.98	-0.87
24.84	2.36	24.94	1.31	-1.05	25.04	2.02	25.14	0.73	-1.29
25.34	2.28	25.42	1.29	-0.99	25.48	1.66	25.64	1.00	-0.66
25.82	2.29	25.92	1.18	-1.11	26.00	1.74			
AVG	2.39		1.34	-1.06	AVG	1.82		0.93	-0.90
% Loss	44%				% Loss	49%			

Data from the Velocity Meter on dolphin kick study, including average trough (slowest) and peak (highest) velocities for down kicks (DT and DP), up kicks (UT and UP) and the average difference between the troughs and peak velocities (ΔPT). It also includes the percentage of loss of velocity during the down kick and up kick, an indicator of how much frontal drag is caused by these motions.

I believe we have been able to identify technical mistakes in every single swimmer that we have tested. I also believe that most of them improved as a result of making the recommended changes. Here are some notable examples.

1. One month after having VM testing, elite butterflier Amanda Kendall changed her head position and the emphasis on her up kick to win the 100-meter butterfly at USA Swimming Nationals in Greensboro, NC in 2018.
2. Weeks after having VM testing, rising swimming superstar Josh Zuchowski learned to widen his breaststroke pull and dropped over two seconds at Junior Nationals to swim 55.9 100-yard breaststroke in 2019.
3. After getting VM testing and changing his start radically (modelling after Olympian Brad Tandy), 9-year-old Kaien Tan from Oregon beat swimmers a year older and weighing 30 pounds more on all of his race starts in 2019.

For each study or comparison on a swimmer that has VM testing done, such as dolphin kick, butterfly or freestyle, we will have from one to as many as five recommendations for stroke technique improvements. Usually the number of recommendations is closer to five.

Now that we have a large enough data base of VM testing on swimmers and understand what is considered good or not so good for various ages and genders and for each metric we measure, we can offer much better advice to swimmers. Just like with anything else, there is a skill to reading the VM studies and videos. An average of about 8 hours is spent on each swimmer's test—recording, editing and compiling the data, then analyzing it, including an hour-long discussion at the end with the swimmer and coach and/or parents. A VM study typically requires a few weeks to prepare and analyze all of the data. We find the VM testing to be invaluable for all swimmers, from beginners all the way up to Olympians. Using VM testing is like looking at a swimmer under a microscope. We can see so much more than we can see from the pool deck. We have yet to find a swimmer with perfect technique, but we will keep looking.

Chapter 4

Race Club Technology

Pressure Meter

The Pressure Meter (PM) provides very different information than the Velocity Meter (VM). While the VM technology offers information that pertains to both propulsion and drag forces, the PM provides data related only to the propulsion.

The PM measures the pressure on the pulling hand during the stroke cycle and can be used in all four strokes: butterfly, backstroke, breaststroke and freestyle. The electronic device of the PM also measures the body rotation (angle and speed) for both shoulders and hips for freestyle and backstroke and the upward and downward rotations for fly and breaststroke. In freestyle and in backstroke, the peak (highest) shoulder and hip rotations occur at two different times, separated by about .2-.3 seconds. The PM measurements include both the angle of rotation (degrees) and the velocity of rotation, or angular velocity (degrees/second). Knowing the speed of the body's rotation is important, as it influences the force of the pulling hand and/or the kick. All of the PM data are synchronized to the swimmer's video as he or she swims across or toward the frame of the camera.

Pressure is the measurement of force/unit area, and is expressed in units of Pascals. Since the PM paddle that fits over the hand is a fixed and known size, the PM is essentially giving us the same information as the force of propulsion. The PM uses pneumatic technology to measure the pressure on the palm side and the back side of the hand. The difference between those two pressures results in a net propulsion measurement.

Although the PM technology does not provide the direction of the force, since it is synchronized to video, we can see the hand and estimate the direction of the applied force. Knowing the peak angular velocities of the body's rotation—whether along the long axis of the body in freestyle and backstroke, or the short axis in fly and breaststroke—and correlating those values to the hand's propulsion is important in the analysis.

There are other technologies in swimming that measure force on the hand. The most notable is the Smart Paddle (TraineSense in Finland), which measures force using plate sensor technology. Force is a vector with both magnitude and direction. The Smart Paddle has the ability to measure the magnitude and the direction of the force, which is very important. When it comes to swimming propulsion, we are interested primarily in the hand's force in the opposite direction to the swimmer's line of motion. Forces in other directions can generate lift, but are less important than propulsion. The current disadvantage of the Smart Paddle technology is that it is not yet able to be synchronized to video, although I understand that they are working on that capability. For accurate analysis, one must be able to see the swimmer's position precisely correlated with the force measurements.

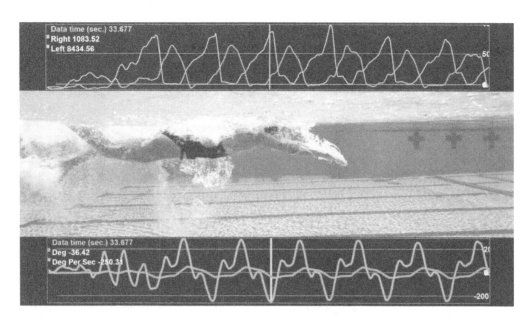

Elite sprint freestyler Margo Geer being tested on the Pressure Meter. The graph above represents pressure on each hand and the graph below represents degrees (smaller curves) and angular speed (bigger curves) of body rotation. Notice the double peaks of body rotation, representing different timing of the shoulder and hip rotations. She is near peak propulsion with her left hand at the end of her pull (graph above) as she simultaneously reaches peak hip rotational speed (graph below).

Pressure Meter Data

Before entering the water, each swimmer to be tested is connected to the PM device by wearing a small hand paddle on each hand. The electronic device (IMU- Inertial Measurement Unit) measuring the pressure, acceleration and angular velocities is attached securely to a belt on the swimmer's lower back. The hand paddles are connected to the device by plastic tubing for the pneumatic measurement of pressure changes, which are kept in place by rubber bands.

American record holder Zane Grothe getting ready to be tested with the Pressure Meter.

While the device looks cumbersome and difficult to swim with, after a few short laps of warm up, the swimmers claim that they can swim with close to their normal technique. The middle finger slips through a central hole in the hand paddles, so the pressure sensors are on both the front sides and back sides of the hands.

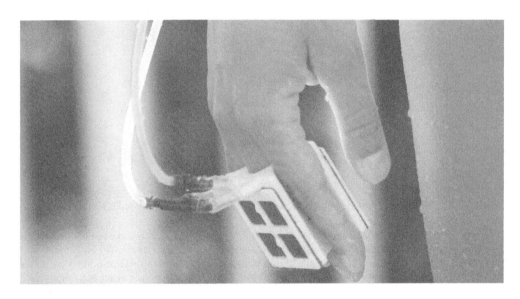

Zane Grothe's fingers squeeze around the PM paddle to secure it in place while swimming.

Once the testing begins, all of the data are collected in the software on a laptop. The laptop connects to the hardware on the swimmer's lower back via Bluetooth connectivity.

Head coach Devin Murphy (red shirt) and PM inventor Nunzio Lanotte (APLab) preparing the data collected from Zane Grothe's testing.

As early adopters of the PM technology, and after performing many tests, we have determined what we believe are the most important data for each of the four strokes. We will typically find two peaks of pulling pressure during the underwater phases of the cycles of the four strokes. The following are the data we collect for each stroke.

Butterfly

- Peak pressure during the front-quadrant propulsion and peak pressure during the late back-quadrant propulsion phase, as the hands near the end of the pull
- Angle and angular velocity of the body along the short axis moving upward (influencing early propulsion pressure) during the pull and downward during the arm recovery (influencing the second down kick)

Backstroke

- Peak pressures for right and left hands correlating to the shoulder rotation (end of the pull) and the hip rotation (beginning of the pull)
- Angle and angular velocities of long axis rotation measured in both directions

Breaststroke

- Peak pressure measured during the out-sweep (lift phase) and propulsion phase of the underwater pull (as hands turn backward and inward)
- Angle and angular velocities measured as the shoulders move upward (influencing propulsion pressure) and downward (influencing kick propulsion) along the short axis

Freestyle

- Peak pressure measured for right and left hands correlating to the peak shoulder (middle of the pull) and the hip (end of the pull) rotations
- Angle and angular velocities of long axis rotation measured in both directions

		Butterfly														
Time	Breath	AV Up	Angle		Time	RP1	Time	LP1	Time	RP2	Time	LP2		Time	Breath	AV Down	Angle
25.09	x	174.86	5.54		25.03	4767.23	25.13	4937.72	25.33	5371.29	25.41	7026.3		25.93	x	202.2	19.82
26.23	x	197.91	10.09		26.27	4695.97	26.29	4836.49	26.49	5134.13	26.55	6552.13		27.07	x	187.75	17.58
27.37	x	240.1	8.18		27.41	4607.06	27.41	4980.36	27.63	5457.97	27.71	6033.29		28.09	x	186.09	15.75
28.55	x	237.96	8.29		28.59	4650.01	28.61	4698.63	28.81	4904.42	28.85	5615.05		29.41	x	196.24	11.78
29.71	x	227.58	7.84		29.77	4416.25	29.79	4539.41	29.99	4851.14	30.07	5661.67		30.59	x	168.97	8.52
AVG		215.86	7.99		AVG	4645.48		4798.22		5135.79		6173.68		AVG		188.25	14.65

		Backstroke														
Time	Hip AV	Angle	RP		Time	Shoulder AV	Angle	RP		Time	Hip AV	Angle	LP		Time	Shoulder AV	Angle	LP
29.37	267.97	39.5	1944.72		28.93	162.32	39.5	5458.54		28.65	238.93	23.18	1640.69		29.67	99.25	23.18	5141.19
30.87	262.39	43.73	1758.24		30.41	145.17	43.73	5099.56		30.17	253.33	20.66	1463.54		31.17	92.69	20.66	4914.75
32.39	255.5	37.34	2372.29		31.97	146.42	37.34	5242.75		31.71	289.92	19.7	1729.94		32.69	113.53	19.7	5508.16
33.85	276.53	38.67	2563.43		33.41	126.09	38.67	5130.86		33.13	248.83	24.62	1947.05		34.15	94.75	24.62	5098.56
35.35	261.67	32.34	1844.15		34.87	127.97	32.34	4203.79		34.59	252.98	24.02	1984.28		35.65	106.86	24.02	4608.99
AVG	264.81	38.32	2006.57		AVG	141.59	38.32	5027.1		AVG	246.8	22.44	1633.1		AVG	101.41	22.44	5052.61

		Breaststroke														
Time	AV Up	Angle		Time	RP Outsweep	Time	LP Outsweep	Time	RP Pull	Time	LP Pull		Time	AV Down	Angle
25.47	113.99	4.16		25.07	2448.22	25.07	2368.63	25.37	6340.99	25.39	6419.91		25.85	112.62	7.47
26.71	207.04	8.13		26.27	2488.18	26.31	2942.72	26.65	6142.52	26.67	5895.16		27.07	126.55	5.82
28.01	203.52	8.87		27.55	2091.24	27.55	2625.04	27.93	6562.76	27.85	5644.68		28.35	130.59	5.95
29.39	205.45	6.62		28.91	1884.11	28.91	2146.85	29.29	6073.92	29.31	5756.57		29.75	112.11	7.22
30.73	202.9	6.16		30.27	1684.98	30.27	2170.16	30.61	5698.96	30.65	5695.96		31.07	103.29	6.81
33.07	190.3	6.05		31.63	2293.7	31.63	2061.6	31.95	5798.86	31.95	5619.38		32.43	115	7.95
33.45	189.45	6.05		33.03	2435.56	33.03	2566.43	33.37	6161.17	33.35	5850.48		33.79	92.34	
AVG	187.52	6.58		AVG	2189.43		2411.63		6111.31		5832.02		AVG	110.36	6.84

		Freestyle All Out														
Time	Breath	Shoulder AV	Angle	RP		Time	Breath	Hip AV	Angle	RP		Time	Breath	Shoulder AV	Angle	LP		Time	Breath	Hip AV	Angle
23.45		193.4	45.07	5542.79		23.79		170.26	60.35	3360.97		24.09		187.44	45.07	5094.23		24.33		210.89	60.35	67
24.75		149.7	43.3	5552.78		25.03		195.59	59.32	3840.49		25.43		141.8	43.3	4613.38		25.65		234.65	59.32	68
26.05		146.33	44.88	5181.15		26.27		190.79	51.36	3569.43		26.75		133.07	44.88	6177.62		26.95		201.65	51.36	6
27.35		141.89	43.43	4902.7		27.83		199.42	50.35	3352.31		28.05		152.87	43.43	4493.5		28.27		239.61	50.35	5
28.69		145.98	49.12	5025.3		28.97		224.75	52	3394.93											
AVG		155.48	45.16	5252.94		AVG		196.16	54.68	3504.02		AVG		153.75	44.17	4684.68		AVG		221.7	55.35	63

PM data file measuring hand pressures, body angles and rotational speeds in all four strokes of a swimmer.

With PM analysis, in swimmers of all ages and abilities, we often find that the pressures are differently applied from the right and left hands. Sometimes we can correlate the difference to the video appearance of the hand slipping or angling inward or outward. Other times not. Nearly always the peak hand pressures are correlated with the peak angular velocities, which are often different in each direction. Often, we find the highest force on the hands being applied when the hands are not in the propulsive phases, but in the lift or release phases of the underwater pull.

With the PM being newer technology, the data are also new. We are learning as we go, collecting a larger data base of swimmers. What we have learned so far is that it is easy to lose the force on the water with either hand. The two hands do not often pull with equal force nor at the optimal time in the pulling motion. In freestyle and backstroke, we may find the maximum pulling force occurring in the front quadrant (in front of the shoulder), back quadrant (behind the shoulder), or right at the shoulder, depending on the technique being used, the body rotational speed and where the swimmer decides to place the most effort. Finally, we have learned how extremely important the body rotation is in developing greater propulsion and that fast body rotation needs to happen in both directions.

Chapter 5

Race Club Technology

Propulsion/Drag Meter

The Propulsion/Drag Meter (PDM) technology is used to measure the force required to tow a swimmer across a pool at a constant speed (drag force) or to measure the force applied by a swimmer to move away from the device (propulsion). In our experience, PDM technology is much more accurate at measuring drag force than it is at measuring propulsion.

The drag force measured by the PDM is called *passive drag*, where the swimmer must maintain a fixed position while being towed. Measuring *active drag* forces, when a person is swimming, is much more complicated and very challenging to measure accurately.

Nonetheless, we have found PDM technology very useful as a research tool to measure the differences in frontal drag that are caused by changing one single technique or parameter at a time.

Coach Devin Murphy using PDM technology to measure drag forces on a swimmer in Islamorada, Florida.

Most of the PDM studies that we perform at The Race Club are done at race speed (2.3 meters/second). Although this velocity is greater than the average speed of all swimmers, except the elite male 50-meter freestyle sprinters, 2.3 m/sec is a speed that many swimmers achieve at their peak velocities in all four strokes, including breaststroke. Since frontal drag force is extremely sensitive to increasing speed, we feel it is most important to understand what is happening with frontal drag force at the highest speeds achieved.

We attach a belt around the swimmer's waist to the PDM device with a non-stretchable thin cord that extends for 50 meters. The swimmer must swim to the other end of the 50-meter pool, maintaining a fairly constant pressure on the towing cord. Once there, the swimmer places the cord on the stomach side (if testing on the stomach). The software and the PDM begin towing simultaneously, with a video camera synchronized to the swimmer's passing motion. The swimmer then assumes the position or technique that is being tested and holds that position for the duration of the tow.

At 2.3 meters per second, it requires only about 20 seconds to tow the swimmer across the 50-meter pool. Most of the testing we do is underwater, but sometimes we will test swimmers on the surface at lower speeds, since the drag force is much greater on the surface. The PDM records the swimmer's speed and drag force (measured in Newtons) at each .05 seconds synchronized to a few seconds of video, as the swimmer passes by the camera. We typically will use the recorded data from the middle 10-12 seconds of the test, including the portion that is in the video. That assures that the swimmer has time to establish and hold the correct position and depth in the water, verified by the video. During those 10-12 seconds, approximately 200 drag and velocity measurements are collected, enough for statistical significance. The average speed and drag force are then derived from the 200 data points. Since the average speeds of two different tests are close, but not exactly the same, and the drag force is extremely sensitive to velocity, the drag forces must be adjusted to the exact same speed before being compared. In so doing, a valid comparison of two different tests can be made.

Gary Hall Sr. being towed across the 50-meter pool at 2.3 m/sec, testing the hand position in front. The graph above indicates the drag force in Newtons. The swimmer's time, speed and drag force are indicated in the top left corner (PDM technology).

Streamline Hammerhead Cap @ 2.3				Streamline Tech Suit Hammerhead @ 2.3		
Time	Force	Speed		Time	Force	Speed
8000	204.33	-2.133		8800	202.62	-1.8
8050	208.37	-2.113		8850	195	-1.784
8100	211.29	-2.092		8900	190.08	-1.811
8150	212	-2.078		8950	188.56	-1.875
8200	210.41	-2.079		9000	189.93	-1.958
8250	207.54	-2.082		9050	193.59	-2.039
8300	204.46	-2.085		9100	198.89	-2.09
8350	202.17	-2.074		9150	204.88	-2.106
8400	201.03	-2.054		9200	210.26	-2.106
8450	201	-2.041		9250	213.77	-2.093
8500	202	-2.041		9300	214.33	-2.082
8550	203.97	-2.065		9350	212.66	-2.079
8600	206.69	-2.101		9400	210.27	-2.082
8650	209.91	-2.131		9450	208.72	-2.089
8700	213.38	-2.142		9500	209.14	-2.104
8750	216.77	-2.12		9550	211.09	-2.119
8800	219.5	-2.083		9600	213.74	-2.127
8850	220.97	-2.043		9650	216.26	-2.122
8900	220.59	-2.016		9700	217.94	-2.106
8950	218.16	-2.011		9750	218.34	-2.084
9000	214.19	-2.018		9800	217.05	-2.065
9050	209.19	-2.026		9850	213.69	-2.052
9100	203.71	-2.025		9900	208.36	-2.057
9150	198.59	-2.016		9950	201.75	-2.067
9200	194.89	-2.011		10000	194.59	-2.074
9250	193.67	-2.014		10050	187.65	-2.078
9300	195.76	-2.037		10100	182.3	-2.078
9350	200.04	-2.074		10150	180.32	-2.073
9400	204.51	-2.118		10200	183.51	-2.065
9450	207.12	-2.157		10250	192.98	-2.058
9500	206.5	-2.182		10300	206.14	-2.054
9550	203.87	-2.199		10350	219.05	-2.049
9600	201.11	-2.204		10400	227.77	-2.04
9650	200.1	-2.204		10450	229.78	-2.037
9700	201.8	-2.2		10500	226.76	-2.035
9750	205.28	-2.193		10550	221.19	-2.037
9800	209.39	-2.185		10600	215.52	-2.054

PDM data include time (.05 second intervals), drag force (Newtons) and velocity (meters/second) for each study. In this particular study, we compared the average frontal drag force between wearing a training suit versus a tech suit at race speed (2.3 m/sec).

The studies we perform on the PDM are a work in progress. As we think of new or different techniques in swimming, we test them with PDM. We are often surprised by the results that we find. Here is a short list of some of our recent PDM test results at 2.3 m/sec. All of these tests below were performed with the swimmer's stomach down. There are many more tests to be run.

1. Wearing a thick silicone race cap (dome cap by Hammerhead) compared to a thinner silicone cap reduced drag by 10.5%.
2. Wearing a men's tech suit (Finis Fuse) compared to wearing a polyester training suit (Funky Trunks) reduced drag by 5.1%.
3. Keeping the feet dorsiflexed (pointing the toes straight down) compared to plantar flexing the ankle (pointing toes backward) increased drag by 41%.
4. *Hyperstreamline* (arms behind the head) compared to streamline (biceps over the ears) reduced drag by 11%.
5. Air bubbles released under the swimmer's body compared to holding the breath reduced drag by 9.1%.
6. Elevation of the core (slight hip flexion 3-5 degrees) compared to horizontal non-flexed body position reduced frontal drag by 10%.
7. Hunching the shoulders (on breaststroke pullout technique) compared to straight or squared shoulders reduced drag by 4%.

8. The head tilted forward (neck extended) compared to holding the head in alignment with the body increased drag by 4%.
9. Spreading the fingers widely in front with a streamline position compared to squeezing the fingers and thumb together added 18% more frontal drag.
10. Keeping the thumbs sticking out on the streamline compared to squeezing them together added 11% more frontal drag.

From this small sampling of the PDM testing we have performed, you get the idea. At race speed, small changes in body position or shape or texture (suits, caps) cause significant changes in frontal drag forces.

The truth is that we live in a detailed sport, where even the smallest mistakes in swimming technique will have dire consequences. Yet coaches aren't paying enough attention to the details. In fairness to coaches, however, unless they have the tools (technology) to get the details, and know how to interpret them correctly, they won't know what they are missing, nor what to advise. Getting the details takes some work and time, but it can make a big difference in performances.

Thanks to VM, PM, PDM and other technology, we now have the ability to look at swimmers under a microscope. It is like looking under the hood of the car for the first time and discovering all of the parts of the engine and how they work. It is indeed an exciting time in the sport of swimming. And it is only going to get better!

Chapter 6

Freestyle Techniques

The Three Styles of Freestyle

In 2007, Mike Bottom, then Head Coach of The Race Club and men's sprint coach at Cal Berkeley, delivered a talk at the American Swim Coaches Association annual meeting on the *Three Styles of Freestyle*. In that talk, Mike described three different freestyle techniques: hip-driven, shoulder-driven and what he called body-driven technique. We had never heard anyone differentiate freestyle techniques before like that, and it was a brilliant talk. There was a question from the audience then about the loping or galloping freestyle technique that was being used by Jason Lezak, Michael Phelps and others, but Mike didn't really consider that a different technique.

After years of observing and analyzing freestyle techniques, using all of our technologies at The Race Club, we would still agree with Mike that there are basically three different freestyle techniques. We classify them a little differently than Mike did, however. We call them hip-driven, shoulder-driven and hybrid techniques. The hybrid technique is another name for loping or galloping freestyle technique. Within each of those three freestyle techniques, there are also other important differences, such as the recovering motion and pulling motion of the arms. Those different techniques will be discussed later.

There are several parameters that differentiate hip-driven from shoulder-driven and hybrid freestyle techniques, but the most important one is stroke rate. Hip-driven freestyle has the slowest stroke rate. Shoulder-driven technique has the fastest stroke rate. Hybrid freestyle, which borrows some of the technique from both hip-driven and shoulder-driven freestyle, has a stroke rate in between those two. The following is a brief description of the three styles of freestyle techniques:

Hip-driven Freestyle

The stroke rates for hip-driven freestyle range from less than 50 per minute (25 right arm and 25 left arm strokes) to around 75 strokes per minutes (using a Finis Tempo Trainer). The arm cycle time (hand entry to hand entry) for a hip-driven freestyler with a stroke rate of 60/minute is two seconds.

Hip-driven freestyle is the most energy-efficient freestyle technique, as we discussed in Chapter 2. It offers the best fuel efficiency, and since it is a distance technique, relies heavily on the aerobic system. It is not the fastest freestyle technique, however. Therefore, hip-driven freestyle is a technique that is primarily used in warm-up and warm-down swimming and distance racing (400 meters or longer). It should never be used for sprinting nor even the 100-meter event. It is simply not a technique that will serve swimmers well in those shorter events.

Besides the slower stroke rate, the other key differentiating techniques of hip-driven freestyle occur at the front end and back end of the underwater pull. At the front end of hip-driven freestyle, the hand pushes forward, not downward, delaying the downward lift phase of the pull. With hip-driven freestyle, the pulling hand should be in the early propulsive phase of the pull by the time the recovering hand strikes the water. In other words, one cannot delay the pulling motion too long using this technique. The hip-driven freestyle is not a *catch-up* freestyle technique, where one hand remains out in front until the other hand strikes the water. Other than perhaps in doing drills, there is no place for a *catch-up* freestyle technique in freestyle races.

At the back end of the hip-driven pull, the swimmer pushes harder and longer, then rotates the hip aggressively as the hand releases forward to the recovery. Thus, it is called hip-driven freestyle. The lead hand pushes forward. The pulling hand pushes rearward, and the swimmer rotates and rides out on top of the hip. Since the swimmer is taking fewer strokes, the objective is to get as much distance per stroke as possible out of each one.

Age Group Swimmer Rachel demonstrates hip-driven freestyle.

Other common techniques that we see being used in hip-driven freestyle racing are a bent arm (lower energy) recovery and a strong kick. The bent arm recovery is used because it is easier and conserves energy for the many strokes to be taken in the longer races. We refer to the bent arm recovery as a *low-octane recovery* and explain why in Chapter 9. The strong kick in hip-driven freestyle is advantageous because with the slow stroke rate, there is a lot of down time on the pull, where neither hand is generating propulsion. Having a strong kick will help sustain the swimmer's speed during the pulling down time. In Chapter 8, we will explain how to build a stronger freestyle kick.

The other swimmers that may benefit from using hip-driven freestyle technique are triathletes that are trying to conserve energy for the bike and run to follow, or swimmers that don't have enough aerobic conditioning or capacity to hold a faster stroke rate.

Curiously, very few elite women swimmers use hip-driven freestyle technique. Notable exceptions are Allison Schmidt (American gold medalist in the Olympic 200 m freestyle in 2012) and Camille Muffat (French gold medalist in the Olympic 400 m freestyle in 2012). Both women had extraordinarily strong kicking propulsion. We see many elite men using hip-driven freestyle in the 800 meters, 1500 meters or longer Open Water events.

Shoulder-driven Freestyle

The stroke rate for shoulder-driven freestyle ranges from around 85 strokes per minute to nearly 150 strokes per minute. In the 50-meter sprint, for example, a swimmer that uses a stroke rate of 120/minute has a one second cycle time. There is a gray area between 75 and 85 strokes per minute, where hip-driven freestyle transitions to shoulder-driven. It is not a black and white sport.

Other than a faster stroke rate, shoulder-driven freestyle is defined by an early downward force of the hand after entry and an earlier hand release at the end of the pull. The swimmer relies on higher stroke rate (RPM) to gain speed rather than maximizing the propulsion from each pull. In one sense, going from hip-driven to shoulder-driven freestyle technique changes the function of the hand from being a paddle to becoming a propeller blade.

The other key technique of shoulder-driven freestyle is the big and aggressive shoulder rotation that occurs with each stroke. The hips rotate also, but much less than the shoulders do. To get the powerful shoulder rotation, the arms need to recover more vertically over the water. In sprinting, the arms often recover with a straighter arm motion, rather than a bent motion. We refer to that arm recovery technique as *high-octane recovery*.

Virtually all elite sprinters use shoulder-driven freestyle technique. Most elite women use shoulder-driven freestyle technique for all events from the 50 to the 1500-meter event. In the men's freestyle events, we see both shoulder-driven and hybrid techniques being used in middle-distance events (100 and 200 meters). In the longer events (400 meters and up), we see all three freestyle techniques being used.

Olympic freestyle sprinter Brad Tandy uses a straight arm (high-octane) shoulder-driven freestyle technique.

Hybrid Freestyle

With hybrid freestyle technique, the stroke rates range from around 70 to nearly 100 strokes per minute, overlapping some with the other two techniques. With the stroke rates in between the other two techniques, hybrid freestyle is a technique that also seems to work best for the middle-distance races, 100 and 200 meters. We often see hybrid freestyle technique also being used in longer events, 400 meters and up, particularly among men.

The key feature of hybrid freestyle technique is the different speeds of the recovering arms. Coming off the breath side, the recovering arm comes down harder and faster than on the non-breath side. After the breath, the head should submerge when the recovering arm strikes the water. Once in the water, the recovering arm on the breath side pushes out the front, similar to a hip-driven technique. The hand on the non-breath side will begin to press downward immediately after entry, similar to a shoulder-driven technique, to help facilitate the breath to the other side. Since each arm borrows a technique from both hip-driven and shoulder-driven freestyle, we call it a hybrid freestyle technique.

Under water, since the recovering arm strikes the water earlier on the breath side, the opposite pulling arm is usually in the front quadrant. By the time the non-breathing side hand strikes the water, the opposite pulling hand is in the back quadrant.

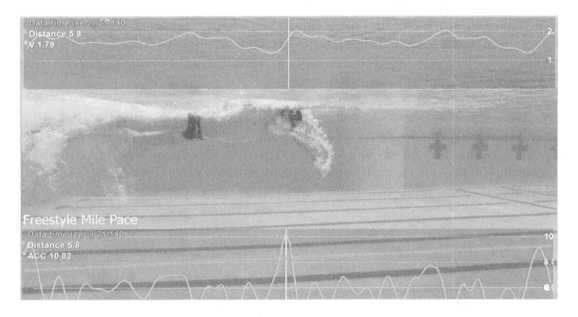

American record holder Zane Grothe uses hybrid-freestyle technique. Coming off the breath to the right side, his left pulling hand is in the front quadrant as the right hand strikes the water. Notice the peak acceleration point (center in graph below) at this same time, coming off quick body rotation, arm recovery and a strong surge kick (VM technology).

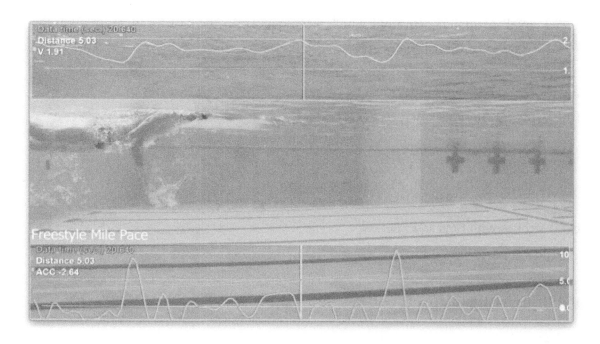

As Zane begins to rotate to the right for his breath, his left arm strikes the water at entry. At that moment, the right pulling hand is well into the back quadrant. His acceleration from this motion is not as great as above, but his resultant velocity is just as high because of less frontal drag at this time (VM technology).

As with hip-driven technique, hybrid freestyle works much better with a strong kick. The rationale for using this technique is to conserve some energy compared to a shoulder-driven freestyle. Swimmers come off of the breath side with as much energy as possible from the head rotation, shoulder rotation, and fast hand/arm entry, coupled with a pull and a strong down kick. After the breath, the head submerges completely under water and the hand is held and pushed out front to help lower the drag coefficient as much as possible. At that point, the swimmer should then accelerate and surge forward, particularly with a strong kick.

In summary, in choosing the right freestyle technique, several factors come into consideration. If it is a sprint freestyle technique the swimmer is looking for, there is only one good option: shoulder-driven freestyle.

In the middle-distance events of 100 and 200 meters, a swimmer may be better served with either a shoulder-driven or hybrid freestyle, depending on the amount of kicking propulsion.

In the events of 400 meters or longer, a swimmer has all three options. Hip-driven and hybrid freestyles are always better with a strong kick, but depending on the level of training, hip-driven freestyle may be the most energy-conserving technique.

Most female swimmers will use shoulder-driven freestyle technique at all ages and distances.

The best way to know which freestyle technique to use is to learn all three techniques and then test them. The test includes both the times achieved with each technique and the amount of energy required to reach those times. Further testing, such as with the Velocity Meter and Pressure Meter, helps us understand more details about each freestyle technique. At The Race

Club, we help all swimmers determine which technique works the best for them for all of the freestyle events.

Helpful Drills for Shoulder-driven Freestyle

6 Kick Switch with Fins and Snorkel

6 Kicks 1 Stroke with Fins and Snorkel

6 Kicks 3 strokes with Fins and Snorkel

Helpful Drills for Hip-driven Freestyle

6 Kick Switch with Fins and Snorkel

6 Kicks 1 Stroke with Fins and Snorkel

6 Kicks 3 Strokes with Fins and Snorkel

Swim with Finis Tick Tock Belt and fins

Swim with Finis Fin Belt and Fins

Wall Swim with snorkel and fins

Catch-up with 3 Second Pause and Fins

Helpful Drills for Hybrid Freestyle

6 Kicks 2 Strokes with Fins and Snorkel

4 Kicks 2 Strokes with Fins and Snorkel

Over the Wave, Under the Wave

Chapter 7

Freestyle Techniques

The Six Phases of the Pulling Cycle

Every aspect or phase of the underwater pulling motion and the arm recovery in swimming freestyle is important. To help understand the contribution of each part of the pulling motion and the recovering arm to a swimmer's speed, we have broken down a single pulling cycle into 6 phases, beginning with the hand entry into the water and ending with the following entry of the same hand.

I.   **Lift Phase**
II.   **Propulsion Phase**
       A. Front Quadrant
       B. Back Quadrant
III.   **Release Phase**
IV.   **Arm Recovery Phase**
       A. Early (upward trajectory)
       B. Late (downward trajectory)

The **lift phase** refers to the predominant forces that occur early in the underwater pulling motion, while the hand is still moving forward and downward in the water. Lift forces elevate a swimmer's body higher in the water which has the benefit of reducing a swimmer's frontal drag.

The **propulsion phase** of the pull begins once the hand starts moving backward relative to the still water it is moving through. The propulsion phase continues until the arm runs out of length and the hand can no longer move backwards in the water, or the hand simply stops pressing backward.

The **release phase** refers to the very brief time after the hand completes its propulsion and the arm and hand begin to move forward again. The hand should slide forward out of the water with the least amount of frontal drag possible to begin the **recovery phase**.

The technique and speed of arm **recovery** over the water determines the amount of work required in this process of getting ready for another pull. It also determines the amount of kinetic energy at the end of the recovery that couples with the other pulling hand and the kick. The speed of the downward trajectory of the arm, along with the shoulder and hip rotational speeds, significantly impact the propulsion and speed of the swimmer.

We will take a journey from hand entry to hand entry, completing a pulling cycle. During this journey, we will explain the importance of each phase of the freestyle pulling cycle and how they differ, depending on the freestyle technique being utilized.

The Lift Phase

Once the hand enters the water directly in front of the swimmer's shoulder, the area we call the front quadrant, the period of time until the hand actually starts moving backwards in the water generating propulsion is referred to as the **lift phase.** The duration of the lift phase is quite varied, depending on the freestyle technique being utilized. With hip-driven freestyle and a stroke rate of around 60 per minute, or a 2 second cycle time, the duration of the lift phase is greater than .6 seconds. With shoulder-driven freestyle at a stroke rate of 120 per minute, or a 1 second cycle time, the duration of the lift phase is less than .3 seconds. During the lift phase, the hand should move forward and downward, just inside the elbow, but not backward, inward (commonly referred to as an in-sweep) or outward (commonly referred to as an out-sweep).

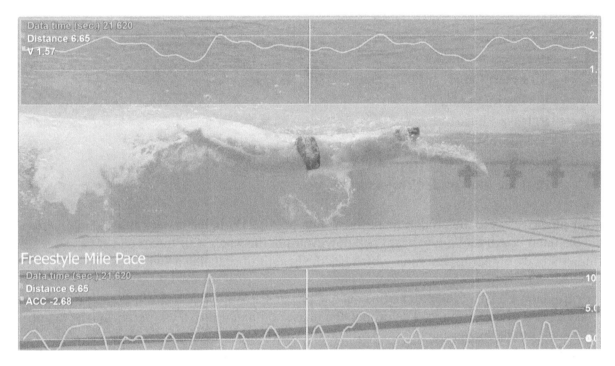

American record holder Zane Grothe in the lift phase of his right arm pulling motion (VM technology).

When observing the motion of the hand from the side during the freestyle swim, imagine an underwater clock which is about two feet in diameter with the top of the clock positioned at the surface of the water. While the arm is longer than two feet, the diameter of the clock is only two feet because as the hand moves around the clock face through the underwater pulling motion, starting at 12 o'clock, the swimmer is simultaneously moving forward. Consequently, by the time the arm completes its underwater pull, the hand moves only about 2 feet from front to back, relative to the water.

As you look at the clock face, 12 o'clock is precisely where the swimmer's hand enters the water. If the swimmer is moving from left to right, during the lift phase, the hand moves forward and downward along the perimeter of the clock until it reaches 3 o'clock on the face. In freestyle, because of anatomical constraints, the hand must move downward considerably before it moves backward. That is the end of the lift phase. From that point, the hand begins moving backward and downward along the perimeter toward 6 o'clock and begins generating propulsion.

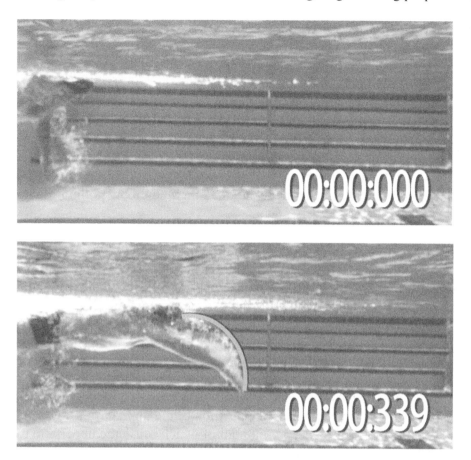

Gary Sr. spends .34 seconds in the lift phase of his right pull, using shoulder-driven freestyle with a stroke rate of 100/minute.

The two primary forces that occur during the lift phase are lift and frontal drag. In general, lift forces, which elevate the swimmer's body more into the air and out of the water, have the benefit of reducing frontal drag. Just as with a boat, the higher in the water and closer a swimmer can get to hydroplaning, the better. Since it is estimated that to hydroplane, a human body needs to achieve a speed of nearly 15 mph, and world record speed in the 50-meter sprint is currently just over 5 mph, we will not be seeing any swimmer hydroplaning soon.

The lift caused by the pulling arm and the hand in the front quadrant occurs for two different reasons, or laws of physics. The first is the Bernoulli effect, which is what accounts for the wings of airplanes lifting the plane off of the ground. The body, arm and hand outstretched in front of the swimmer acts like a wing, causing a certain amount of lift from the flow of water around it. The taller and faster the swimmer, the bigger the arm and hand, and the longer the flattened hand is held out front, the more the lift from the Bernoulli effect occurs. The second lift force is mechanical and occurs once the hand begins to press downward in the water, what is referred to as the *catch*. When the swimmer begins to press downward with the hand, the fingers and thumb should separate slightly to maximize the lift and they should remain spread during the propulsion phases that occurs later. A slight separation of the fingers and thumb will increase the drag caused by the moving hand, effectively increasing the surface area of the hand. Given the speed of a swimmer and the configuration and size of the arm and hand in the water, the Bernoulli effect likely causes significantly less lift force than the Newtonian mechanical effect of pressing downward.

The other important force that comes into play during the lift phase in freestyle is frontal drag, which has the effect of slowing the swimmer. One objective of swimming fast is to minimize the drag forces whenever possible. When the hand strikes the water, it is actually moving forward at a greater speed than the swimmer's body, since it is moving away from the body. Once in the water, however, with the arm completely submerged and fully extended, all parts of the arm are moving forward at the same speed as the swimmer's body. Once the hand begins to move downward in the water, the upper part of the arm is moving forward faster than the hand. This fact is important in understanding why the technique of a high-elbow pulling motion reduces frontal drag.

The drag caused from any part of the body in the water at a given time is proportional to the shape of that part of the body (drag coefficient), its surface characteristic (slipperiness) and the square of its forward speed. With respect to improving freestyle technique for reducing frontal drag during the lift phase of the pulling cycle, the two most important anatomical parts that deserve our attention are the upper arm and the hand/wrist.

Using a high-elbow pulling motion has the effect of keeping the upper part of the arm, which is the largest part, out of harm's way. By keeping the upper arm pointing more in the swimmer's line of motion, as we initiate the downward motion of the hand, we reduce the frontal drag caused by the upper arm. When comparing the position of the upper arm using an out-sweeping motion, an in-sweeping motion or a deeper pull, all of which cause the upper arm to stick out more from the body's line of motion, the high-elbow pulling motion is the most desirable with respect to lowering frontal drag.

Much has been written about the importance of using a high-elbow pulling motion, particularly in longer freestyle events. Little has been written about the position of the hand and wrist at entry, yet that is also important. When the hand enters the water and is moving forward, we want to minimize the frontal drag from the hand and the arm. We do so by initially keeping the arm straight with the wrist and the hand in alignment with the forearm, all of which are pointing forward. The fingers and thumb should be squeezed together before the hand enters the water and they should remain squeezed together, once they enter the water. To reduce frontal drag maximally from the hand during this early lift phase, the little finger should be rotated downward in hip-driven and hybrid freestyle techniques (on the breath side). Mykhailo Romanchuk demonstrates using this pinky-down technique in the 1500 meter final of the World Championships in 2018. Turning the pinky down will reduce lift, but more important, it will also reduce frontal drag. The *pinky-down* technique in freestyle can be used only with hip-driven or hybrid freestyle technique. With shoulder-driven freestyle technique, the downward force of the hand should begin immediately, so there isn't time to rotate the small finger downward after hand entry.

Here are some results of our studies using the PDM (APLab Italy) on how drag forces (measured in Newtons) at race speed (2.3 m/sec) are affected by different hand positions with one arm held out front under water. The results are compared to a palm-down with fingers and thumb squeezed together position, stiffened wrist with hand in alignment with the forearm. The lowest frontal drag hand position is with the little pinky down.

Hand position	Change in frontal drag force (adjusted for speed)
Fingers and thumb spread slightly	+ 2%
Wrist bent with hand flared to side	+ 2.3%
Wrist bent backward slightly	+ 13%
Wrist bent downward slightly	+ 12%
Little finger rotated downward (vertically)	-9.5%

Some coaches advocate angling the fingers downward and bending the wrist at hand entry with the palm down, which, according to our data, is not a good idea. That hand entry technique will add significant frontal drag. The best technique is to position the hand in the water with fingers and thumb squeezed together pointing forward, either palm down or, preferably, if time allows, pinky down.

Once the pulling or lift motion of the hand begins with a downward force (the *catch*), the swimmer should go from the palm-down, fingers-pointing-forward position to fingers-pointing-downward position as quickly as possible, with the hand just inside the elbow. The fingers and thumb should separate slightly to maximize the pulling force. When the hand begins moving downward or backward quickly through the water, the flow of water through the small spaces separating the fingers becomes turbulent, effectively increasing the surface area of the hand. If the fingers spread too far apart, the flow between them becomes laminar or smooth and results in a loss of propulsion. The larger the effective surface area of the hand, the more potential there is to increase propulsion.

The Propulsion Phase-Front Quadrant

As we observe the path of the swimmer's hand from the side, with the swimmer moving from left to right, the hand continues along the perimeter of the two-foot clock face going from 3 o'clock toward 6 o'clock. Now, the swimmer's hand is moving backward (and some downward) relative to the still water and begins generating propulsion. During the early (front quadrant) part of the propulsion phase, the hand and the forearm move backward relative to still water, while the upper arm continues moving forward. There is absolutely no contribution to propulsion coming from the upper arm in the front quadrant. Rather, the upper arm is a source of frontal drag during this phase.

Gary Sr. finishes the front quadrant propulsive phase in .21 seconds and moves into the back quadrant.

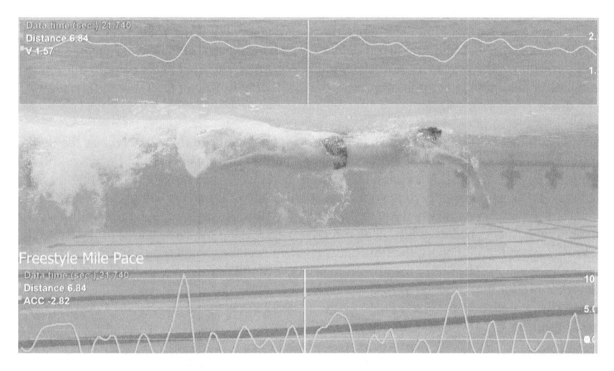

Zane Grothe is in the front quadrant phase of his right arm pulling motion. Notice the very high elbow to reduce frontal drag from the upper arm (VM technology).

During the early propulsion, it is correct to think of the hand and forearm as being a single unit, connected by a stiffened wrist. However, there is a widely held belief among swimmers and coaches that in this early propulsion phase, the forearm is responsible for as much or more of the propulsion as the swimmer's hand. That is not true. While we are not able to measure the propulsion coming directly from the forearm during the pull, there are three very good reasons why we believe that the hand contributes the large majority of propulsion from the pulling arm.

First, the hand is a relatively flat surface. While the forearm may be long and may have more surface area than the hand, it is rounded in shape. In fluid mechanics, the shape of the object is more important than the surface area in determining drag force. The flow of water around a flat surface will produce much more frontal drag than the flow around a rounded surface. To

52

generate the most propulsion, we want to maximize the drag force of the hand and arm moving backward to result in more speed of the body moving forward. Newton's third law of motion states that the swimmer's hand pushes backward against the water with the same force that the water pushes against the swimmer's hand. This results in the swimmer moving forward. One action will result in a reaction. This is a perfect example of Newton's third law.

Second, the hand is moving backward in the water at a greater speed than the forearm. The propulsive drag force is principally related to the type of surface (flat vs rounded), the total surface area and the speed at which that surface moves backward. The hand moves a farther distance backward under water than any other part of the arm in the same amount of time.

Third, and perhaps the most convincing, if you have ever tried swimming with your fists closed, you will find that the amount of propulsion generated from the pulling arm is greatly diminished. Even then, you are not eliminating the hand completely. You are simply making it smaller. Yet, with the same sized forearm moving at the same speed backward, the amount of propulsion a swimmer can generate from the small, tight-fisted hand is small. The full, flattened hand, with fingers and thumb slightly separated, is where most of the pulling propulsion comes from.

The swimmer's shoulder represents the boundary between the front quadrant and the back quadrant. When the pulling hand is in front of the shoulder, it is in the front quadrant. Once it passes the shoulder on its way backward, it enters the back quadrant. Since the hand does not enter the propulsion phase until it is about 1 – 1.5 feet in front of the swimmer's shoulder, the hand spends very little time in the propulsion phase while it is in the front quadrant (approximately .15-.21 seconds). Yet, it is an important phase.

Before we had Pressure Meter technology (PM from APLab Italy) that measures pressure (force/unit area) on the hand, we engaged in several debates with coaches over where the pulling hand generated the most propulsion—front quadrant vs back quadrant. From a biomechanical perspective, it would seem that the maximum force should be generated as the hand is somewhere near the shoulder on its way back. It turns out, the maximum force of the pulling hand can occur in either quadrant, or right at the shoulder, depending on where the swimmer puts more effort and how well the swimmer utilizes two important coupling motions of the body, shoulder rotation and hip rotation. In other words, it also depends on the freestyle technique being used.

These two rotational motions of the body have a profound influence on the propulsion of the pulling hand. They occur at different times. The peak shoulder rotational speed typically occurs when the hand is in the front quadrant, at, or just past the shoulder, depending on what freestyle technique is being used. The hip rotation occurs about .2-.3 seconds later when the pulling hand is nearing or is at the end of the back-quadrant phase and during the release phase. Whether you consider that the hip rotation occurs first or second depends on whether you are measuring from the start of the underwater pull or from the start of the arm recovery. Either way, it is important to recognize that these two parts of the body rotation do not occur simultaneously.

If the swimmer is rotating more aggressively with the shoulders, but maintaining a more stable hip position, we will find the greatest pulling propulsion occurring in the front quadrant or near the shoulders. If the swimmer pushes the hand hard out the back and rotates the hip aggressively, we can find the peak hand pressure or force occurring toward the end of the pulling propulsion phase or even in the release phase. The three different techniques of freestyle, shoulder-driven, hip-driven and hybrid, all result in different locations of maximum pulling force.

Finally, we would like to clarify one other point. We often hear coaches speak about swimmers finding 'clean water' with the pulling hand. To us, this implies that a swimmer somehow needs to move his hands from side to side, to get away from swirling water, to maximize pulling propulsion.

As the hand moves backward in the water, since water is incompressible, the water on the palm side of the hand is motionless until the hand reaches it. Then it must flow around that surface, forming a vortex behind it. The swirling vortex on the back side of the hand results in a small slipstream behind the hand, but not in front of it. Because the hand is a less-streamlined shaped object than the forearm, a larger vortex will be formed behind it. The pressure differential between the palm side and the back side of the hand or forearm is what determines the amount of propulsion. Since force is a vector, which has magnitude and direction, we want the direction of the force vector to remain as straight backward as possible during the pulling motion. Any in-sweeping, out-sweeping or sideways motion of the hand, which is typical of the S-shaped pulling motion that some swimmers use, will simply result in less magnitude of force pressing backward.

Distance freestyler Zane Grothe (left) uses a high-elbow pull with less propulsion and less frontal drag, while sprinter Margo Geer (right) pulls deeper with more propulsion and more frontal drag.

Once the hand passes the shoulder, or the 6 o'clock position on the perimeter of the clock, it enters the back quadrant and must take a little detour to keep pressing backward. Let us explain why.

The Propulsion Phase-Back Quadrant

As we follow the path of the hand relative to the still water on the imaginary 2-foot clock face, and with the swimmer moving from left to right, the hand reaches the back quadrant right around 6 o'clock. From this point, the hand takes a slight detour and leaves the perimeter of the clock. Instead, the hand and arm elevate some, cutting a little bit of the clock off and take a shorter path, more of a straight line, toward 9 o'clock. The reason the hand takes this detour is to continue pushing backward in the water for as long as possible. There is no advantage to a swimmer pushing upward in the water.

From 6 O'clock backward, Gary Sr.'s hand cuts the corner of the circle to continue pressing backward. He completes his back-quadrant propulsion in .21 seconds.

Zane Grothe is in the back quadrant of his pulling motion. To help keep the hand pushing backward the upper arm elevates and is now moving backward, also generating a small amount of propulsion (VM technology).

The amount of time that the hand spends in the **propulsion phase** in the back quadrant varies, depending on the stroke technique being used. With hip-driven or hybrid freestyle technique, which have slower stroke rates and where the swimmer pushes the hand harder out the back, the duration in this phase is longer, ranging from .28 -.34 seconds. With shoulder-driven freestyle, where more emphasis is placed on a faster stroke rate and an earlier release of the hand, the duration is approximately .21-.26 seconds.

With any freestyle technique, however, it is important for the swimmer to maintain the maximum force possible pushing backward with the hand and forearm in all four quadrants, two on the right arm and two on the left arm. Coaches refer to this as *holding water* for as long as the stroke rate permits. Most swimmers don't do that. At some point along the path backwards, they allow the hand to turn in, turn out, slide upwards or they overextend the wrist backwards (feathering), all of which lead to a loss of propulsion and speed. When a strong propulsive force is applied to the hand moving backward, it is virtually impossible to maintain the path in a perfectly straight line. The force applied to the hand will normally cause some excursion of it from side to side, but that lateral movement should not be much. Also, the upper arm must elevate in the back quadrant to avoid pushing upward with the hand.

At The Race Club we spend a great deal of energy and time trying to get the pulling motion right. From the hand entry all the way through the release phase of the pulling arm, we want to find the right balance between frontal drag and propulsion. The ideal pulling motion for a 50 sprint will be deeper than it is for an endurance event (high-elbow pull). For a short duration, a strong swimmer can sustain more frontal drag, while gaining more propulsion from the deeper pulling motion, and end up swimming faster. For any event longer than a 50 sprint, the importance of reducing frontal drag takes precedence over increasing the propulsion. The frontal drag forces of an incorrect pulling motion will wear a swimmer out very quickly. Drills such as the one-arm pulling drill, the high-elbow sculling drill, snap-paddle drill and six-kick-one-stroke drill all help swimmers to develop the correct pulling motion.

The amount of force or pressure applied with the hand in the back quadrant is also profoundly influenced by the speed of the swimmer's hip rotation. The hip rotation occurs .2-.3 seconds after the shoulder rotation, just after the end of the back-quadrant propulsion phase. Even if the two events do not coincide precisely, the hip rotation occurs so soon after the end of the back-quadrant propulsion that it can still augment that force. Pushing the hand harder out the back and rotating the hip more aggressively will slow the stroke rate resulting in more of a hip-driven or hybrid freestyle technique, rather than a shoulder-driven freestyle.

In the back quadrant, for the first time, the upper arm begins to move backward, although not at great speed. Therefore, the amount of propulsion generated by the backward-sweeping motion and elevation of the upper arm in the back quadrant is small.

Using Pressure Meter technology (PM from APLab Italy), which measures the pressure on the pulling hand, we have discovered that some swimmers will complete the propulsion phase by turning the hand upward, rather than continuing to press backward. In some cases, this upward pressure can be greater than all of the other time during the propulsive phase of the pull. There is no benefit to applying a strong force in an upward direction with the hand. The swimmer would be better served to put more effort into the propulsive phase with the hand moving backward.

Once the arm runs out of length, the propulsion from the pulling arm is completed. The next step in the pulling cycle is to bring the arm and hand forward out of the water, getting ready to take the next pull in front. We call this final under water arm motion the **release phase**.

The Release Phase

Once the propulsion phase of the pulling arm is completed, the objective of the swimmer is to release the arm and hand from the water, bringing them over the surface for another pull. Since the hand and arm start moving forward again, reducing frontal drag through this motion becomes a primary concern, particularly while they are still under water. On the face of the imaginary 2-foot clock, with the swimmer moving from left to right, the hand moves from the 9 o'clock position at the end of propulsion back to very near 12 o'clock, precisely where it began its underwater journey moments ago. The duration of the release phase is brief, .10 to .15 seconds, yet it is important.

Gary Sr. completes the circle with the release phase in .12 seconds, finishing right where he started the pull.

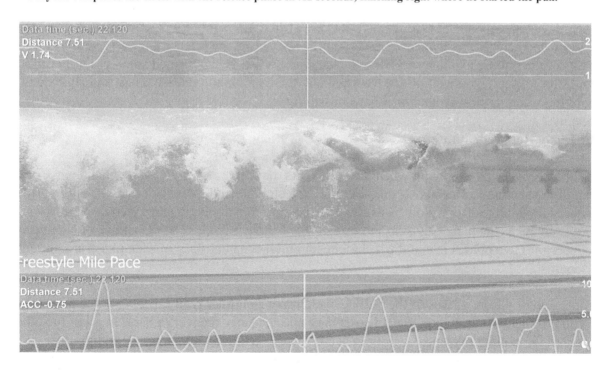

Zane Grothe is in the release phase of his right arm. He turns his little finger upward and slides the hand and arm forward, leading with the elbow, to cause as little frontal drag as possible (VM technology).

Depending on the type of arm recovery, there are two different release motions typically seen in elite freestylers. With a bent arm recovery (low octane), the elbow tends to lead the hand as it moves forward. With a straight arm recovery (high octane), the entire arm tends to leave the water as one unit and at the same time. In either release technique, once the propulsion phase is completed, the hand should turn sideways with the thumb down (or vertically) in the water to reduce frontal drag as it moves forward and leaves the water.

Not infrequently, we see swimmers try to hang on to their *grip* on the water too long and continue pressing upward with the hand as they release it. When this happens, from the deck, one can observe the swimmer's hand throwing water upward and to the side behind them. While pushing hard at the end of the propulsion phase is important, particularly with hip-driven and hybrid freestyle techniques, it is also important to know when to let go. At that point, the hand should turn sideways with the little finger up to release it with the least amount of frontal drag as it slides forward. From the time the release phase begins to the end of the early recovery (upward trajectory), the hand and wrist should go into a relaxed position. The relaxation of the wrist and hand during these two phases of the pulling cycle, no matter how brief they are, is important in allowing the muscles of the arm and back to recover for another pulling cycle.

We often refer to the technique of relaxing the hand and wrist during the release and early recovery phases as *the magic of the relaxed wrist.* Every elite freestyler, even sprinters, do that. Yet we find most beginner adult swimmers or triathletes are unable to let go and relax their wrists during these two important phases. Their arms look as if *rigor mortis* set in on the recovery, stiff and contracted. As a result, their pulling arms fatigue more quickly. They cannot sustain the strong forces through the pulling motions for long, which demand a lot of energy.

When done properly and at race speed, not every stroke offers any true recovery time. Freestyle, butterfly and backstroke do offer some brief arm rest during the release and early recovery phases of the pulling cycle, by relaxing the hand and wrist. When offered some vacation time, take it. It will serve you well. Relax the wrist and the hand on the release phase and slide them out of the water as cleanly and quickly as possible.

The Early Recovery Phase

The arm recovery phases begin when the hand exits the water and end upon the hand entry out in front of the swimmer. Depending on the freestyle technique and the stroke rate, the entire arm recovery time ranges from about .3 to about .4 seconds. We divide the arm recovery into two phases: **early,** as the hand elevates, and **late**, as the hand descends. The reason we divide the arm recovery into two phases is that the technique and biomechanics used in each phase are quite different.

In only two of the six phases of the pulling cycle can a swimmer really recover some from the exertion of the pulling motion, the release phase and the early recovery phase. In all of the other phases of the pulling cycle, the swimmer needs to be exerting a lot of force or energy to maximize propulsion. Great freestylers will take advantage of these two rest or recovery phases of the pulling cycle with some important techniques that are often not recognized nor replicated by less successful swimmers.

Zane Grothe demonstrates the *magic of the relaxed wrist* and hand during the early freestyle recovery phase. As a distance swimmer, Zane uses a bent elbow (low-octane) recovery technique.

In the release phase, we start the *magic of the relaxed wrist,* which continues through the early recovery. We cannot overemphasize the importance of relaxing the hand and wrist during the release and early recovery phases of the pulling cycle. Virtually every great freestyler does that. In fact, it is the relaxed hand and wrist during these two phases that are largely responsible for the effortless appearance of fast swimmers. Yet, under the water, they are anything but effortless.

The skeletal muscles of the human body have the ability to recover at an incredibly fast rate, hundredths of a second, if given the chance. That simply means if relaxed, the muscles can get ready quickly for another strong contraction. The release and early recovery phases combined, which range in duration from .25 seconds to .35 seconds, are more than enough time for the important pulling muscles to recover.

However, if the wrist and hand remain stiff and contracted during these two phases, the arm muscles will not recover as well nor as fast as when the hand and wrist are relaxed. This is a concept that is so natural to an adept swimmer, yet so difficult for a beginner swimmer or an early triathlete to learn. To become a great freestyler, a swimmer needs to know when and how to stiffen the hand and wrist to reduce frontal drag, how to *hold* the water with the hand pushing backward to maximize propulsion, and when and how to *let go* with the hand and wrist to hasten the arm muscle recovery.

To help teach swimmers how to relax their hands and wrists on the release and early recovery, we like using the *six-kick, one-stroke drill* with fins on. During this drill, we have the swimmer draw the elbow up vertically to an imaginary string extending directly upward from the swimmer's shoulder. Once the arm elevates to the string, with the shoulder rotated backward, the hand is at the peak height of its arched recovery motion. We then have the swimmer stop the motion of the arm at that imaginary string and simply dangle the wrist a few times. The dangling wrist, with the hand falling downward from gravity and fingers separated, is a sign that the swimmer has learned to *let go* with the hand and wrist. It is a sign of arm relaxation.

Once swimmers learn to chill out with the hand and wrist on the early recovery phase, they will appear more effortless, because they are using less effort. More important, they will recover and swim faster.

Both the path of the arm motion and the length of the arm during the recovery are important. The easiest way to recover the arm over the water is by bending the elbow and swinging the arm around to the side, with the hand barely clearing the water. This is the technique that many beginner swimmers use to conserve energy, but it is not the fastest way to swim.

If the arm takes a more vertical path, it is working against gravity on the way up, but it benefits from the gravitational force on the way down. If a swimmer straightens the arm on the recovery, doubling the length of the recovering arm compared to the bent elbow, it will require four times more energy or work to recover the arm at the same arm recovery speed. Why would we want to work against gravity or quadruple the amount of work on the arm recovery? There is only one reason and that is to increase speed.

To increase propulsion of the pulling arm, the most important time to increase the kinetic energy of the recovering arm is not in the early phase, but toward the end of the late phase, as the hand nears striking the water. It is not until the late recovery phase that the other hand is in the propulsion phase. Using a more vertical trajectory, increasing the downward arm speed (angular velocity) and lengthening (straightening) the arm will all result in an increase in the kinetic energy of the recovering arm at this critical moment. A more vertical recovering arm will also lead to greater shoulder rotation, which has the potential to increase the propulsion from the pulling arm.

At The Race Club, we like to use the analogy of comparing the length of the arm during the recovery with the additive used in gasoline for cars, octane. Octane at the gas station comes in three different levels, low (regular), medium (mid-grade) and high (premium). Arm recoveries also come in about 3 forms, completely bent (lowest energy), partly straightened or bent (middle energy) and straight (highest energy). High octane fuel, which is the most expensive gasoline, is designed to make high-combustion engines go faster. _High-octane_ recovery (straight arm) is designed to make high combustion swimmers (fast-twitch sprinters) swim faster. It also costs more in terms of energy requirement. _Low-octane_ recovery (bent arm) requires less energy but delivers less power (propulsion). Although not absolute, in general, _high-octane_ freestyle is a better recovery technique for sprinting and _low-octane_ freestyle recovery is a better technique for distance events. _Medium-octane_ recovery technique seems to be more suitable for middle distance events, like the 100 or 200 meters.

The Late Recovery Phase

The **late** phase of the arm recovery starts when the hand is at its highest point and is completed once the hand enters the water. It is the final phase and one of the most important in the complete pulling cycle. It is important because the technique used at the end of the arm recovery has a profound influence on the propulsion generated from the pulling hand. The technique used for the arm recovery also influences the amount of frontal drag that occurs during the lift phase that follows, once the arm enters the water.

Historically, there has been a misunderstanding about the best technique to use for the hand entry at the end of the arm recovery. Most of that misunderstanding stems from the misconception that air bubbles surrounding the hand under water are increased as a result of a forceful hand entry. Air bubbles behind the hand will certainly reduce the propulsion during the pull and should be avoided, if possible. The fewer the air bubbles surrounding the hand, the more potential to *hold water,* and get a stronger pull.

For years, in an effort to reduce the numbers of air bubbles behind the hand, many coaches have advocated a slower, delicate hand entry into the water. We call this technique the *modern toilet seat syndrome,* as the hand tends to slow down before entry, as if the arm had a spring hinge like the toilet seat that comes down very slowly. Others have advised sliding the hand into the water just above the head and then moving it forward under water to rid the hand of any air bubbles prior to the important lift and propulsion phases. We don't believe that either suggested technique is advisable.

The number of air bubbles surrounding a swimmer's hand underwater seems to have little to do with the speed of the hand entry. Some of the fastest swimmers in the world, swimming at very high speeds with aggressive hand entries, manage to avoid having many air bubbles at all behind the pulling hand. Poor swimmers, trying to be as delicate with their hand entries as possible, often end up with a virtual bubble bath behind the pulling hand.

How fast swimmers manage to avoid causing many air bubbles to form behind their pulling hands is one of the great mysteries of our sport. Many theories have developed, but the most plausible one is that fast swimmers have better proprioception (feel) for the water with their fingers. Nort Thornton, retired Head Coach from Cal Berkeley, believes that it is more specifically the proprioception from the Ulnar nerve, supplying sensation to the ring and little fingers, that determines a swimmer's ability to feel the water. Because of this extraordinary sensitivity in the fingers, or for whatever reason, elite swimmers instinctively get rid of air bubbles around their hands on nearly every stroke they take. Lessening the air bubbles following the path of the hand helps them to increase propulsion during those phases of the pull, to *hold water.*

Entering the hand earlier by sliding it into the water above the head is not a good idea, either. There is an enormous difference in density between air and water (some 800 times greater in water), so to reduce frontal drag, the hand and arm should be kept in the air for as long as possible. The best place to enter the hand into the water is with the arm fully extended and directly straight in front of the shoulder. Do not enter the hand just in front of the head, which causes more drag, nor fully extended forward in front of the head, which will lead to an out-sweeping pulling motion. An out-sweeping pulling motion causes more frontal drag, less propulsion and a zig-zagging body motion down the pool.

Now that we have dispelled those two myths, there are two very good reasons why swimmers should drive their recovering hands aggressively down through the water at the entry. First, the amount of kinetic energy found in the arm and hand as they approach the water directly impact the pressure or force of the pulling hand. We call this a coupling motion. As the recovering hand nears the water, the pulling hand with any freestyle technique (other than a catch-up freestyle) will be in the propulsion phase. The more energy there is in the recovering arm at that moment, the more propulsion can be generated by the pulling hand. Second, the speed at which the recovering arm strikes the water (angular velocity) is linked to the speed of the shoulder rotation. The faster the arm drives down to the water, the faster the shoulders will rotate. Because of the amount of mass in the upper body compared to the arm, a fast shoulder rotation will positively impact the pulling force more than the fast recovering arm. Since the two motions are linked together, however, a swimmer doesn't really need to worry about body rotation. By concentrating on driving the arms and hands hard down to the water from a more vertical recovery, the fast shoulder rotation will happen automatically. Slow the hand down at entry and so goes the shoulder rotation, slow. When used together with good technique, these two powerful coupling motions of arm recovery and shoulder rotation can turn an average swimmer into a much faster swimmer.

Finally, once the hands and arms enter the water, they should cause the least amount of frontal drag. That means that the hands should enter the water with the thumb down or the palm down and the thumb and fingers pointed forward, not tilted downward at the wrist. The fingers and thumb should be squeezed together with the wrist stiff, so the hands and arm stay in the same line as the body's direction of motion. The stiffening of the wrist and squeezing together of the fingers needs to happen before the hand enters the water, not after. In other words, the hands and wrist need to be relaxed on the way up, during the early phase of arm recovery, and stiffened with fingers squeezed together on the way down. If the fingers and wrist are relaxed at hand entry, the flow of water will cause the fingers and thumb to spread wider, or the wrist to flare to the outside or even worse, to bend backward. Contrary to what is often taught, the fingers should not be relaxed nor pointed downward toward the bottom of the pool at entry. The change in hand position from fingers-pointing-forward to fingers-pointing-down should occur during the transition from the lift phase to the propulsion phase, and as quickly as possible.

Zane Grothe starts to squeeze the fingers together and tighten the wrist during the late phase of his freestyle recovery. His hand will enter the water with his arm fully extended directly in front of his shoulder with his fingers pointing forward. His head will be under water to help reduce drag by the time the hand reaches the water.

In one complete pulling cycle, from hand entry to the following hand entry, the hand and arm have gone through six different phases. Each phase has a different purpose in the overall quest to find the ideal balance between pulling propulsion and frontal drag and get the swimmer the farthest down the pool possible with each stroke taken.

When learning the correct freestyle pulling and recovery techniques, please don't try to think of performing all six phases of the cycle at one time while you are swimming. If you do, you are likely to get them all wrong. Instead, focus on drills and swimming that will correct one or two phases at a time, perhaps using one arm at a time. Start with the lift and front-quadrant propulsion phases, then the back-quadrant propulsion phase, then the release and early recovery phases, then finally, the late recovery phase. In that manner, you will more likely end up with a great freestyle pulling and recovery technique.

In baseball, when a pitcher throws the ball at 90+ mph, with or without a certain amount of spin on it, there are an inordinate number of complex motor movements of the entire body that are required for that ball to arrive at the plate with pinpoint accuracy. The skill to accomplish that great pitch does not happen overnight. Neither does the skill to swim with perfect arm pulling and body motion for sustained speed and efficiency.

Get some coaching help and then practice, practice, practice. Fast swimming starts with great technique.

Helpful Drills for the Lift Phase

Snap Paddle Drill with fins, paddles and snorkel

One arm drill with small paddles, focusing on keeping the hand inside the elbow

Helpful Drills for the Propulsion Phases

One arm drill with fins and small paddles, focusing on holding pressure on the pulling hand straight backwards

6 Kick 1 Stroke drill with fins, focusing on getting as much distance per stroke possible

High-elbow sculling drill with snorkel, small paddles and fins

Helpful Drill for the Release Phase

One arm drill with fins, focusing on turning and releasing the hand at the end of propulsion

Helpful Drills for the Recovery Phases

Body rotation drill using fins and snorkel

6 Kick 1 Stroke drill focusing on vertical arm recovery and hard strike to the water for hand entry

Chapter 8

Freestyle Technique

Building a Faster Freestyle Kick

There are four basic functions of the freestyle kick. The first, and most important, is to generate **propulsion** for the freestyle swim. The second is to generate **lift** forces. Lift is also an important function because the legs do not float, at least for most people. Keeping the legs pointed backward in the line of the swimmer's motion and out of harm's way with respect to causing drag can help with overall speed, even when most of the propulsion is coming from the arms. The third function is to take advantage of the law of **inertia** by maintaining a more constant speed. A six-beat kick is needed to do that. The fourth is to provide some **balance** to the pulling motion and work in harmony with the pull.

We consider the kicking speed to be the baseline speed for the freestyle swimmer. In other words, the swimmer's speed starts with the kicking speed for whatever distance he is racing. A 50-meter kicking time determines the baseline freestyle speed (yards or meters per second) for a 50 sprint. A 1500-meter kicking time determines the baseline freestyle speed for the 1500. Once a swimmer determines his or her kicking speed for the race distance, he or she can calculate the contribution to the freestyle speed from the pull and coupling motions by subtracting the kicking speed from the swimming speed. Perhaps that is an over-simplification, but we think it is pretty close. Here is a story that defends that theory.

Several years ago, we were coaching a 34-year old sprinter from Northern Ireland, Andy Hunter, who was trying to qualify for the Commonwealth Games. His goal was to reach 23.0 for the 50-meter freestyle. His personal best time was 24.6 and we had 6 months to try to help him reach his goal. Dropping 1.6 seconds in a 50-meter sprint is like trying to drop a minute off of one's 1500 time. We were committed to try, and so was he.

He arrived from Ireland overweight, out of shape, not having trained seriously for seven years, and with a 50-meter kicking time of 50 seconds. We told him he wouldn't reach his goal of 23.0, unless he could kick 50 meters in 35 seconds or faster.

In one of the first swimming meets in Ft. Lauderdale after he had arrived, Andy swam the 50 meter free long course in the same heat as the world record holder, Cesar Cielo. Cesar swam a 22.0 that day and Andy finished the race about seven meters behind him, in 25.2. Andy left the pool feeling pretty dejected. He felt even worse after we showed him the video of the race, where he was around seven meters from the wall when Cesar finished.

"How in the world can he beat me by seven meters in a 50-meter race?" he asked. "How can that happen?"

We explained it to him this way. By the time he raced in Ft Lauderdale, Andy's kick time had dropped to 45 seconds, which is 1.1 meters per second. Cesar could kick the same distance in around 30 seconds, which is 1.67 meters per second. After adding in the pulling and coupling motions (stroke rate of 120/minute), Cesar boosted his swimming speed to just under 2.3 meters per second to swim 22.0. Andy boosted his swimming speed with a stroke rate of 140/minute to 1.98 meters per second to swim the same race in 25.2 seconds. In other words, Cesar added .6 meters per second to his baseline speed while Andy added nearly .9 meters per second to his baseline speed.

Good for Andy! Unfortunately, because his baseline speed was so low, he was still over .3 meters per second slower in overall speed than Cesar.

So I asked Andy, "How long was Cesar swimming?"

"22 seconds," he responded.

"And what is 22 x .3?" I asked.

"6.6 meters", he answered. That is precisely how far Andy was away from the wall when Cesar finished the race.

After 5 months of training and lots of ankle stretching and hard kicking sets, Andy improved his kicking time for 50 meters to 38 seconds, not quite what we wanted. In his shaved, tapered Championship meet, he swam a 23.2 for the 50 freestyle, just off of his goal time and narrowly missing making the Commonwealth Games. In spite of that, we were pretty proud of him and that bit of coaching.

In swimming, the kicking speed is often a game changer. The relative importance and overall contribution of the kick to a swimmer's total speed increases as the race event shortens. Virtually every elite sprinter has an awesome kick. Not all great distance freestylers do. However, it is important to try to improve your kicking speed in all freestyle races. It only makes you better. It is also the part of the freestyle technique that usually stands the most to gain.

Of course, like most things, kicking has a cost/benefit ratio. It is not easy to kick fast. Nor is it easy to kick slowly for those swimmers that don't have good kicking tools. If you're going to expend a lot of energy with the kick and not get much propulsion out of it, what is the point? You might as well pull your way through the race.

If you are serious about becoming a better swimmer, however, another option is to learn how to develop better kicking tools. Then, work really hard on getting your kicking legs fit. Neither of those tasks is easy, but we will try to point you in the right direction. It starts with understanding how the freestyle kick works.

Propulsion

Technically, there are really only two types of freestyle kicking techniques, a two-beat or a six-beat kick. Within each stroke cycle (hand entry to hand entry), the legs will either form a down kick once (two beat kick) or three times (six beat kick). However, there are many variations of the two beat and six beat kicks that often get used. For example, some swimmers will alternate stroke cycles between using a two-beat kick on one cycle, followed by a six-beat kick for the next cycle. A wider, more knee-bending two-beat kick is referred to as a *scissors* kick.

Some swimmers that use a six-beat kick, particularly in longer races, choose to accentuate only one of the three down kicks. That one, which we call the *surge kick*, typically occurs after the opposite hand has entered the water, and helps propel the swimmer forward. In between the surge kicks, the other two down kicks may be very soft or non-existent. In the middle of the 1500, Olympic champion Sun Yang from China was renowned for using two strong surge kicks with his hip-driven freestyle. One surge kick was followed by two very soft down kicks, and after the second surge kick, virtually no kicks at all were taken. Some would consider that a four-beat kick, but I believe it is just a variant of the six-beat kick.

Most elite freestylers today will use a six-beat kick for all races, particularly in shorter races. A two-beat kick is less propulsive, generates less lift and is less efficient. The only real advantage of it is that it requires less energy or work to do.

The mechanics of generating propulsion from the kick are very different from the pull. Unlike the water in front, beneath or to the side of the swimmer, where the water is perfectly still (at least in the pool), the water directly behind the swimmer, where the kicking propulsion takes place, is not. The flow dynamics of the kick and pull are very different. To generate propulsion, the hands must move backward relative to a fixed point in the pool. The feet do not need to move backward to generate propulsion. The motion of the feet in freestyle kick, where nearly all of the propulsion is taking place, is upward, forward and downward, but not backward. The reason that the feet, and to a smaller degree, the back of the calves, generate propulsion without moving backward in the water is because they play off of the vortices or eddy currents formed by the swimmer's body and feet moving through the water.

As the swimmer's body moves through water, as a non-streamlined object, a vortex or slipstream will follow the swimmer's path. The swimmer's feet also form vortices behind them as they move up and down and forward through the water. The feet of the swimmer change directions quickly going from down kick to up kick and pass through the two vortices formed by the body and the feet in their path.

Since the slipstreams are moving forward or toward the feet, the feet do not need to be moving backward to generate propulsion. In effect, relative to the water moving forward, the feet are moving backward. The greater the surface area of the feet and the faster they move through or against the vortices, the greater the propulsion.

In freestyle kick, there are two potential points in the kicking cycle where propulsion is generated leading to acceleration. The first is at the initiation of the down or up kicks, as the feet quickly reverse directions and push back against the vortices they caused. The second and greater potential propulsion is generated as the two feet pass each other through the body's vortex. The amount of the propulsion generated from the down kicking foot can be augmented greatly by the swimmer having extraordinary plantar flexibility and inversion of the ankle. If the ankle is able to turn inward (inverted or pigeon-toed), then the downward kicking foot traverses the slip stream at more of a right angle, which improves propulsion even more. One of the essential tools of developing a fast freestyle kick is having this extraordinary inverted or pigeon-toed plantar ankle flexibility.

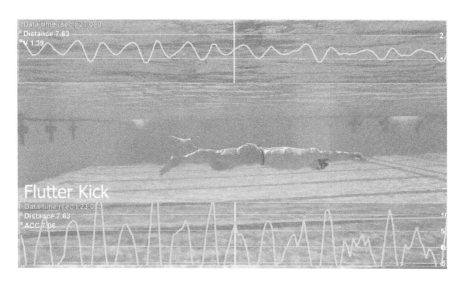

Elite swimmer Josh Zuchowski accelerates at the initiation of the up and down kicks (graph below at center line using VM technology).

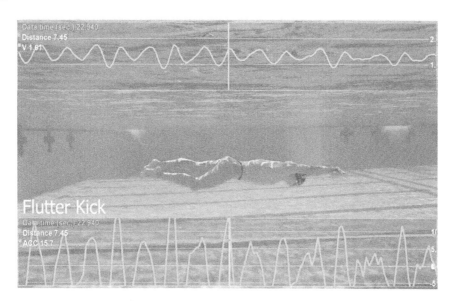

Josh Zukowski accelerates even more (graph below at center line) as the two feet pass each other and traverse the body's vortex (VM technology).

In freestyle kicking there is also one point where there is significant deceleration, where the drag forces are maximized from the kicking motion. The drag forces increase as a result of the lower leg drawing forward with the knee bent and foot hanging at the end of the down kick. Both of these motions occur at the same time and cause considerable deceleration. Unfortunately, when swimmers do not have enough ankle flexibility, their tendency is to over-bend the knee to get more propulsion. We call that kicking technique, *trying to hit the 50-yard field goal.* It doesn't work out well.

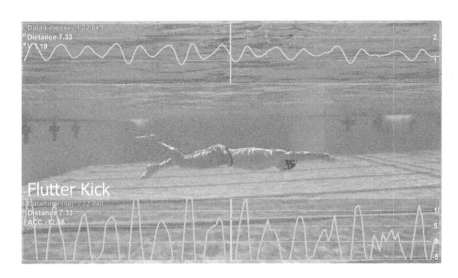

Josh Zuchowski decelerates significantly (graph below at center line) from drawing his right leg forward and allowing his left foot to hang too long (VM technology).

In looking at the velocity curves on the graph above and the acceleration and deceleration curves on the graph below, we found that with the drawing of the right leg forward, Josh's knee bend was about 5 degrees greater on that side than with the left leg. That led to greater deceleration and loss of velocity. When the knee bend goes much beyond 70 degrees, the deceleration is usually too great, leading to loss of efficiency and speed. A few times during the test, his slowest velocity fell below 1 m/sec. While the acceleration was also greater on the subsequent right down kick, it was not enough to offset the loss of speed. The average difference between Josh's trough (slowest) and peak (fastest) velocity with the right leg (ΔPT) was much greater than with his left leg. The greater swing in velocity caused by excessive knee bend in Josh's right leg is a slower and less efficient kicking technique.

	Flutter Kick									
Time	RT	Time	RP	Difference	Time	LT	Time	LP	Difference
21.80	1.15	21.88	1.66	0.51	21.98	1.15	22.08	1.75	0.60
22.16	0.86	22.24	1.66	0.80	22.32	1.16	22.42	1.67	0.51
22.52	0.83	22.58	1.76	0.93	22.66	1.05	22.78	1.70	0.65
22.88	0.94	22.94	1.61	0.67	23.02	1.16	23.14	1.58	0.42
23.24	1.01	23.32	1.53	0.52	23.40	1.19	23.54	1.62	0.43
23.62	0.88	23.70	1.50	0.62	23.82	1.18	23.94	1.41	0.23
24.04	0.97	24.10	1.48	0.51	24.20	1.16	24.30	1.42	0.26
24.42	0.92	24.50	1.48	0.56	24.60	0.96	24.70	1.48	0.52
24.82	0.97	24.90	1.46	0.49	24.96	1.05	25.10	1.41	0.36
25.20	0.81	25.28	1.52	0.71	25.38	1.00	25.48	1.37	0.37
25.60	0.89	25.68	1.52	0.63	25.78	0.97	25.86	1.43	0.46
AVG	0.93		1.56	0.63	AVG	1.09		1.53	0.44

Josh Zuchowski's freestyle kick VM data. RT is Right Trough velocity. RP is Right Peak velocity. Difference (ΔPT) is between the peak and trough velocity and is related to the amount of propulsion generated from that kick. LT and LP is the data for the Left Trough and Left Peak velocities.

Lift

The propulsion generated by the down kick is greater than that generated by the up kick when the swimmer is on his stomach. The lift force of the down kick is also greater than the opposing force of the up kick. The net effect of those two unequal forces is to maintain the legs at the surface while swimming. When the legs are kept in line with the upper body the frontal drag force caused from the swimmer's body position will be lessened, compared to when the legs are hanging down some.

Inertia

To maintain a more even and steady velocity, which improves the mechanical efficiency of the kick, the legs must work in both directions. The two major causes of excessive deceleration, overbending of the knees and allowing the foot to hang too long after the down kick, will result in a loss of mechanical efficiency in freestyle kicking.

Balance

The propulsion generated by the swimmer's kick and pull are not centered on the long axis of the body. Rather they are off-centered slightly on each side. As a result, to keep the forward motion more linear, the pulling propulsion coming from the left arm must be balanced to some degree by the propulsion coming from the opposite leg. In breaking a world record in the 200-meter backstroke by several seconds (the record still stands today), Aaron Piersol spoke of the synchronous balance and harmony that he experienced in his body during that extraordinary swim. Because the arms and legs in freestyle and backstroke do not move in unison, some balance of the forces is needed with both strokes.

Building a Faster Freestyle Kick

To kick freestyle fast requires that the swimmer have extraordinary pigeon-toed, plantar flexibility of the ankles. The foot needs to not only be extremely pointed from the ankle, but also turned inward (inverted). A bigger, wider foot with that type of ankle flexibility is also advantageous, but not essential. Elite women, without having giant feet, have recorded some of the fastest kicking times. One other anatomical tool that is characteristic of fast kickers is hyper-extension of the knees. The hyper-extension of the knee joint enables the kicker to continue the motion of the down kick farther than normal, generating more propulsion. The only way we know of to develop hyperextension of the knees is from years of kicking in the pool, often with laxity in the knee joint.

In addition to these anatomical tools, a fast freestyle kick requires tremendous strength in the hip flexors and extensors, as well as the knee extensors. There is really not a single leg muscle, nor lower back muscle, nor core muscle that is not used in the freestyle kicking motion. It is just that we don't use that same kicking motion in almost anything else we do on land. One can improve the strength of the kick with dryland exercises and strength training. However, to develop a faster kick, there is no substitute for lots of kicking in the water.

Finally, to kick fast, the legs need to be extremely fit. When using a six-beat kick, the legs are constantly moving up and down, with no rest in-between. With a pulling stroke rate of 60 strokes/minute (hip-driven) using a six-beat kick, the kicking stroke rate is 360 kicks/minute, including both up and down kicks. If the stroke rate is 90/minute, then the kicking stroke rate is 540 kicks per minute. That is a lot of kicking motion. To keep that going for long, the legs had better be fit. To develop that kind of fitness in the legs, there is again no substitute for lots of kicking.

Building the anatomical tools, leg strength and leg fitness to become a faster kicker takes time and commitment. But it can be done. If you want to make that commitment, here are some suggestions on how to do it.

Developing Freestyle Kicking Tools

Increasing plantar flexibility and inversion of the ankles is not as difficult as it may sound. The ligaments in the anterior ankle joint are small and can be stretched quickly with appropriate dryland exercises. We have seen swimmers with very stiff ankles develop reasonably good ankle flexibility within a few weeks with the right stretches.

To test the plantar ankle flexibility, get into the freestyle squat position. On a heavily padded mat, place your lower legs on top of the mat with the toes pointed back and inward (pigeon-toed). The tops of your feet should be resting on the mat. Your upper legs and body should be erect. Now bend your knees maximally and allow your bum to go back as far as possible toward your feet. Ideally, you want your bum to be touching your heels. If you get pain in your knees doing this, then create a spacer, such as a big pillow, kick board or towel, to go between your heels and your bum.

With your hands in your lap (not touching the ground), lift your knees off the ground as high as you can and balance them in the air, while keeping the tops of your feet on the mat. The angle formed between the ground and your bent legs in the air is a good measure of your plantar flexibility. Fast freestyle kickers will have their knees high in the air, forming an angle greater than 50 degrees. The highest angle that we have seen formed in this position is about 80 degrees.

You could be like some swimmers that will not be able to elevate their knees into the air at all in this squat position. That means we have a lot of work to do to develop your freestyle kick. If that is the case, while doing the static stretches, lean your upper body backwards and place your hands on the ground behind you. By supporting yourself with your arms, you should now be able to keep your knees off the ground. You may not be able to endure for 2 minutes on the static stretch, but start with as long as you can and build up to 2 minutes in this position. Soon you will be able to elevate your knees without any help from your arms.

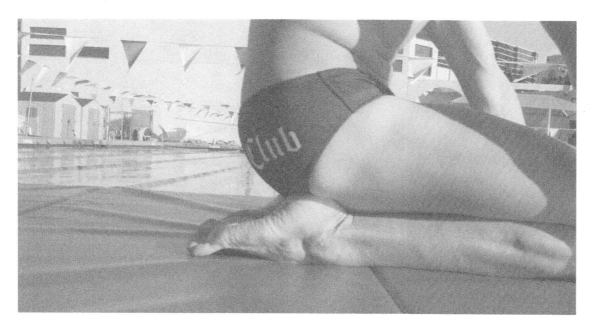

Elite swimmer David Gamburg demonstrates the freestyle squat position.

Test of plantar flexibility by balancing with knee elevation off the mat. Fast kickers, like David, will get the knee angle over 45 degrees off the mat. Hold this static position on the tops of your feet for 2 minutes to improve plantar flexibility.

If your knees hurt in the freestyle squat position, then use some spacers like these two kickboards to alleviate the stress on the knees.

You may even need to support yourself with your hands behind you to get your knees off the ground. Try to hold the position for as long as possible.

Static stretch: In the freestyle squat position, with knees elevated as high off the ground as possible, hold the position for 2 minutes. If you feel pain in the tops of your feet, you are doing the right stretch. If you should feel pain in the knees, however, be sure to place a spacer between your bum and heels until the knee pain disappears. If you do this stretch daily, you will begin to see improvement within days.

Dynamic stretches: There are two dynamic stretches that we like to use at The Race Club to increase plantar flexibility of the ankles. One is called *freestyle squat pushups* and the other is called *freestyle squat standups*. The latter should be done only with those that have developed extreme plantar flexibility.

Freestyle squat pushups start with you on a padded mat in the freestyle squat position. Place your hands on the mat palms down in front of your knees. The closer you get your hands to the knees, the more difficult the exercise becomes. If you aren't sure, start with your hands farther away from your knees on the mat. You can always bring them closer, if you are able to.

Start the stretch by elevating your bum off of your knees while simultaneously placing more weight on your hands. Continue elevating your bum higher until your legs are completely straightened, while still remaining on the tops of your feet on the mat. Don't allow your feet to flip over. The idea is to create an A position supported by your hands and the tops of your feet. If you are unable to completely straighten your legs, then move your hands farther away from your knees until you can. After reaching the A position, bring your bum all the way back to your heels and repeat the process. We recommend doing 20 freestyle squat pushups daily in addition to the 2-minute static stretch.

Freestyle squat pushups. David pushes up from the squat position to having his legs completely straight, resting on the tops of the feet, supported by the arms.

To be able to do this freestyle pushup with the hands so close to the feet requires extremely (plantar) flexible ankles.

The *freestyle squat stand-up* is a challenging exercise and should not be attempted without having extreme ankle plantar flexibility. In this exercise, the swimmer starts in the freestyle squat position. Using the tops of the feet as the source of pressure, the entire body is elevated vertically off of the ground into a standing position. If the arms are held above the head in a streamline position, it becomes even more difficult. This exercise adds additional stress on the ankle plantar flexion and also builds strength in the knee and hip extensors.

Freestyle squat standups. Only those swimmers with extremely flexible ankles should attempt this stretch/exercise. It also requires and builds leg strength to do properly.

Dryland

While replicating the exact kicking motions in the gym are difficult, any exercise that builds power in the knee and hip extensors and hip flexors or core will help your kicking. Examples include knee extensions (from 60 degrees, not 90 degrees), prone straight leg lifts (up kick), straight leg and bent knee fast leg kicks (flick kicks, supine on back) and balance ball freestyle kicks.

Doing one minute of flick kicks builds core strength and leg strength and loosens ankles.

One minute of balance ball flutter kicks from plank position closely replicates the kicking motion in water.

Biomechanics and Fitness

Try to avoid the two most common causes of excessive frontal drag (deceleration) in freestyle kicking—over-bending of the knees before the down kick and letting the feet hang too long at the end of the down kick. Without having much plantar flexibility in the ankle, you won't get much propulsion on the down kick without excessive knee bend, so you must try to develop that first. For the up kick, point the toes backward as soon as you can at the end of the down kick and work the leg and bottom of your foot upward to gain propulsion. The faster you can move your feet and body through the water, the stronger the vortices that you have to push against or through. To learn to kick with a tighter motion, try placing an elastic band around both legs below the knees. It may slow you down some, but hopefully, it will motivate you to get more ankle flexibility.

There are literally hundreds of kicking sets and strategies in the pool to develop your kicking fitness. They are all good. In general, based on the higher energy demands of a steady, propulsive six-beat kick, compared to the pulling arms, the legs are often undertrained. In training elite swimmers, we insist on doing two complete kicking-focused workouts per week. The only swims we will do in those sessions are warm up, recovery and warm down. The rest is hard kicking. We are not big fans of using a conventional kick board, as it puts the swimmer into a poor body position, yet we will take any kick sets we can get. Instead, we prefer kicking with an alignment board and snorkel, as they create better body position and help the streamlining. We also like to get creative with kick sets, so our swimmers don't get bored. Here are five of our favorite creative kick sets.

Kick Set #1 Alignment Board and Snorkel

20 x 75 meters hard freestyle kicking using alignment board and snorkel. Hold a tight streamline. Take 15 seconds of rest between each hard 75 meters.

Using an alignment board and snorkel improves the body position for kicking work.

Kick Set #2 Wall Kicks

5 x 45 second hard wall kicks using a snorkel. Place the head down and with arms straight and hands holding the wall firmly, kick into the wall as hard as you can. After each 45 seconds of hard kicking, take 15 seconds rest and start again. You should feel the quadriceps burning in the final 15 seconds of each set.

World class swimmer Zach Hayden pounds hard freestyle kicks against the wall for 45 seconds.

Kick Set #3 Vertical Kicks

5 x 45 second vertical kicks with fins on, arms either held in streamline position above the head or elbows at the surface of the water. Take 15 seconds rest after each 45 second kick and go again. You will need a pool at least 6 feet deep to do this one.

Using fins, Zach Hayden keeps his chin above the water in a streamline position for 45 seconds.

If you can't manage a streamline position, then place your elbows at the surface for the 45 seconds of vertical kicking.

<u>Kick Set #4</u> Tug-o-War Kicking

5 x 45 second tug-o-war kicking competition. Cut a ¾ inch PVC pipe to 18 inches. With snorkels on, one swimmer grabs the center of the PVC pipe, while the other swimmer places the hands on the outside of the PVC pipe. Starting in the middle of the pool, the two swimmers kick toward each other, while holding the arms straight and keeping the PVC pipe at the surface. After 45 seconds, the swimmer that kicks the other backwards is the winner of that match. The two swimmers have 15 seconds to return to the middle of the pool to start the next one. Best out of five is the winner. Regardless of the age or size of the swimmers, the match can be evened between the two by adding one fin or two for the weaker kicker.

Olympian Roland Schoeman and World Champion Junya Koga get after it in a kicking tug-o-war.

The kicking tug-o-war set will bring out the best competition in swimmers, kicking to exhaustion.

Kick Set #5 Kicking with Weights

20 x 25 meters using a snorkel, holding 5-10 pounds of weights in both hands under your chest. Kick hard 25 meters with head down. Try to keep at the surface so you can breathe through your snorkel. Take 15 seconds of rest after each 25 kick.

World Champion Junya Koga uses 10 pound weights clutched to his chest for 25 meter sprint kicks.

In summary, remember that kicking speed is the game-changer in freestyle. Test your kicking speed at least once per month for a 50-meter, 100-meter or longer race. Get motivated, get working and start building a better freestyle kick for a faster swim.

Chapter 9

Freestyle Techniques

Arm Recovery Techniques

In freestyle, we often see three very different techniques of arm recovery. One is with the arm bent completely. The second is with the arm bent partly. The third is with a straight arm. We also see some swimmers swing the arm around to the side more on the recovery, while others recover with their arms more vertically, coming over the top.

How the arm recovers will determine how much energy or work is required to bring the hand back in front of the swimmer, readying for another pull. It also will determine how much kinetic energy the arm has at impact with the water, which is delivered or coupled with the underwater pulling hand and kick.

It would seem logical that we would want to expend the least amount of energy possible to bring the arm and hand over the water in freestyle. After all, there is no propulsion in that motion. Or is there? It turns out, the energy of the recovering arm in the late phase of the recovery, as it nears the water, has a profound influence on the propulsion of the pulling hand and the kick.

The amount of kinetic energy in the rotating arm, moving in a circular motion, is proportional to its mass, its length (squared) and its angular velocity (squared). We cannot change the mass of our arms very easily, but we can change the length and angular velocity of the recovering arm.

If we go from a completely bent arm, also called a high-elbow recovery, to a straight arm on the recovery, we are effectively doubling the length of the arm (radius of the circular motion). That will increase the amount of work in the recovery by four times. If we double the angular velocity (rotational speed) of the recovering arm, that would also increase the amount of work by four times. If we make both of those changes, it will increase the work in the recovery by 16 times!

There is only one reason to make the arm recovery harder and that is to increase our swimming speed. We are back to the cost/benefit ratio involved in the arm recovery. In sprint events that depend on greater speed, it absolutely makes sense to maximize the kinetic energy of the finishing recovery arm by lengthening it and increasing the stroke rate. In distance freestyle events, it would make more sense to conserve energy on the recovery by bending the elbows, perhaps just popping the hand into the water with a little more force at the end when it really helps the propulsion. In middle distance events, like the 100 and 200 meters, both the length of the arm and the rotating arm speed should be somewhere in the middle.

For the most part, that is precisely what we see among the elite freestylers. Sprinters use straight arm, or nearly straight arm, fast recoveries. Distance swimmers bend the elbows and slow their recovering speed. Middle distance swimmers are somewhere in between. Of course, there are exceptions. Janet Evans and Lea Smith, two elite distance freestylers, used or use straight arm recoveries all the way up to the 1500 meters, for example. Other elite swimmers have used different recovery techniques with each arm. Lotte Friis from Denmark and Cesar Cielo are two good examples.

At The Race Club, as I explained in Chapter 7 on the phases of the arm pulling cycle, we like to use the analogy of octane levels found in gasoline to describe the recovering arm motions. A completely bent elbow is referred to as *low-octane* recovery. Straight arm is considered *high-octane* recovery. Some bend in the elbow is considered *medium to medium-high-octane* recovery.

The amount of work in the arm recovery is also influenced by the angle of the arm as it comes around to the front. The lower the arm angle has to the water, the easier the recovery becomes. Many swimmers swing their arms around to the side during the recovery because they know it is easier. We don't recommend that technique for any distance of race for two reasons.

When we recover the arm more vertically, we are working against gravitational force on the way up, but on the way down, we get to use gravity to our advantage. Since we are trying to maximize the energy of the recovering arm at the water's impact, using gravity will help us do that.

Second, regardless of how much we bend our arm during the recovery or what the distance of the race is, if we bring the arm more vertically on the recovery, we must rotate our shoulders back more in the process to accomplish that motion. When we come down hard with the recovering arm, we will now rotate the shoulders faster and farther to prepare for the next arm recovery. The speed of the rotating shoulders has even more influence on the propulsion of the pulling hand and kick than the arm recovery does.

The vertical arm recovery increases our speed at any distance. The energy/propulsion (cost/benefit) ratio for using vertical arm recovery compared to swinging the arm forward to the side is well worth it at any distance.

The following is a brief summary of which octane level we believe freestylers should use with their arm recoveries. All of these recoveries should be done more vertically.

Low Octane Recovery

Low-octane recovery is best suited for distance events, 400 meters or more. It can be used in hip-driven, shoulder-driven or hybrid freestyle technique. The stroke rates used with low-octane recovery may range from 50 to 100 per minute, but even with a slower stroke rate using this recovery, the swimmer can accelerate the hand speed right before the entry to accentuate the coupling energy. That is an excellent way to get more benefit from a more energy-conserving recovery technique.

American record holder Zane Grothe uses a low-octane vertical recovery on his distance freestyle technique.

Medium to Medium High Octane Recovery

We like using this arm recovery technique for the 100 meter and 200-meter freestyle events, where more power and speed are required. The arm should still recover vertically, with the hand being somewhere above the height of the elbow, not below it. Coming from this higher vertical position will enable the swimmer to strike the water with greater energy than a lower hand position.

Olympian Jimmy Feigen uses a vertical medium-octane arm recovery in powering his way to the 100-meter freestyle.

High Octane Recovery

The high-octane freestyle recovery is used primarily as a sprint freestyle technique. We also believe it is an excellent technique to finish any freestyle race, regardless of the distance. In 2008, Coach Mike Bottom taught Olympic gold medalist Nathan Adrian to use medium-octane freestyle through 90 meters of his 100-meter race. At 90 meters, he then had Nathan switch to high-octane freestyle with no breath to the finish. His stroke rate also went higher at the finish. Nathan has won more close races, including his Olympic gold medal in 2012, by using that finishing technique than any swimmer we know. Many other swimmers have since adopted the technique of finishing their races with high-octane freestyle recovery.

Olympian Brad Tandy uses a powerful high-octane, vertical arm recovery to sprint a 50-meter freestyle.

In summary, while there are rationales for using different freestyle arm recovery techniques, in the end, you should choose the recovery technique that works best for you. In swimming technique, there are always exceptions to the rule. There is no rule, however, that states you must use the same arm recovery technique with each arm in any race. Nor is there a rule that states you cannot change arm recovery techniques during the race.

Whatever arm recovery technique you decide to use, be sure to practice with drills and training, so that you are confident in your ability to sustain it.

Helpful Drills - these can be done for every octane level and should be done with fins and snorkels:

6 kick switch drill

6 kicks/1 stroke drill

6 kicks/3 strokes drill

Chapter 10

Freestyle Techniques

Coupling Motions

A term swimming coaches often refer to when discussing good technique is *connecting*. In fact, it is not just in the sport of swimming that the word *connecting* is used. Coaches of baseball, golf, tennis, gymnastics, soccer and many other sports use the same term. When coaches explain the term *connecting* to their athletes in whatever sport, they are typically demonstrating one motion of their body, such as a pulling motion or arm swing, while referring to the simultaneous motion of another part of the body, such as the shoulders, hips or core.

Athletes understand what *connecting* means. They understand that when they are *connecting* with certain body motions, they somehow harness the energy from these other motions to get more power, more speed, more distance per stroke than when they are not. Why *connecting* works, however, is a little more mysterious. From a physics standpoint, we'd like to provide an explanation of why *connecting* in swimming really works.

In the real world, we all live in an open system. That simply means that our bodies can interact with and respond to external forces. In swimming, for example, our arms come down more easily on the recovery because of gravity. We leave the wall on a turn or a starting block quickly by pushing off forcefully with our feet. We slow in the water almost as quickly as we leave the wall because of the drag forces acting on us. Those are examples of external forces, but what about inside our own body?

Inside our body, there is also interaction of all of the parts, since they are all connected. It wouldn't seem possible that by lifting your right arm that would have any effect on your left toe, but it does to some small degree. Though it is a long way from your right arm to your left toe, they are connected through the body.

In Chapter 1, in our discussion about physics, we explained that nearly all of the propulsion of a swimmer comes from the surface of the hands and feet moving through the water. Swimmers only have so much strength in their arms and legs to push their hands and feet through the water and generate propulsion. The question is, with the given strength that a swimmer has in the arms and legs, can he or she somehow increase propulsion by moving other parts of the body? The answer is *yes*.

We call these motions of our body that augment the propulsion *coupling motions*. For them to work, these specific coupling motions must be timed or coupled closely with the propulsion. If they are not, they don't work.

Second, the coupling motions by themselves generate no propulsion, whatsoever. If swimmers perform coupling motions on the surface of the pool or underwater, they can do them all day long and they won't move one inch down the pool.

Finally, the coupling motions cannot do excessive harm, like increase frontal drag, that would cause the swimmer to slow down. It wouldn't make sense to put energy into motions that made a swimmer slower, would it?

There is a cost to using coupling motions. It is called work. The more work we put into the coupling motions, or the more kinetic energy we create in those motions, the more coupling effect we will get with the propulsion. Now, we must not only train the muscles that generate propulsion, we must also train the muscles that create coupling motions. Swimming just got harder, not easier. Yet, it also got faster.

When explaining coupling motions in our Race Club camps, the example we like to use is in walking. While walking, our arms don't hang down by our sides. They swing back and forth. The arm swinging does not generate any propulsion for the walker. That all comes from the feet pushing off of the ground. However, as the arm swings backwards, it always reaches its peak energy level (at the bottom of the swing) precisely as the foot pushes off the ground. The result is that the kinetic energy from the arm swinging actually increases the propulsion from the foot pushing off the ground. We get farther down the path with each step by swinging our arms than by letting them hang. When we run, we swing our arms even harder, generating even more propulsion from the feet.

In freestyle, there are two principal coupling motions, body rotation and the arm recovery (late recovery phase). The body rotation is separated into shoulder rotation and hip rotation, as the two parts of the body rotate at different times. Each rotation influences the pulling propulsion at a different phase of the pulling motion.

Arm Recovery

In Chapter 7, with the six phases of the pulling cycle, we discussed how the amount of kinetic energy in the recovering arm during the late phase of the recovery impacts the pressure in the pulling hand. Since the pulling hand does not get into the propulsion phase until the recovering arm is approaching the water, the amount of energy in the recovering arm prior to that point is far less important. We also discussed the important and direct link between the speed of the recovering arm and hand, as they approach the water, and the speed of the shoulder rotation. The faster the hand is moving when it strikes the water, the faster the shoulder rotates.

Because these two motions occur simultaneously, we cannot be certain how much contribution each individual motion is making to the added pulling pressure, but it doesn't really matter. It is a package deal; buy one get one free. That is good, because a swimmer doesn't need to worry about trying to accomplish two things at once. Of the two motions, we find it much easier to concentrate on driving the hand down hard to the water than to concentrate on rotating the shoulders quickly. **If a swimmer drives the hands down hard,** the fast shoulder rotation will happen automatically. Working together, if the energy is significant, the two motions will make a considerable difference in a swimmer's propulsion and speed. In the cost/benefit ratio analysis, this one is definitely worth the extra work involved.

Elite sprinters will drive their hands to the water so forcefully, they will create a 3-foot high splash at entry.

Shoulder Rotation

In Chapter 7, we also discussed the importance of recovering the arms vertically in freestyle, as opposed to swinging them lower and around to the sides. One of the main reasons for doing so is to force the shoulders to rotate backwards farther on each side. If the shoulder rotation is farther, faster and lasts longer, then more kinetic energy can be coupled with the pulling hand and kick.

Using Pressure Meter technology, we are now able to measure simultaneously the pressure on the pulling hand, the amount of body rotation to each side and the speed of the body rotation (angular velocity) in both directions. This technology enables us to correlate the speed of both shoulder and hip rotation to the pulling propulsion.

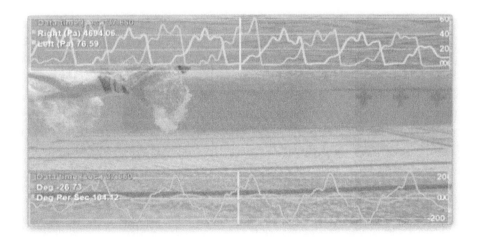

American record holding freestyler Zane Grothe, using PM technology, shows the nearly simultaneous peaks of shoulder rotation (graph below at center line) and right-hand pulling pressure (graph above at center line).

At The Race Club we have a series of progressive drills teaching faster body rotation and more aggressive arm/hand entry. Our favorite drill is the six kick/one stroke drill with fins on, where we emphasize the vertical arm recovery and driving the recovering hand quickly down to the water. This drill helps improve the arm recovery motion and the shoulder rotation.

Hip Rotation

The peak hip rotation occurs after the peak shoulder rotation. The two events are separated by about .2-.3 seconds. They are both important and, depending on how much energy is put into each one, they can largely influence the pulling pressure at that moment. Typically, we will find greater hip rotational speed while using the hip-driven or hybrid freestyle techniques. With the slower stroke rates of those two freestyle techniques, there is simply more time to rotate the hips than there is with the faster stroke rate of shoulder-driven freestyle.

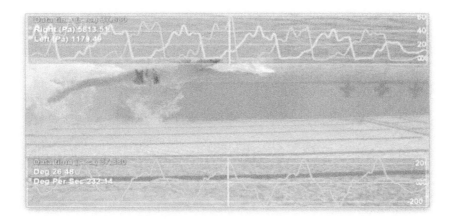

Zane Grothe uses a hybrid freestyle technique pushing hard out the end of each stroke. His peak hip rotational speed (graph below at center line) coincides exactly with the peak pressure of his right hand (graph above at center line).

There are many drills and training devices that will help increase hip rotational speed. Unfortunately, unless a swimmer really focuses on rotating the hips aggressively and pushing the hand backwards firmly at the end of the pull, neither will likely happen.

One of our favorite drills for improving hip rotational speed is a 30 second freestyle swim against the wall at the end of the pool. While one hand is held in front pushing against the wall, the other hand takes a freestyle stroke under water. At the end of that stroke, the hip snaps completely vertically to the same side. After one stroke, the hand recovers over the water toward the wall. Then another stroke is taken with the other arm, snapping the hip aggressively at the end.

After 30 seconds of wall swimming, snapping the hips from one side to the other, the swimmer makes a turn and swims a 50 freestyle, emphasizing the hand pushing hard out the back of the pull and rotating the hips quickly. This drill is preferably done with a snorkel and fins.

In summary, the next time you hear someone talk about *connecting* in freestyle, we hope that you will think about the two important coupling motions of arm recovery and body rotation. They are the parts of your body that are doing the connecting to your pull and kick.

If you are focusing on shoulder-driven freestyle technique with a higher stroke rate, don't worry so much about your hip rotational speed. Instead, focus on a vertical arm recovery with an aggressive driving of the hand down to the water with your arm fully extended at impact. That technique will increase your shoulder rotational speed.

If you are focusing more on a hybrid or hip-driven freestyle technique, then utilize some drills that will increase your hip rotational speed and the propulsion at the end of your pulling stroke. You will also need to spend some time working on the aggressive hand entry from a vertical position, which will also give you faster shoulder rotation. With either technique, your stroke rate will be slower than with shoulder-driven freestyle, so you must get as much propulsion from each stroke as you possibly can. That means using a fast finish to the arm recovery, quick shoulder rotation and aggressive hip rotation with a strong finish to your pull.

Regardless of the freestyle technique you choose, recognize the value of using strong coupling motions. Once you train freestyle using them, you will be able to swim much faster.

Chapter 11

Freestyle Techniques

Head and Body Positioning

In freestyle, the head and body positions will have an effect on frontal drag and propulsion forces. As is typical in swimming, the ideal head and body positions that will minimize frontal drag are not the same as those that maximize propulsion. Unlike other freestyle techniques, such as pulling motion, where we must choose between a high-elbow pull with less drag and less propulsion versus a deeper pull with more drag and more propulsion, when it comes to head and body position in freestyle, we can have our cake and eat it, too.

Head Position

In all four swimming strokes, the peak propulsion always occurs before the peak velocity is reached. Usually, the peak velocity in freestyle results just after one hand enters the water and the other hand is in the pulling propulsion phase. If the swimmer is breathing every cycle, after one hand enters the water, the head will be turned for the breath and partially above the water. After the other hand enters the water, when the head has turned back down after the breath, it needs to get underwater. In most of the freestyle swimmers, the head never gets underwater.

In fluid mechanics, the human head would be considered anything but streamlined. It is pretty big, round in shape and the leading body part in the swimmer. The head accounts for most of the surface drag of a swimmer.

Using our Propulsion/Drag Meter (PDM), we found that at 1.9 m/sec, a swimmer in a fixed, straight body position with hands at sides and head in alignment, the frontal drag increased by 62% on the surface compared to the exact same speed and body position beneath the surface. We also calculated that 38% of the total frontal drag forces at that speed and with that body position could be attributed to surface drag.

PDM technology towing a swimmer at an average of 1.9 m/sec on surface with hands at sides.

The point is that being on the surface really slows us down. Since surface drag is proportional to the fourth power of our speed, the faster we swim freestyle, the more advantage it is to get the head underwater, particularly at the peak velocity point. Very few swimmers do that, however. The question is: why?

There are two good reasons why most freestylers tilt their heads forward after the breath, with the tops of their heads protruding above the surface. The first reason is safety. If a swimmer buries the head underwater after the breath, then the neck must be flexed slightly and the swimmer's view is straight down. The swimmer would have no clue what is in front of him or her. Of course, during the breath, unless the swimmer lifts the head out of the water in the forward direction, as is done in open water swimming for sighting, which causes a tremendous increase in frontal drag, he or she will not be able to see forward either. In other words, with the proper head position in freestyle, a swimmer is always blind to what is in front.

In competition, that is acceptable, as swimmers have the entire lane to themselves. If we can see the black line on the bottom of the pool and the T signaling that the wall is coming, that is enough. In training, where there are 4, 5, 6 or more swimmers to a lane, workouts can become a bit of a frenzy. Swimmers push off the walls crooked or inadvertently veer over into the wrong side of the lane all of the time. To avoid a nasty collision, swimmers tilt their heads forward, keeping a careful watch out. We call that defensive freestyle.

The second reason that freestylers have their heads tilted forward is that they are more powerful in that position. Remember that swimmers do not feel the frontal drag forces, but they do feel positions of power and greater propulsion. By arching or extending the lower back some, swimmers can pull with more power than when their backs are straight, similar to doing a pull up. Swimmers feel stronger in the power position, so that is where they like to swim, with the head tilted forward.

When we come back to the cost/benefit analysis of head position, it is a tougher call. Is the extra frontal drag of the higher head worth the benefit of more power? Some great swimmers, like world record holders Ian Thorpe (Australia), Federica Pellegrini (Italy) and World Champion Florian Wellbrock (Germany), think so.

Freestyle swimmer with the head in a tilted-forward position. The top of his head is above the surface.

However, among today's elite freestylers, we see most of them opting for getting the head under water after the breath. They arch their back some on the breath-stroke, gaining more propulsion as the head breaks the surface for the breath. Then, they drop the head underwater after the breath, trying to surge forward with lower drag. In a way, by doing so, they have their cake and eat it, too.

American record holder Zane Grothe submerges his head after the breath using his hybrid freestyle technique.

Among elite male and female 50-meter freestyle sprinters, where no breath is usually taken, none of them tilt their heads forward. That is not surprising when you consider the impact of surface drag on the swimmer's speed.

How the head is lifted for the breath also has a huge impact on frontal drag forces. In the next chapter, when we discuss breathing techniques in freestyle, we will describe how to take a low-profile breath, minimizing the frontal drag forces.

There is one other important point regarding the swimmer's head. Since the head is in the lead position for the swimmer, the friction (drag force) encountered with the head moving through the water is significant. Recently, using PDM technology, we compared the average drag force underwater of a swimmer in a streamline position, towed at race speed (2.3 m/sec). In the first test, he was wearing a normal silicone cap with many small folds formed over the head. In the second test, he wore a thicker silicone racing dome cap (Hammerhead cap) that retained a very smooth surface, but everything else was the same. We found an astonishing 10.5% reduction in frontal drag wearing the smoother, thicker racing cap compared to the normal silicone cap.

Body Position

The straighter the human body, the less the frontal drag. Unfortunately, we must flex or extend our cervical, thoracic and lumbar spine in freestyle to gain propulsion, although less than with the other strokes. The spine is never quite perfectly straight. Also, when a well-conditioned swimmer relaxes the core in freestyle, the hips tend to sink down, as the lift forces come from the hands and feet. Without a tight, elevated core, there is nothing to keep that part of the body straight.

When the human body is horizontal and relaxed, the gravitational force will cause the lumbar spine to extend some (like a horse's back). In that position, if a swimmer elevates the core and flexes at the hip slightly, perhaps 3-5 degrees, the frontal drag force decreases. Using our PDM technology at race speed (2.3 m/sec), we found that the frontal drag force decreased by 10% by elevating the core and slightly flexing at the hip. Those two techniques of elevating the core and slightly flexing the hip actually help to straighten the horizontal body position of the swimmer.

Keeping the body in a straighter line requires core strength. Because of the extraordinary body speed on the start and turns, it is particularly important to hold a tight body line at those times. We will discuss the best way to streamline your body in Chapters 23, 24 and 25 on starts and turns.

The lift that is generated by the down kick also helps to keep the body in a straighter horizontal position. To help reduce drag, the kicking motion needs to be tight and the legs kept at the surface. Keeping the legs at the surface will also make it easier to keep the head down.

In freestyle, we have advocated rotating the body both at the shoulders and hips to generate more propulsion through coupling. Some have advocated body rotation as a means of reducing frontal drag. Using PDM technology, measuring the frontal drag of a swimmer under water in a streamline position, and on the surface with hands at the sides, we compared the relative drag force of the swimmer on his stomach versus his side. In both tests, under water or on the surface, the frontal drag of the swimmer was greater when he was on his side than it was on his stomach. The amount of increase in frontal drag on the swimmer's side compared to the swimmer's stomach on the surface was only 1.8%, so the difference is small. Rotating to the side, however, does not reduce frontal drag.

Body rotation is an important technique to increase propulsion, but not to reduce drag. The correct head and body positions at the right time, however, do reduce drag and help to increase propulsion. Swimmers just need to know when to make the adjustments.

Suggested Drills for Head/ Body Position to be done with snorkel and fins:

Sculling hands in front with head out of water

Sculling hands in front with head lifted slightly

Sculling hands in front with head submerged just under surface

Swimming freestyle slowly ensuring head is submerged as hands enter water

Chapter 12

Freestyle Techniques

Breathing

Unlike in backstroke and breaststroke, where the air is more readily available to breathe, taking a breath in freestyle and in butterfly is problematic. It requires changing the head and body positions, which result in an increase in frontal drag. Second, in shorter races where higher stroke rates are needed, taking a breath can also slow the stroke rate and the swimmer down.

In freestyle, using the word *breath* is probably a misnomer. It is more of a quick air exchange, getting a little more oxygen in and getting rid of a little carbon dioxide. Getting the oxygen helps supply the aerobic energy system. Getting rid of some CO_2 helps keep the body's pH closer to neutral.

In any event longer than 50 meters, and even during the 50-meter sprint in young swimmers, breathing becomes essential for the above two reasons. If a breath has to be taken, then besides the two functions of breathing above, two other major objectives of the breath are to minimize any additional drag and not to slow the stroke rate appreciably.

To meet those objectives, there are two important questions regarding breathing technique used in freestyle: How should a swimmer breathe? How often should a swimmer breathe? Let us try to answer both questions.

How to Breathe

To take a breath in freestyle, without using a snorkel, the head must break the surface. Once it does, frontal drag begins to increase rapidly. The higher the head is lifted out of the water and the longer it stays out of the water, the more drag is caused.

Breaking the surface with the head in swimming freestyle also causes a bow wave to form. The bow wave has a crest (high point) and it has a trough (low point). By the time the head turns for a breath, the crest is usually around the forehead of the swimmer. The trough of the wave is more posterior to the crest, located closer to the swimmer's neck.

To take a breath in freestyle, the swimmer should neither turn the head nor lift the head any more than is necessary. To that end, the swimmer needs to breathe in the trough of the bow wave, not the crest. That means turning the head back toward the collar bone and to the side, not just to the side. In doing so, the swimmer will reach the air with less rotation than when breathing straight to the side. Also, the swimmer should think about maintaining the crown of the head, the very top of the head, pointing forward during the breath, to prevent lifting it.

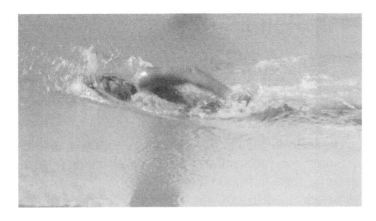

Freestyler Ashton King keeping the crown of his head pointing forward and breathing in the trough of the bow wave.

When both of these techniques are used, breathing in the trough and keeping the crown of the head pointing forward, we refer to it as a *low-profile* breath. Among the elite swimmers of today, Nathan Adrian has the lowest profile breath we have seen. It is so quick, one almost cannot tell that he has taken a breath at all.

A good way to tell that a swimmer is not over-rotating the head for the breath is by keeping both eyes open with the goggles on. If the breath is taken correctly, the lower eye should be under water, not above the water. If the swimmer is seeing the blue sky or an above-water view with both eyes, he or she is turning the head too far.

Once the swimmer brings the head back down after the breath, he or she should keep the chin tucked down close to the chest and try to get the head under water, looking down, not forward. He or she should avoid the temptation to look forward, as it will keep the head above the surface of the water. The swimmer should be looking at the bottom of the pool after the breath, not forward.

With this lower-drag head position, swimmers are not able to see where they are swimming. To help prevent any physical harm from a collision, they should stay close to the lane line on their side, leave ten seconds or longer behind the swimmer in front, transition quickly to the other side of the lane after turning and wear a cushioned, padded swim cap, such as the Hammerhead cap, to protect the head, in case of a collision. But they should keep the head down.

With the face planted back in the water, most swimmers will hold their breath. Then, they will burst out a small exhalation as they turn the head for the next breath, just in time to get another small air exchange. That is not what the elite swimmers do, however.

In freestyle, butterfly and breaststroke, elite swimmers release a quantity of air from their noses right after the face is down. The air released from their noses forms a considerable number of air bubbles that follow along the path of their bodies, under the chest and abdomen. Eventually, those air bubbles find their way around or behind the swimmers back to the surface. In the meantime, they have served the swimmers well.

Air bubbles released from the nose of freestyler, Isabella Arcila, flow backwards under her chest and body.

Under a swimmer's body, the released air bubbles reduce frontal drag. Since the bubbles are underneath the swimmer, the swimmer's buoyancy does not appreciably change compared to holding the breath, either.

Using PDM technology, we measured the drag force of a swimmer being towed in a streamline position at 2.3 m/sec. First, we tested him holding his breath. Then we tested him at the exact same speed releasing air from the nose under his body. With the air bubbles released, it reduced his frontal drag force by 9.1%!

Measuring the frontal drag of a swimmer being towed in streamline at 2.3 m/sec, releasing air bubbles through the nose.

In researching this concept of air bubbles, we found two other interesting examples of using air bubbles to reduce frontal drag. The first is with cruise ships. By emitting air bubbles along their massive hulls, the ships reduce drag and improve their fuel efficiency tremendously.

Cruise ships reduce frontal drag and improve fuel efficiency by emitting air bubbles along their hulls.

The second example of using air bubbles to reduce drag is with Emperor Penguins in the Antarctic. These birds will trap air bubbles under their plumes and keep them there while swimming around in the ocean. When being chased by Leopard seals or other predators, they release the air from under their feathers under water, reducing frontal drag. That enables them to spurt forward and upward on to the ice and out of harm's way. The air bubbles surrounding their small bodies at a crucial time enable them to survive in nature.

Emperor Penguins, surrounded by air bubbles, rocket upward and on to the ice to escape predators.

How Often to Breathe

In Chapter 2, while discussing the energy systems in physiology, we explain the rationale for the different respiratory rates in different events. The fact that we have two energy producing systems, aerobic (requiring oxygen) and anaerobic (not requiring oxygen), that work at very different rates and with different consequences, means that we need to understand how often to breathe in each different event, since breathing is our only source of oxygen.

The relative contribution of energy to the total required that is provided from the aerobic system increases from about 5% in the 50-meter sprint races to about 95% in the 1500-meter race. Races in between those two distances split the energy contribution more evenly. In the 100-meter race, for example, about half of the energy required comes from each system. Therefore, the respiratory rate or breathing pattern needs to be different in the various races.

In the 50-meter sprint, the objective is to breathe as little as possible. At the higher stroke rates used in the 50-meter sprint, a breath will likely slow the stroke rate considerably. The oxygen gain and carbon dioxide release from a breath taken will come into play only at the end of the race. The question of the trade-off between slowing the stroke rate and increasing drag with a breath and gaining the additional energy and keeping a lower pH is a good one. Some elite sprinters feel that they do better by taking one breath, rather than none.

With almost all elite swimmers, either no breath or one breath is taken in the 50-meter sprint. The majority of elite swimmers will take no breath. In young swimmers, depending on their age and aerobic capacity, 2 to 6 breaths may be needed. Once the race starts and the energy demand has begun, the aerobic system doesn't even contribute energy for about 20 seconds. It takes that long for the aerobic energy system to get going. If a breath is needed or taken, it will only help for the final 5-10 seconds of the race. That is also the most crucial time in the race.

In the 100-meter freestyle race, we find a different breathing pattern among most elite men and women. The men typically breathe every cycle, while the women more often breathe every fourth stroke (two cycles), or alternate breathing every cycle for two cycles followed by breathing every two cycles. In other words, they take four strokes without a breath, followed by a breath each cycle for two cycles. Why the difference?

The most likely explanations are that men have more muscle mass, a higher percentage of fast twitch (type II) muscle fibers and produce lactate at a higher rate than women. In an effort to maintain more pH neutrality, they need to rid their bodies of carbon dioxide faster. Women train more aerobically than men and likely develop better aerobic energy systems for this race. They can get away with breathing less. Diaphragmatic differences also exist between men and women that may come into play in the ability to deliver oxygen to the muscle.

In swimming races of 200 meters or longer, where the contribution of aerobic energy reaches 75% or more, the respiratory rate needs to be as close to what is maximally efficient on land as possible. With land exercises, air is readily available to be taken as needed. With maximal effort at any distance, the ideal respiratory rate is about 50-60 breaths per minute. At rates higher than that, the breaths become too shallow and less efficient at delivering oxygen. The demands of energy for swimming are certainly no less than with land-based exercises, so the respiratory rate should be similar.

Stroke rates of elite swimmers in the races from 200 to 1500 meters vary from about 60 per minute at the lowest to around 100 per minute at the highest. At a stroke rate of 60/minute (30 cycles per minute) a swimmer who breathes every cycle is getting 30 breaths per minute, or actually less, including the turns. This is far from the ideal respiratory rate of 50-60 breaths per minute. At a stroke rate of 100/minute, a swimmer breathing every cycle is getting 50 breaths per minute, physiologically ideal.

To improve the delivery of badly needed oxygen, swimmers with slower stroke rates of 60-80/minute, for example, need to learn the technique of taking consecutive breaths. That is not the same as bilateral breathing, which is one breath for every 3 strokes. That breathing pattern even lessens the delivery of oxygen, when compared to breathing every cycle, and makes matters worse. Taking consecutive breaths means taking two breaths or even three breaths in a row to each side, one with each stroke. The most common place to do so is going into and out of each turn.

Sun Yang (world record holder from China), with a stroke rate of 60/minute, famously did this in the 400 and 1500 races going into and out of each turn. Occasionally, in the 1500 race, he would breathe 3 times in a row in the middle of the pool, also. Those extra breaths enabled him to get closer to the ideal respiratory rate.

Breathing Before a Race

The question *Should I hyperventilate before race?* is often asked. According to exercise physiologist, Trever Gray, the answer is yes, but not too much! In a small study, he found that hyperventilating for 30 seconds before a race improved the performance of swimmers, compared to no hyperventilation or hyperventilating for 2 minutes. Apparently, putting the body into mild respiratory alkalosis by hyperventilating for 30 seconds gets the anaerobic energy system working earlier. It gives that energy system a sort of kick start. Using the anaerobic energy system causes metabolic acidosis, which is trying to neutralize the pH from the respiratory alkalosis caused by the hyperventilation. While the hyperventilation may be of more benefit in shorter races, please don't overdo it. Too much hyperventilation can make you giddy or even cause you to black out (shallow water black out), so be careful! It may also trick you into not breathing often enough early in the race.

In summary, learn to breathe quickly with a low-profile breath to reduce frontal drag. Release some air from your nose after the breath, while looking down, not forward. Adopt the breathing pattern (respiratory rate) that is appropriate for the event, your age, aerobic fitness level (VO2 max), and your freestyle technique (stroke rate). Once you do all of that, you will find that the breath in freestyle doesn't have to be so problematic after all.

Suggested Drills to be Done with Fins:

One arm freestyle breathing toward the inactive arm focusing on low profile breath

Normal freestyle focusing on one goggle lens in the water, one goggle lens out

Normal freestyle focusing on exhaling through the nose and taking a quick breath every cycle

Chapter 13

Backstroke Techniques

Fundamentals

The fundamentals of backstroke are essentially the same as for freestyle. The priorities are different and there are other subtle nuances of backstroke that are different. In general, we believe that those swimmers that can swim freestyle well, so long as they apply the same fundamentals equally, should also be able to swim backstroke well. That is not always the case.

Our approach at The Race Club to teaching backstroke is from a *Newtonian* mechanical perspective. How do we reduce frontal drag? How can we increase propulsion? How do we increase efficiency by taking advantage of the law of inertia? Let's start with reducing drag.

Frontal Drag

The most common causes of excessive drag in backstroke are poor head and body position, improper pulling technique and improper kicking technique. In backstroke, the head should remain in alignment with the upper body. It shouldn't be tilted forward (flexed) or backward (extended). We often see both of those mistakes being made.

Most swimmers make the mistake of tilting the head forward. We call it the *reading in bed* position. To swim straight in backstroke, swimmers need to have some awareness of where they are in the lane. It is much easier to have that awareness if the head is up and tilted forward.

The problem with having the head tilted forward and too high is the dramatic increase in frontal drag that it causes. Not only is there more surface drag from the protruding head plowing through the water, but the high head position tends to push the hips and legs lower in the water. The entire body is now swimming with a slight angle, adding considerably more drag.

As in freestyle, the best technique with the head in backstroke is to have it go back at the right time and elevate at the right time. That is not achieved by using the neck to extend the head back and flex or tilt it forward. Rather, the head should remain in alignment with the upper body and allow the shoulders to move back and upward. Swimming backstroke correctly, one is performing a mini-crunch all the way down the pool.

Most swimmers are good about bringing their shoulders up. They are just not good about getting them back. They like reading in bed because they are more aware of their position in the lane and are more powerful in that position. Yet, to reduce drag, once the recovering arm and hand are on the way down, the shoulders need to angle back just enough to allow a small stream of water to come over the face of the swimmer. Unlike freestyle, where the swimmer hopes to have the head down far enough for the bow wave to go over the top of the head after the breath, in backstroke, the swimmer actually gets to see the bow wave. It is a clear end point. No stream visible through the goggles when the shoulders go back? The shoulders are not far enough back.

Once the backstroker gets the shoulders back before the recovering hand hits the water, he or she needs to bring them back up quickly. The reason the swimmer brings the shoulders back up, doing a sort of mini-crunch, is to gain propulsion. The swimmer is more powerful pulling from the shoulder-up position. In the shoulder up position, it is also a time when the swimmer can gain some awareness of where he or she is in the lane, not by turning the head, but by using peripheral vision. Similar to freestyle, by shifting the shoulder position in the water at the right time, with respect to propulsion and drag, the backstrokers can have their cake and eat it, too.

Because backstroke is correctly performed with faster stroke rates, there may not be time to get the shoulders up and back for each stroke. Particularly in the shorter races, the shoulders will usually come up on one cycle and back on the next cycle, causing a mini-crunch type motion down the pool.

Occasionally, we find swimmers that swing their heads from side to side in backstroke. That extra motion of the head may not add any significant frontal drag, but it is essentially wasted motion. The head really shouldn't move much, other than the slight up and down movement from the shoulders. One good technique to fix the problem of excessive head movement is to place a Styrofoam cup half filled with water on the forehead of the swimmer. Then have the swimmer swim backstroke for 25 or 50 meters, trying not to spill the cup of water. It works like a charm! After learning how to do that, most swimmers will keep their heads still.

The lift generated by the down kick also helps to keep the legs in line with the body, lessening drag. In backstroke, the lift is generated by the weaker side of the kick, rather than the strong side as in freestyle and butterfly. However, as we will discuss in the kicking chapter, the flow dynamics change with a swimmer on his back, so that the down kick (weak side) becomes much more propulsive compared to a swimmer's weak side up kick on his stomach.

A significant amount of frontal drag in backstroke is caused by poor pulling technique, using a straight arm motion, rather than a bent elbow. It is one of the most common problems we encounter in backstroke. The reason that it is so common is that most backstrokers under-rotate their bodies. In so doing, if they were to bend their elbows as they should, the hand would break the surface on the pulling motion (which often occurs), once past the shoulder, and they would lose propulsion. To fix the problem, they simply keep the arms straight or straighter during the pull. That technique keeps the hand under water, but results in an increase in frontal drag and a loss of propulsion.

It is the upper arm in backstroke, as it is in freestyle, that causes most of the frontal drag on the pulling motion. The upper arm is moving forward in the water at the beginning and at the end of the underwater pull. It is at the beginning of the pull when most of the drag damage is done.

When the backstroke hand enters the water, if the pulling motion is begun with a straight arm, the upper arm immediately jettisons out to the side. There is no turning back. The drag goes up quickly. If the swimmer bends the elbow immediately after entering the hand in the water to start the pulling motion, he or she can keep the upper arm more in line with his or her motion and out of harm's way. The difference in these two techniques may seem trivial, but it is not. Later, in propulsion, we will explain how the swimmer can avoid breaking the surface of the water using this bent-elbow pulling motion.

In Chapter 15, we will discuss the important kicking technique for backstroke. For now, it is important to recognize that overbending the knee before the up kick is perhaps the most serious cause of frontal drag in the backstroke. It happens often.

Propulsion

The propulsion in backstroke is derived almost completely from the hands and the feet, with the back of the lower leg providing some small propulsion on the down kick. The propulsion of backstroke is augmented by the energy from the coupling motions, body rotation and the arm recovery, the same as in freestyle.

Because the biomechanics of the swimmer are quite different in backstroke pull compared to the freestyle pull, a swimmer is able to get into the propulsion mode sooner with the pull and remain in propulsion mode longer than with most freestyle techniques. The swimmer does not need to pull as deep to reverse the direction of the hand motion, either. However, the biomechanics of the backstroke pull do not generate as much force as with the freestyle pull, so backstroke is not as fast a stroke as freestyle.

Body rotation for backstroke is not only a powerful coupling motion, it also has a beneficial effect on the biomechanics of the pulling motion. The more a swimmer rotates to the side, the less negative the angle of the shoulder is at the initiation of the pull. The shoulder is in a negative angle when it is extended backward, a position of less strength. In freestyle, more body rotation puts the shoulder at a greater negative angle, weakening the initiation of the pulling motion. In backstroke, the rotation does the opposite. It puts the pulling arm in a stronger biomechanical position.

Given two very good reasons to rotate the body aggressively in backstroke, increasing coupling energy and biomechanical strength, one would think that everyone would be rotating in backstroke. They don't. The body rotation just requires too much work.

The backstroke kicking propulsion is also different from the freestyle kick. In Velocity Meter (VM) testing, we see a much more uniform velocity curve on the backstroke kick compared to on the stomach. The weaker down kick becomes more propulsive by pressing down with the help of gravity against a larger vortex caused by the upward moving foot. As in freestyle kicking, the peak acceleration occurs as the two feet pass each other in opposite directions.

Elite backstrokers learn to take advantage of the vortices, using the weak side of their kicks by pressing down hard with the bottoms (soles) of their feet. They do the same thing on their starts and turns, using the underwater dolphin kick to increase propulsion and speed. In short course races, in the 50 meter and 100-meter events, elite backstrokers will spend more time underwater dolphin kicking than they will on the surface swimming. Having a fast, underwater dolphin kick becomes essential to swim fast backstroke, particularly short course.

World Champion Junya Koga, kicking on his back, shows very little change in his velocity curve (above graph). His peak acceleration near the yellow line (graph below) occurs as the two feet pass each other.

Inertia

Of all four strokes, backstroke is the most mechanically efficient. Elite backstrokers will hold a much more consistent speed than they do with the other three strokes, similar to what happens in the backstroke kick.

Having the mechanical efficiency of the backstroke kick is part of the reason why backstroke itself is a more efficient stroke. The other reason has to do with the timing of the coupling motions. In freestyle, the shoulder rotation will increase the propulsion somewhere near the middle of the propulsion phase, when the pulling arm is in a strong biomechanical position. That will cause an abrupt acceleration and increase in velocity. In backstroke, the peak shoulder rotational speed doesn't occur until the pulling arm is at the end of the pull, a biomechanically weaker place. The hip rotation in backstroke augments the propulsion at the very beginning of the backstroke pulling motion. Again, that is biomechanically a weaker place.

Effectively, with the body rotation in backstroke, the weaker parts of the pull get a little boost in power, while the middle of the pull, which is the strongest, does not. The result is a more even velocity throughout the entire pulling motion.

Using PM technology, the peak shoulder rotation (graph below) occurs when the recovering right arm strikes the water. This increases the pressure toward the end of the pull of the left hand (graph above).

The peak hip rotation (graph below) occurs as the left hand leaves the water and augments the pulling pressure of the right hand (graph above) at the very beginning of the pulling motion (Pressure Meter technology).

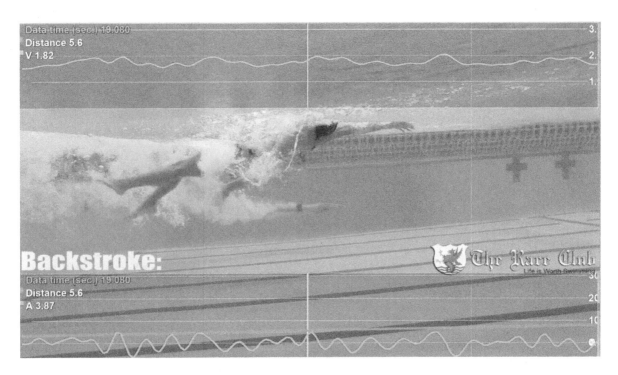

The timing of the two body rotations and their effect on the pulling pressures, plus the fluid mechanics of the backstroke kick lead to a more consistent velocity curve (graph above), as illustrated by this VM study on World Champion Junya Koga.

Of all the fundamental techniques we teach for backstroke at The Race Club, we believe that stroke rate is the most important one. A swimmer can have a beautiful looking backstroke, but if the stroke rate is too slow, he or she probably won't win. There is no hip-driven or hybrid backstroke technique that is effective. It is all shoulder-driven. Consequently, there are three acceptable stroke rates—fast, faster and fastest. Because the propulsion phase in backstroke is longer than in freestyle, there is less down time, when neither hand is in propulsion mode. A faster stroke rate will shorten the down time even more, taking advantage of the law of inertia.

The stroke rates that we most commonly see among elite backstrokers are the following:

- 200 meters 85-90 strokes per minute
- 100 meters 95-105 strokes per minute
- 50 meters 110-130 strokes per minute

Taller swimmers may have slightly slower stroke rates in backstroke, but not by much. Even Matt Grevers, at 6 feet 8 inches, held a 95/minute stroke rate in winning the gold medal in the 100-meter backstroke in the London Olympic Games of 2012.

In the 2019 World Championships, Regan Smith, set a new standard in stroke rate by winning the 200 meters with a 92/minute stroke rate (finishing the last 25 meters at 95/minute stroke rate) and the 100 meters with a 108/minute stroke rate. Both swims were in world record time.

If done well, backstroke can be a really enjoyable and fast way to swim. Pay attention to Newton's three laws of motion by reducing drag, increasing propulsion and increasing your stroke rate. If you do, you will see great results.

Helpful Drills for Improving Your Backstroke Coupling Motions

Body Rotation Drill

6 Kick 1 Stroke Drill

6 Kick 3 Stroke Drill

Helpful Drills for Improving Your Pulling Motion

One arm pulling drill with fins

Helpful Drills for Increasing Stroke Rate

Backstroke Spin Drill

Dolphin kick Backstroke

Chapter 14

Backstroke Techniques

The Six Phases of the Pulling Cycle

The pathway of the hand in backstroke with the correct pulling motion is different than it is in freestyle. In freestyle, the hand travels in a circular pathway under water through the pulling cycle. In backstroke, the hand takes a more linear pathway under water through the pulling cycle.

There are a couple of reasons for this difference. First, because of biomechanical differences in the shoulder when a swimmer is on his back compared to his stomach, he or she doesn't need to pull as deep to get the hand into a position to push backwards with force. In freestyle, the hand is at least two feet under water before the propulsion phase begins. In backstroke, propulsion can start at a depth of eight to ten inches. Second, when a swimmer pulls deep in the backstroke, he or she puts the shoulder into more of an extended position, which is called a negative angle, a biomechanically weaker position. Either a deeper pull, or an S-shaped pull, where the vectors of force are not all primarily backwards, will lead to a loss of propulsion.

For these two reasons, in backstroke, a swimmer is able to get into propulsion mode more quickly than in freestyle. The shortest time a freestyle swimmer can get his hand into propulsion from the hand entry is about .28 seconds. A swimmer is able to get the hand into the propulsion phase in backstroke in about .16 seconds after hand entry. He or she is also able to maintain a relatively strong propulsive force with the hand in a very linear path backwards, which is desirable.

Because the propulsion in backstroke is less than in freestyle, the hand will exit the water slightly behind the entry point. With elite backstrokers, that amounts to just a few inches behind its entry point.

We classify the backstroke pulling cycle with the same six phases we use in the freestyle cycle: lift, front-quadrant propulsion, back-quadrant propulsion, release, early recovery and late recovery. We will describe these six phases and how they differ from freestyle.

Finally, and this is the most important advice we can offer, start to teach or learn the correct backstroke techniques by having the swimmers stand on the deck first. In ten minutes on the pool deck, a swimmer can learn how to use proper backstroke pulling and recovery motions, as well as shoulder rotation. In the process of learning great backstroke technique, lots of time and frustration can be saved if the swimmer starts out on the pool deck.

World Champion backstroker Junya Koga demonstrating perfect backstroke pulling and recovery motions with excellent body rotation on the beach in Islamorada.

Lift Phase

When the arm and hand enter the water after the recovery, they enter the lift phase of the pulling cycle. Although we call this earliest phase in backstroke the lift phase, that is probably not a very good name for it. There is very little lift force going on during this brief period, although there is some.

This phase should not last very long, .16-.24 seconds, depending on the stroke rate. The slower the rate, the longer the hand is held above the head before initiating the pulling cycle. Nonetheless, it is an important phase. It should start with the little finger first crashing forcefully into the water directly above the shoulder, not the head, with the fingers and thumb squeezed together and pointed forward. We still find many backstrokers that plop the back of their hands into the water, but we don't believe this a good idea. Using Propulsion/Drag Meter (PDM) technology, we found that the frontal drag with the arm extended forward with the hand vertical and the pinky down was 9.1% less than with the palm down at race speed (2.3 m/sec). Admittedly, we have not measured the frontal drag with the back of the hand down, but we presume it would be similar to having the palm down. Regardless, since the hand is moving forward in this phase and will cause some frontal drag, we recommend that swimmers should enter the water with the little pinky down and the thumb and fingers squeezed together. With the pinky down, they can get into propulsion mode a little bit faster.

It is also very important to enter the hand directly above the shoulder. Far too many backstrokers over-reach with their hands, entering them above their heads. When this happens, as in freestyle, the first motion of the hand will be a significant out-sweep. The force applied to the outer side will result in the body moving in the opposite direction—action and reaction. If a swimmer is over-reaching on one side only, he or she will invariably run into the lane line on the other side. If the swimmer over-reaches on both sides, the result is a zig-zagging motion down the pool. Neither outcome is desirable.

Once the hand and arm are in the water, the next step is perhaps the most crucial one in the entire underwater backstroke pull. The elbow should bend immediately. If it doesn't bend right away, the pulling motion will begin with a straight arm. When that happens, the damage is done. There is no turning back. The upper arm begins to stick out like a sore thumb, throwing the brakes on from frontal drag.

The pulling objective in swimming backstroke is not unlike that in swimming freestyle during the first phase—keep the upper arm in line with the swimmer's line of motion for as long as possible. In freestyle, we refer to that technique as the high-elbow pull. In backstroke, it is not really a high-elbow pull. It is a bent-elbow pull where the elbow drops deeper into the water. In either technique, the swimmer should try to keep the upper arm closer to the line of motion.

One of the most useful ways we have found to communicate this important technique of early elbow bend in backstroke to swimmers at The Race Club is by asking them to begin the pulling motion by keeping their elbow pointed toward the far end of the pool. That is a concept that seems to resonate well with swimmers.

Bending the elbow immediately after the arm entry not only reduces frontal drag, it will also set up the swimmer for the next important concept—to feel as if he or she is pushing the water backwards with the hand, rather than pulling or scooping the arm and hand backwards. Pushing water, rather than pulling water, is an important differentiating concept.

Once the arm is in the water and the elbow starts to bend, the hand immediately begins to change direction and apply pressure (the catch). It transitions quickly from the palm facing to the side with the pinky down to pointing the fingers directly to the side with the wrist slightly flexed and fingers separated. Since the hand drops down only a few inches in the water to make this turn, it generates a little bit of lift and is now ready to start the propulsion phase.

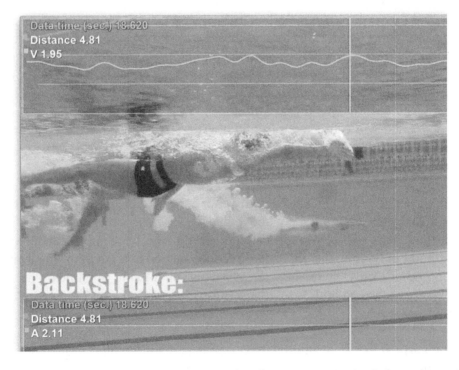

Junya Koga enters the short lift phase with the little finger down and palm facing to the outside.

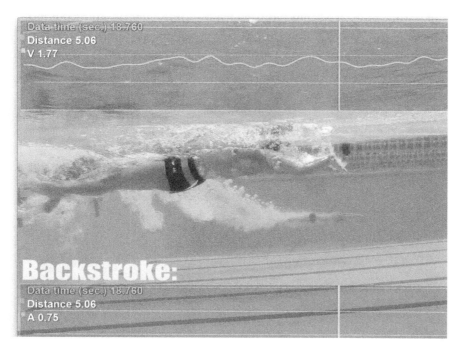

Data time (sec.) 18.760
Distance 5.06
V 1.77

Backstroke:
Data time (sec.) 18.760
Distance 5.06
A 0.75

After just .16 seconds, Junya has completed the lift phase by bending the elbow and turning the fingers to the side, flexing the wrist slightly, and is ready to start the propulsion phase. The hand is only about 10 inches under water.

Propulsion Phase Front Quadrant

When the hand starts moving backwards in the front quadrant, it begins the propulsion phase. The position of the hand should be above the elbow, but well below the surface, with the fingers and thumb pointed to the side and separated slightly Now the objective is quite simple. Keep the surface of the hand perpendicular to the body's motion and accelerate it backwards as much and as far as possible and in as close to a straight line as possible. While maintaining this linear path, the swimmer should feel as if he is pushing the water backward, rather than pulling the arm like an oar, or scooping the water, which assuredly means the hand is too deep.

During the front-quadrant propulsion phase, the elbow continues to bend and drop lower as the hand moves backward, reaching a maximum bend (from the upper arm) of 100-140 degrees. The more the elbow bends, the closer the hand will be to the swimmer's body. If the arm remains straighter (greater than 140-degree angle), too much drag is caused in the early part of the pull. If the arm bends too much (less than 100-degree angle), the hand loses too much propulsion.

Since the hand gets into the propulsion phase earlier than in freestyle, the time it spends in the front-quadrant and in the back-quadrant propulsion phases is pretty even. It takes Junya Koga, swimming backstroke with a cycle time of 1.06 (113/minute stroke rate), .19 seconds to reach his shoulder, the boundary between the front and back quadrants. He will spend about that same time in the back-quadrant propulsion phase. The range of time in the front quadrant ranges from about .16 -.24 seconds. The path of the hand should be nearly a perfectly straight line backwards.

Just before the hand and arm reach the shoulder, the upper arm no longer continues moving forward. Neither does it move backward. It remains in more or less a neutral position in the

109

water, neither generating propulsion nor causing frontal drag. Nearly all of the drag caused from the upper arm occurs in the first .25-.35 seconds of the underwater pull. After that, the upper arm is out of harm's way.

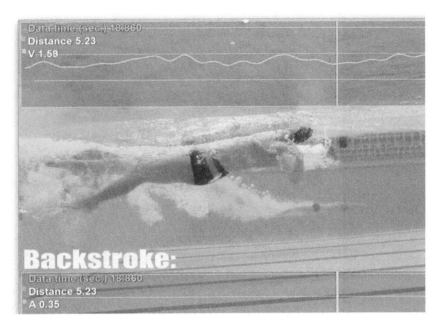

Junya's hand remains in the front-quadrant propulsion phase for about .19 seconds, before reaching the shoulder. With the fingers pointed to the side, the hand remains perpendicular to his body motion in nearly a straight line back.

Propulsion Phase Back Quadrant

Once the hand passes the shoulder and enters the back quadrant, it should continue in a linear pathway backward at a depth of around 8-10 inches, midway between the elbow and the surface, until it nears the end of the pull. Because of the amount of force applied on the hand, there will always be some vertical movement of the hand during the propulsion phase, usually upward, but it should not be much. The time the pulling hand spends in the back quadrant pulling phase ranges from about .19-.25 seconds

The hand should not break the surface of the water on its way backward, either. If it does, propulsion will be lost. Two different errors can cause the hand to break the surface during the pull. First, creating a wide S-shaped motion of the hand, where the hand goes deep at the beginning, then moves upward toward the surface, and then back down again, can cause it to break the surface at the top of the curve. When a swimmer changes the vector angle of force of the pulling hand to any direction other than straight backward, he will lose propulsion, with or without breaking the surface. Second, by not rotating the body enough during the pulling motion, it puts the hand at risk of breaking the surface when the elbow is bent. We will discuss more about shoulder rotation in Chapter 16 on coupling motions. A quick, full body rotation in backstroke has the benefits of increasing the biomechanical advantage of the pulling arm (less negative angle), increasing the coupling energy, and reducing the risk of breaking the surface with the hand. All three advantages are related to increasing propulsion.

While the propulsion generated by the pulling hand is augmented to some degree by the coupling energy of the shoulder (end of pull) and the hip (beginning of pull) rotations, it is still greatest in the middle, near the shoulder. It is lowest at the beginning and just less than its peak at the end. As it nears the end of the back-quadrant propulsion phase, near the waist, the hand starts to turn downward. The hand then flips its direction from sideways to either fingers pointed backward or downward. If the fingers point backward, then the thumb remains upward for the release. If the hand flips farther, the fingers drop toward the bottom and the back of the wrist faces upward for the release. We are not certain which technique is better. With either technique, there is likely just a last bit of propulsion that is generated from flipping the hand over or downward at the end of the pull. The hand should complete the back-quadrant propulsion just below the suit level, but no deeper.

The recorded pressure on the right hand (graphs at vertical line) is lowest at the beginning (left), highest in the middle (center), near the shoulder, and slightly lower at the end (right) of the backstroke pulling propulsion phase.

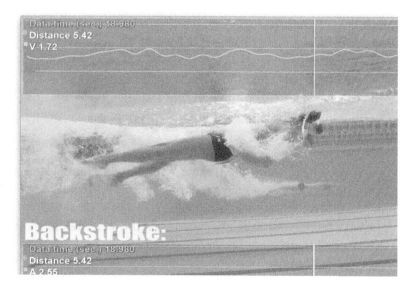

Junya completes the back-quadrant propulsion phase with a down turning of the hand. Once the hand stops moving backward, propulsion from that hand ceases.

111

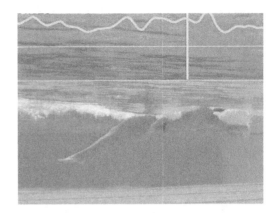

Junya finishes his pull with thumb up. **Backstroker Josh Zuchowski finishes with fingers pointing down.**

Release Phase

During the release phase the hand and arm are drawn upward and forward with the least amount of drag possible. If the hand finishes the propulsion phase too deep, it takes too long to get the hand back out of the water for the recovery. The release phase should last about .15-.20 seconds. If it takes longer than that, then the hand finished too deep or the stroke rate is too slow.

There are two techniques of releasing the hand cleanly and quickly. One is with the thumb upward and the hand in a vertical position. The other is with the wrist bent and the fingers pointing downward. In theory, the thumb up release may cause less drag, but with either technique, the arm should be straight and the drag very low.

Early Recovery Phase

There is only one good technique for arm recovery in backstroke and that is with a straight arm (high octane) in a vertical path. The arm should exit the water vertically with the wrist and fingers relaxed. Since the arm should be coming upward quickly, the centrifugal force will keep the hand in line with the forearm, even when the wrist is relaxed. Some swimmers try to take a less vertical path with the recovering arm, coming around the side more. By doing so, they will not get enough body rotation, nor shoulder elevation, nor will they get as much help from gravity during the late recovery phase.

One might wonder why in backstroke we find only one arm recovery technique, straight (high octane), while in freestyle we see three arm recovery positions—completely bent (low octane), somewhat bent (medium octane) and straight (high octane). The last elite backstroker to use a bent-arm recovery might have been Adolph Kiefer, who won the gold medal in the 1936 Olympic Games. We believe that there are three main reasons for using a straight-arm recovery in backstroke. First is that the anatomical ability to flex the shoulder joint (move the arm forward) is much better than the ability to extend the arm (move it backward), making it easier to bring the arm vertically over the top in backstroke compared to freestyle. Second, backstroke has only one effective technique, which is shoulder-driven with a faster stroke rate. Straight arm freestyle is most commonly used with a faster stroke rate. Third, the longest backstroke race is 200 meters, considerably shorter than with freestyle events. Without a hip-driven or hybrid version or a longer event, and with the ease of shoulder flexion, the higher-energy producing straight-arm recovery is the best option for backstroke.

As in freestyle, the relaxation of the hand and wrist during the release and early recovery phases is an important process in the muscle recovery of the arm. Keeping the wrist stiff and the fingers squeezed during the early recovery will lead to earlier arm fatigue and loss of pulling power.

When the recovering hand leaves the water, the hip will then rotate at its maximal speed. The angular velocity of the hip rotation will influence the propulsion of the opposite hand, which is just beginning its propulsion phase overhead. We will discuss this important technique in Chapter 16 on coupling motions.

One of the most important techniques that needs to happen during the early recovery phase is the elevation of the recovering shoulder. In freestyle, the shoulder rotation is symmetrical or square. In backstroke, it is not. The recovering shoulder rolls forward (upward) more than the opposite shoulder rotates back. It is almost a unilateral forward roll or hunch of the recovering shoulder to get it as high above the water as possible during the recovery. The shoulder should roll upward far enough to nearly touch the swimmer's chin. Getting the shoulder up and over the water will reduce frontal drag from this motion and will force the pulling shoulder deeper into the water, a biomechanically advantageous pulling position. It makes perfect sense. Yet, most swimmers don't elevate the shoulders (enough), as it requires a lot of work to do so.

Junya Koga doing shoulder elevation exercise on the Yoga ball in Islamorada

Late Recovery Phase

When the hand passes directly over the elevated shoulder vertically and reaches its highest point on the recovery path, it enters the late phase of the recovery. With the assistance of gravitational force, the speed and energy of the arm should increase all the way down through the water, not just to the water. Many swimmers tend to slow the hand before it enters the water, when it should be travelling at high speed, hoping to avoid making a splash. That is a mistake.

The speed and kinetic energy of the arm at the end of the recovery will influence the propulsion of the opposite hand at the end of the pulling motion, in the back quadrant. The hand rotates on its way down so that the hand should enter the water vertically with the little finger down. Even at high speed, the hand in a vertical position can enter the water cleanly, without producing an excessive amount of air bubbles.

If the arm accelerates all the way down through the surface of the water, the centrifugal force will tend to pull the arm out of the shoulder joint, a position that is called subluxation or hyperextension. Swimming may be the only sport in the world where we actually want a joint to become destabilized, in a subluxated position, albeit temporarily. The faster the swimmer drives the arm down on the recovery, the greater the force pulling the shoulder joint apart. Of course, once the swimmer stops the angular motion and the centrifugal force ceases, the shoulder will move right back into its normal stabile position to start the pull.

The duration of the arm in the entire recovery phase will vary, depending on the stroke rate and the length of the recovering arm, ranging from around .30 - .40 seconds.

In summary:

- Use a vertical, straight arm (high-octane) motion on the recovery, driving the arm hard and aggressively downward through the water's surface.
- Elevate the recovering shoulder high out of the water, nearly touching the chin.
- Enter the hand with the little pinky down and bend the elbow immediately after the arm enters the water, keeping the elbow pointed toward the far end of the pool.
- Get into the catch (propulsion phase) as quickly as possible and continue pushing the hand backward in nearly a straight line, keeping the hand a few inches below the surface.
- Finish with a quick downward turn of the hand, but don't let the hand finish too deep.
- Release the hand quickly with either the thumb up or the wrist bent with fingers down.
- Then snap the hips up aggressively to help the other hand get started with a stronger pull.

Although the pulling motion is different in backstroke compared to freestyle, the fundamentals are the same. Make the adjustments. Pay attention to minimizing drag, maximizing propulsion and maintaining a fast stroke rate. You will see your backstroke begin to improve right away.

Recommended Drills for Backstroke Pulling Motion to be Done with Fins:

6 kicks 1 stroke focusing on the connection between the pulling motion and rotation (helps with coupling of shoulder rotation to the end of the back-quadrant propulsion)

6 kicks 3 strokes focusing on the connection between the pulling motion and rotation (helps with coupling and establishing faster stroke rate)

One Arm Drill with fins (for correct pulling motion)

Spin Drill focusing on high stroke rate

Chapter 15

Backstroke Techniques

Kicking

The biomechanics of backstroke kick are very similar to freestyle kicking. Backstroke kick also serves the same four functions as freestyle kick: propulsion, lift, inertia and balance. There is one important difference, however. That pertains to the weak-side kick, which in backstroke is the down kick. When a swimmer is on his or her back, the down kick becomes much more propulsive both in backstroke kick and in dolphin kick. In the Velocity Meter (VM) study below, elite backstroker, Amy Bilquist, demonstrates the difference in the velocity meter curves between freestyle kick and backstroke kick on the surface. In the backstroke kick, she maintains a much more even or consistent velocity than in her freestyle kick. This flatter velocity curve in backstroke kick has occurred in all of the backstrokers that we have tested.

The angle of knee flexion is nearly the same in freestyle kick and backstroke kick, yet the velocity curves (graphs above) for Amy Bilquist differ. Kicking on the back may not be faster, but it is more efficient than kicking on the stomach.

As in freestyle kicking, the peak acceleration (propulsion) in backstroke typically occurs just after the two feet pass each other. The weak side of the kick becomes more propulsive on the way down because of a bigger vortex to push down against and the assistance of gravity.

The two feet play off of the two vortices caused by the body moving through the water and the feet moving up and down. During the up kick, the more pigeon-toeing (inversion) and plantar flexion of the foot, the more propulsion can be generated. During the down kick, it is the bottom of the foot pointed straight backwards and the back of the leg moving downwards that generate the propulsion. Since the two feet are moving in opposite directions, they use both the vortices they created and the one behind the swimmer's body to reach the maximum propulsion as they pass each other.

The ideal knee flexion in backstroke kick seems to be similar to freestyle and dolphin kicks, which is in the range of 60-70 degrees from the surface. That may seem like a lot of knee bend, but it is not. The swimmer needs to reverse direction of the foot quickly to keep the knee from over-bending. Once the up kick begins and the knee joint begins extending, the hip flexes some.

During this early up kick, the knees should just reach near the surface of the water, or barely break the surface. It is very common to see too much hip flexion in backstroke kick, with the knees coming too far out of the water, resulting in excessive frontal drag. We call this poor technique, *riding the bicycle.*

On the up kick, the toes should break the surface, but not by much. With the knee flexion in backstroke kick occurring as the feet are moving toward the bottom of the pool rather than upward, we wouldn't expect to see the feet come out of the water as much as in freestyle kicking. They don't. As the foot moves upward, the swimmer needs to accelerate it aggressively through the body vortex. During this time, the hip goes from its slightly flexed position to a more neutral position at the end of the up kick. Even so, the toes should just break the surface of the water, particularly when the swimmer has hyperextension of the knees. With a strong backstroke kick, one should see a small disruption or boil form at the surface from the toes breaking the surface. If the feet remain underwater, the maximum propulsion will not be reached.

In backstroke kick there is very little hip flexion, perhaps 10-15 degrees, which begins at the start of the up kick. Too much hip flexion at that time will result in the knee coming too far out of the water. Once the hip flexion reaches 10-15 degrees during the early up kick, it remains there until the foot reaches the body vortex behind the swimmer. Once the foot enters the body vortex on the way up, the hip flexion begins to decrease. When the foot passes through the body vortex completely, it reverses its direction quickly to start moving downward, just breaking the surface. The foot position changes from pigeon-toed, plantar flexion to pointing the toes straight backward. At the start of the down kick, the hip is still flexed slightly.

The motion of the leg in the early down kick is caused by the hip extensors. As the foot moves through the body vortex on the way down, the hips go from slightly flexed to a neutral or minimally extended position. Once the foot passes through the body vortex, the knee flexion begins and continues as the foot moves in its downward path through the full amount of flexion (60-70 degrees).

All of the propulsion from the down kick occurs with the straight leg and bottom of the foot pressing downward from the hip extensors. Since the surface of the bottom of the foot is also generating propulsion on the way down, the foot plantar flexors (gastrocnemius muscles) are involved in this motion. Once the foot passes through the body vortex on the way down and the knee begins to bend, there is no more propulsion gained from the foot during the knee flexion, only drag. Yet the knee flexion is necessary to get the foot into a position of generating more propulsion during the next up kick. It is a necessary evil. One cannot get significant propulsion from the up kick without bending the knee. With little plantar flexibility, to gain more propulsion, the knee needs to bend even more. It is a *Catch 22.* A swimmer cannot get carried away with the knee flexion and try to kill the next up kick, what we refer to as the *50-yard field goal* kick. If so, the deceleration from the frontal drag caused by the excessive knee bend will outweigh the additional propulsion from the giant kick. Even so, we see this mistake being made often, even among elite backstrokers.

Virtually all of the elite backstrokers of the world, male or female, use a six-beat kick. Since all fast backstroke is shoulder-driven and the race distance stops at 200 meters, using a six-beat kick makes sense. There really is no viable two-beat kick in backstroke. The shorter the race, the more important is the kick propulsion. In a six-beat kick, within each stroke cycle, there are three up kicks per leg and three down kicks per leg. Because of the extraordinary body rotation that is required to swim backstroke well, when the swimmer is rotated to the left, the up kick is directed toward the left side. When the swimmer is rotated to the right, the up kick is directed to the right side. In between these two kicks, the swimmer is transitioning from one side to the other, so the up kick is straight upward.

As in freestyle, however, not all of the strong-side kicks in backstroke (up kicks) are always equal in propulsion or effort. It is very common to see backstrokers use the over-bended knee kick, the *50-yard field goal* kick, on every third up kick. We often refer to this as the *surge* kick, because it happens right after the opposite hand enters the water and causes a sudden surge in speed. The temptation to use the *surge* kick should be avoided in freestyle and backstroke, as the increase in frontal drag caused from the extra knee bend will do more harm than good.

Besides the inconsistency of the up-kicking effort, we also see some variations in the traditional six-beat kick. Elite Australian backstroker, Mitch Larkin, for example, will cross the left leg over the right leg after the up kick. Others may use soft or almost non-existent up kicks in between the strong surge kicks.

We believe that the best kicking technique in backstroke is with a steady six-beat kick that is tight enough to generate good propulsion, yet not cause too much frontal drag. That means there cannot be excessive knee bend or hip flexion on any of the up kicks. The effort used in all up kicks should be relatively equal, and the effort used in all of the down kicks should be relatively equal. Most important, however, is that more emphasis is placed on the weaker side (down kick) in backstroke than the swimmer would put into the up kick in freestyle.

If we were to pick an elite swimmer today that has close to the ideal backstroke kicking technique, we would pick Regan Smith. Her kick is tight, uniform, strong in both directions and relentless. All of that contributes to her ability to break world records.

Dolphin Kick On the Back

In backstroke races, the underwater dolphin kick speed on the start and turns is an extremely important part of the swimmer's strategy. In fact, in short course races (25 yard or 25 meter pool), elite backstrokers will spend more time in the race doing dolphin kick on their backs than they will swimming backstroke. Therefore, to become a great backstroker, a swimmer needs to develop excellent under water speed of the dolphin kick on the back.

In Chapter 25, we will discuss the dolphin kick in great detail. Now, it is important to point out that differences in propulsion that exist between freestyle and backstroke kicking also exist between dolphin kicking on the stomach and back. In either case, the down kick becomes more propulsive on the swimmer's back. In most of the swimmers that we have tested with the Velocity Meter dolphin kicking on their backs, the highest velocity is achieved on the down kick, not during the stronger up kick.

Junya Koga kicks dolphin on his stomach (left) and on his back (right). The top graphs indicate velocity (each white horizontal line is 1 m/sec) and the graph beneath it indicates acceleration and deceleration (each white horizontal line is 10 m/sec2). The velocity is much more consistent on his back and his average velocity is greater on his back.

We find the biomechanical movements of the dolphin kick on the stomach and the back to be very similar. Hip flexion should be in the range of 20-35 degrees and knee bend in the range of 60-70 degrees. One difference between dolphin kicking and backstroke or freestyle kicking is that in dolphin kick, the propulsion is generated from the chest downward. There is more hip flexion involved in dolphin kicking. While the same important ankle plantar flexibility is required to kick fast with either dolphin kick or backstroke kick, there is little or no motion of the upper body in backstroke or freestyle kick. The power is generated from the hips down, not the chest down.

In summary, although the biomechanics of the kicking motion are very similar in backstroke and freestyle kick, there are some nuances to the backstroke kick that are different. Learning to press downward forcefully with the bottom of the foot on the down kick is a technique that should be used in backstroke kick and dolphin kick on the back. Therefore, to significantly improve the backstroke kicking speed, a swimmer cannot rely on practicing with freestyle kick only. Practicing with lots of backstroke kicking and dolphin kicking on the back is essential to increase backstroke speed.

Develop extreme ankle plantar flexibility, then work on strength for knee and hip flexion and hip extension, using a straight leg motion. Keep the kick as tight as possible and learn to kick hard in both directions. If you can do all of this, you will begin to see results in kicking speed and backstroke speed right away.

Helpful Kick Set for Backstroke or Freestyle.

If you over bend your knees in backstroke kick, try using the Finis elastic band placed below the knees to help keep your kick tighter.

Chapter 16

Backstroke Techniques

Coupling Motions

The coupling motions of backstroke are the same as they are for freestyle—body rotation and the arm recovery. Because they occur at different times in the pulling cycle and influence different parts of the pull, we separate the body rotation into two components, shoulder and hip rotation, just as we did in freestyle. In Chapter 10, in our discussion on freestyle, we defined coupling motions and how they work. For backstroke, let's start with the arm recovery.

Arm Recovery

There is a tremendous amount of potential energy from a straightened arm, held high above the water, that is about to be unleashed with all of its mass and speed upon the water's surface. Harnessing all of that potential energy, now turned into kinetic energy as the hand crashes to the water, and transforming that energy into greater propulsion is, more or less, the art of coupling.

The recovering arm in backstroke should always be straight (high octane). The path of the arm in the backstroke recovery should always be vertical, coming directly over the shoulder. The shoulder in the backstroke recovery should always be elevated as high as possible, in effect, making the hand reach an even higher point in the recovery than it would have without elevating the shoulder.

All three of these techniques will help to increase the kinetic energy of the arm as it strikes the water, but we haven't mentioned, yet, the biggest difference maker in this entire process—how much effort swimmers put into driving the hand and arm downward. Swimmers have two options. They can either rely on gravity to help bring the arms down to the water, using the momentum of the rotating arm that is already in motion, or they can be assisted by gravity, using their own muscles to drive the arm down to the water even harder. The latter is what the elite backstrokers do.

They do not worry about making air bubbles with the hand. They do not worry about making a splash. They do not try to be delicate. They drive the hand and arm down to the water because they know it makes them faster.

Elite backstrokers have also figured out that if they drive their arms down hard to the surface, they will also get faster shoulder rotation along with it, just as they do in freestyle. Yes, it is the same two for one deal. Since the arm is coming down with the highest level of octane possible, the stakes are even higher. The elite backstrokers not only drive their hands downward hard, they also extend the arm as far down the pool as possible, sub-luxating or hyperextending their shoulder joint in the process.

Shoulder Rotation

The speed of the shoulder rotation has a profound influence on the pulling propulsion and the kicking propulsion. Of course, as we just pointed out, the speed of the shoulder rotation is directly linked to the speed of the arm coming down on the recovery motion. One difference in backstroke compared to freestyle, however, is that the coupling energy from the shoulder rotation in backstroke impacts the end of the pulling motion, not the middle.

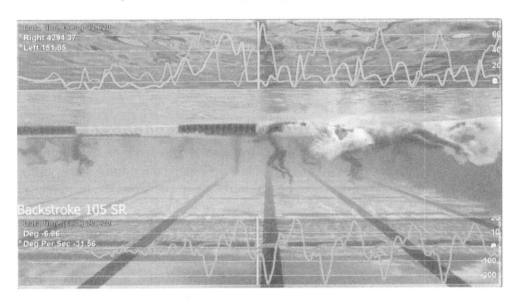

Elite backstroker Amy Bilquist reaches her peak shoulder rotational speed (graph below at vertical line) just before the left hand strikes the water. The smaller peak represents the shoulder rotation and the larger peak represents the hip rotation. The shoulder motion and arm energy lead to greater pressure with her right pulling hand (graph above at vertical line) toward the end of her pull. (Pressure Meter technology)

At almost the exact same point in her stroke cycle, using the same stroke rate, Amy is near a peak acceleration point (graph below at vertical line) which will be followed by a peak in her velocity (graph above at vertical line). (Velocity Meter Technology)

Finally, the amount of the shoulder rotation is influenced by how far upward or forward the recovering shoulder is elevated. By bringing the recovering shoulder higher, the pulling shoulder goes deeper, effectively increasing the amount and speed of the shoulder rotation, as the body rotates from one side to the other.

Hip Rotation

The speed of the hip rotation, as the hand and arm enter the release and early recovery phases of the cycle, also influences the propulsion from the pulling hand and the kick. Instead of on the same side, however, the hip rotational speed impacts the pulling hand of the opposite arm, as it begins the front-quadrant propulsion phase.

There is not quite the same link with the speed of the hand leaving the water with the hip rotation as there is with the hand entry and shoulder rotation. The swimmer really needs to concentrate on rotating the hips quickly in backstroke and in freestyle, to increase that coupling energy.

At the peak hip rotational speed (graph below at vertical line), the pressure on the left hand (graph above at vertical line) starts increasing. The pulling hand is in a biomechanically weaker position, so the propulsion is not as high as it will become (PM technology).

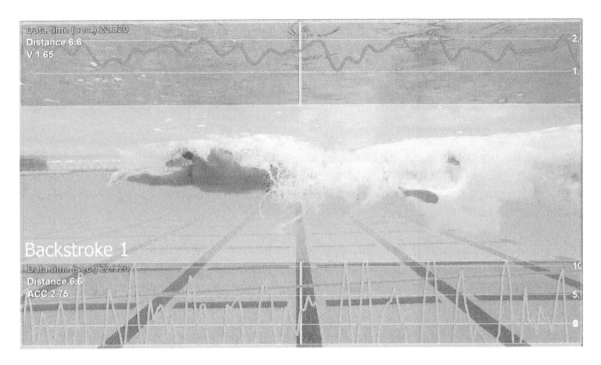

Data time (sec.) 22.920
Distance 6.6
V 1.65

Backstroke 1

Data time (sec.) 22.920
Distance 6.6
ACC 2.75

In almost the exact same point in the stroke cycle, the left hand begins the early propulsion phase, the hip rotates and the swimmer accelerates some (graph below at vertical line). As a result, the velocity begins to increase (graph above using VM technology).

In summary, the coupling motions of quick hip rotation and a strong finish to the arm recovery (shoulder rotation) can help propel you to a faster backstroke swim. To increase coupling energy in backstroke, the most important two points to concentrate on are to drive the hands and arms hard down to the water and to snap the hips up after the pulling hand releases and elevates in the early recovery.

Helpful Drills for Backstroke Coupling Motions to be Done with Fins:

6 kick switch with focus on rotation

6 kicks 1 stroke

6 kicks 3 strokes

Dolphin Kick Backstroke if swimmer is struggling with tempo

Chapter 17

Breaststroke Techniques

Fundamentals

Breaststroke is the most challenging stroke to learn and to teach. One reason for that challenge is that swimming breaststroke well requires a different set of anatomical tools than freestyle, backstroke or butterfly. Second, breaststroke is the most timing-sensitive stroke. If the timing is off just a little bit, breaststroke doesn't function nearly as well.

When compared to the other strokes, there are several other unique features of breaststroke. Here are just some of them:

1. Breaststroke is a stop-and-go stroke

Mechanically, breaststroke is the least efficient stroke. It does not take advantage of the law of inertia. Even among the Olympian breaststrokers, when the large thighs are drawn forward for the kick with the shoulders elevated out of the water, the velocity of the swimmer drops to, or nearly to, zero. While swimming, the breaststroker goes from the lowest drag coefficient to the highest drag coefficient with each stroke cycle. We call breaststroke the *standing dunk* of swimming. The swimmer doesn't get to run and dunk the ball. Each time the swimmer drives forward with the kick, he is doing so from a dead stop.

2. The breaststroke kick and pull occur independently

Breaststroke is the one stroke where a kick and pull are not going on simultaneously. They occur independently. That means as the kick happens, the arms and upper body (and legs at the completion of the kick) need to stay out the way (reduce drag). When the pull happens, the legs need to stay out of the way (reduce drag). While that independence may make it easier to estimate the propulsion that is generated from the kick and the pull, it will result in some down time, when neither arms nor legs are generating propulsion. That further adds to the huge variations in velocity.

3. There is no true recovery time in breaststroke

With freestyle, backstroke and butterfly, there is a brief period of time during the release and early recovery phases where the wrist and hands get to relax. In breaststroke, if the swimmer tries to relax at any point during the kick or pull cycles, the frontal drag force increases tremendously. Except for a very brief time when the upper arms and part of the hands break the surface of the water, the arms and legs remain under water the entire time. That means the swimmer must be on guard against causing excessive drag or not generating enough propulsion at all times. To swim fast breaststroke, the swimmer cannot take any *vacation* time.

4. In breaststroke, harnessing the coupling energy for the kick is the most difficult to achieve of all strokes

This fact goes back to the timing sensitivity of breaststroke. To be able to couple the kinetic energy of the upper body with the kick demands that the kicking cycle becomes extremely fast. To use the fast-stroke-rate, power breaststroke technique, such as that of Adam Peaty or Lilly King, one must develop a fast, propulsive kick. The *drop-and-shoot or shoot-kick-glide* breaststroke technique of the past simply does not enable a swimmer to develop enough speed in the shorter races.

5. The body position in breaststroke, prior to the kick propulsion, has the least regard for the drag coefficient

Because the swimmer's velocity in breaststroke approaches zero, the swimmer (at that time) need not be concerned about maintaining a low-drag body position. There is no frontal drag caused from any object that is not moving, regardless of the medium it is in. Unlike other strokes, where the swimmer is always moving forward at some speed, the breaststroker comes to nearly a complete stop prior to the kick. At that moment, the position of the swimmer is irrelevant, as there will be no drag. Therefore, the swimmer can and should assume the body position that will result in the greatest propulsion from the ensuing kick to move him or her forward. It is for that reason that we see the elite breaststrokers elevate their backs and shoulders completely out of the water and draw their legs far forward prior to the kick.

Watching breaststrokers compete at all ages, one sees what appears to be a wide variety of stroke techniques. Being *lumpers,* rather than *splitters,* we like to keep things simple. We categorize breaststroke into two stroke techniques, related to the difference we find in the pulling cycle and stroke rate. One is *fast arm recovery* breaststroke. The other is *delayed arm recovery* breaststroke.

Much of the difference in technique is determined by the event. You will find few elite breaststrokers in the 50 or 100 events using anything other than a fast arm recovery breaststroke technique. In the 200-meter breaststroke, however, many swimmers convert to a delayed arm recovery technique with a much slower stroke rate. The delay in the arm recovery can come with the arms pulled back fully (Rebecca Soni, USA), or, more commonly, on the way forward (Daniel Gyurta, Hungary). Often, in swimming the 200 meters, the stroke rates of elite breaststrokers will start out very slow (30/minute or less) with a *delayed arm recovery* and end the race in final 25 meters with a *fast arm recovery* technique using a stroke rate of 55/minute or higher.

Although some may believe it is wrong to do so, we believe that one can consider that all forms of breaststroke are some variants of these two techniques. That is not to say that everyone uses the same kicking or pulling motions. They don't. We don't consider those to be different stroke techniques any more than we consider using a different pulling motion in freestyle a different freestyle technique.

In analyzing breaststroke, we like to take the same *Newtonian* approach that we do with the other strokes, looking at frontal drag and propulsion forces, and then inertia.

Frontal Drag

Immediately after the two propulsive moments in breaststroke from the pull and the kick, it is extremely important for the swimmer to immediately get into a streamlined position with the lowest drag coefficient possible. In breaststroke, a swimmer doesn't get as many propulsive opportunities as with the other strokes, so he or she better be ready to take advantage of each one after it happens. That requires streamlining both ends of the body.

During the pull, the legs should be straight back and the toes pointed. Using our Propulsion/Drag Meter technology (PDM), we found that the feet hanging straight down will increase frontal drag at race speed by 41% compared to the feet pointed backward. During the kick propulsion, the upper body should get into what we refer to as *racing* streamline position. Others refer to this as breaststroke streamline. In this streamline position, the chin should touch the chest with the arms placed behind the head, just like in *hyperstreamline.* The arms should be hyperextended straight forward as far as possible, even with the hips slightly flexed. The fingers should be pointing straight ahead, squeezed together with palms down, thumbs underneath and index fingers touching side by side. We call this breaststroke streamline *racing streamline.* Unlike *hyperstreamline,* where the wrists are stacked on top of each other, in *racing streamline,* the hands are placed side by side. To avoid causing drag from the legs and feet, the legs should be lifted and the feet pointed back at the end of the kicking cycle, while the legs are still moving backward. If a swimmer waits until the legs are completely straightened after the kick to lift them and point the toes, it is too late. The frontal drag has already happened.

Olympian Rebecca Soni keeps her legs straight behind and toes pointed as she completes her kick and nears her peak pulling propulsion.

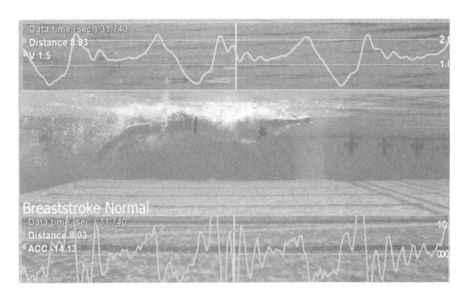

Elite swimmer Josh Zuchowski lets his legs and feet hang too long at the end of his kick, leading to a 47% loss of velocity (graph above). The deceleration at this point is excessive (graph below at vertical line), caused by poor technique at the back end of his body, not the front end. In front, he holds a good *racing* streamline position (Velocity Meter technology).

Breaststroke Normal SR 47

Time	T1	Time	P1	Difference	Time	T2	Time	P2	Difference
30.68	1.19	31.06	2.25	1.06	31.40	0.24	31.60	2.17	1.93
31.78	1.12	32.36	2.10	0.98	32.64	0.14	32.88	2.21	2.07
33.26	1.18	33.62	2.28	1.10	33.94	0.22	34.16	2.24	2.02
34.44	1.20	34.84	2.12	0.92					0.00
AVG	1.17		2.19	1.02	AVG	0.20		2.21	2.01

Breaststroke II

Time	P2	Time	T1	Difference
31.60	2.17	31.78	1.12	-1.05
32.88	2.21	33.26	1.18	-1.03
34.16	2.24	34.44	1.20	-1.04
AVG	2.21		1.17	-1.04
% Loss	47%			

Breaststroke Wide Outsweep SR 45

Time	T1	Time	P1	Difference	Time	T2	Time	P2	Difference
20.64	1.17	21.22	2.02	0.85	21.56	0.16	21.74	2.33	2.17
22.08	1.19	22.54	2.11	0.92	22.82	0.23	23.04	2.12	1.89
23.40	1.09	23.92	1.95	0.86	24.22	0.19	24.40	1.99	1.80
24.70	1.12	25.22	2.02	0.90	25.56	0.12	25.74	2.01	1.89
AVG	1.14		2.03	0.88	AVG	0.18		2.11	1.94

Breaststroke II

Time	P2	Time	T1	Difference
21.74	2.33	22.08	1.19	-1.14
23.04	2.12	23.40	1.09	-1.03
24.40	1.99	24.70	1.12	-0.87
25.74	2.01			
AVG	2.11		1.13	-0.98
% Loss	46%			

Data taken from Josh Zuchowski's Velocity Meter study. T1 and P1 refer to the Pull Trough (slowest) and Peak (fastest) velocities. T2 and P2 refer to the Kick Trough and Peak velocities. The difference between the two gives us an indication of the amount of propulsion the swimmer is generating from the kick and the pull. In this study, we compared Josh's technique of using a wide pulling motion versus a narrower pulling motion. The wider pull turned out to be better for him, resulting in greater average speed.

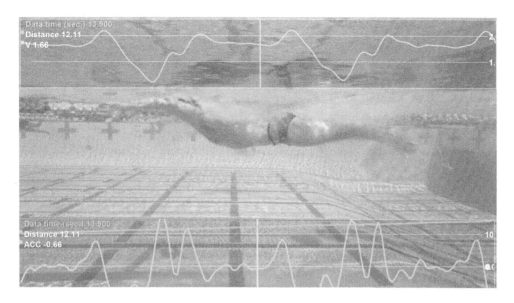

Olympian Mike Alexandrov finishes his kick in a much better streamline position and loses only about 20 - 25% of his speed (graph above at vertical line) from his peak velocity after the kick (VM technology).

Breaststrokers will often not streamline either end of their bodies after the kick. In front, this swimmer's arms are in a relaxed position with fingers pointing upward. Her head is protruding well above her biceps. Behind, her feet are hanging rather than pointing backward. As a result of not streamlining well at either end, she loses 41% of her velocity before the next pull (VM technology).

127

Rebecca finishes her kick with a slight hip flexion. A small hip flexion has about 4% less drag than a straight body at race speed (2.3 m/sec). This position also enables her to generate some small amount of propulsion from an up kick prior to the next breaststroke kick.

Another technique for reducing frontal drag in breaststroke is during the arm recovery. The shoulders should be elevated as high above the water as possible prior to the kick. At this moment, the swimmer's velocity is near zero, so the position of the upper body being vertical will not cause any significant drag. The height of the shoulders should be enough so that when the hands are driven forward from the chest to the water, most of the hand will clear the water. Keeping any part of the arm out of the water as it drives forward will help reduce drag.

After some recent studies with varying hand positions using PDM, we believe that the hands should drive forward in the breaststroke arm recovery and pierce through the water with the palms facing together and the little fingers down (*prayer* position). This hand position reduced drag by 9.1% compared to having the palms down. Once in the water and with the arms fully hyper-extended, the hands should rotate inward to a palms-down position in preparation for the next out sweeping motion.

Rebecca drives her hands forward with little fingers down to reduce drag. Once they are in the water, with arms fully extended, she rotates them back to the palms down position for her next pull.

To achieve maximum propulsion with the breaststroke kick, a swimmer must be able to attain significant surface area with the instep of the foot and ankle and the inside of the leg pressing backwards. To get that, the swimmer must flex the knees (knee bend), flex the hips (draw thighs forward), pronate the ankle (dorsiflex, abduct and evert—pull the toes back and turn the foot out) and internally rotate the hip (point the toes outward). Swimmers that have extraordinary flexibility in those areas, particularly with internal rotation of the hip, will not need to draw their legs forward (hip flexion), nor bend their knees (knee flexion), nor widen their knees as much as others to reach the maximal surface area with the instep and inner leg for the kick. As a result, they will cause less frontal drag to occur during the kicking cycle, yet still end up with great propulsion. Other swimmers, with less flexibility, will need to draw the legs and feet up farther and widen the distance between their knees to attain their maximal instep surface area, both of which are disadvantageous.

Olympic gold medal breaststrokers, Adam Peaty and Rebecca Soni, for example, are able to initiate the kick from a maximum angle of about 120 degrees between their thigh and upper body. Most other breaststrokers need to draw the legs up farther, creating an angle of between 100 and 110 degrees, to get the surface area and propulsion they need (the smaller the angle, the farther the thighs are drawn forward). Being able to achieve strong propulsion with less hip flexion not only reduces frontal drag, it also enables them to get through their kicking cycle faster and increase their swimming tempo (stroke rate), compared to other swimmers. Drawing the legs forward with the knees closer together reduces frontal drag compared to wider knees. It also enables the swimmer to push back with their instep against the vortex they caused by drawing their legs forward and gain more propulsion.

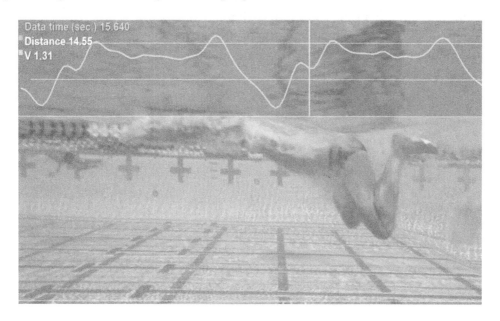

Mike Alexandrov draws his legs forward to about 110 degrees to initiate kick propulsion. With less flexibility, Mike has to draw the legs forward farther and with the knees slightly wider. Even so, with such strong legs, he can get through the kicking cycle quickly (VM technology).

129

Rebecca Soni draws her legs forward to about 120 degrees to initiate her kick propulsion. Her kick is narrower so she is able to push back against some of her vortex, increasing her propulsion.

Propulsion

The propulsion from the breaststroke pull is generated mostly by the hands as they turn the corner, changing direction from an out sweeping motion to pressing backward, then to an in sweeping motion. The time spent in propulsion with the hands in breaststroke is very brief, around .15 seconds. There is also a small amount of propulsion that is generated from the inside of the forearm and upper arm during the in sweeping motion, as the elbows press back and down toward the sides of the chest.

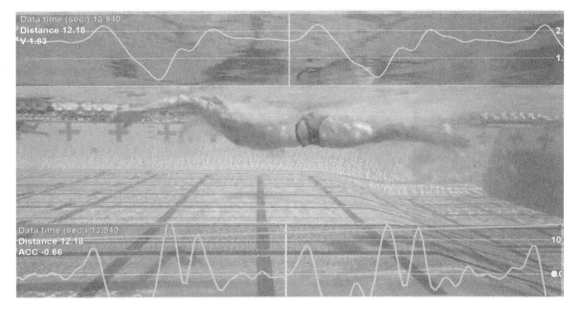

Olympian Mike Alexandrov reaches his trough velocity (slowest velocity) of 1.63 m/sec before his pulling propulsion begins (graph above, using VM technology).

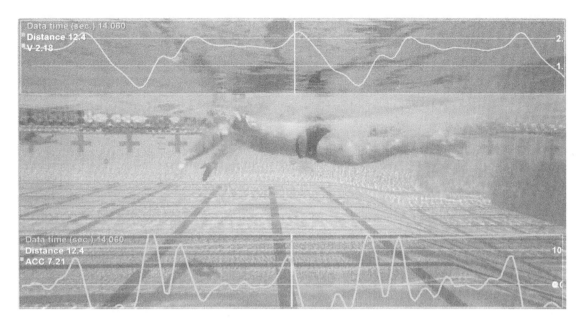

After turning the corner and a quick pulling propulsion phase, Mike reaches a peak velocity of 2.18 m/sec, a ΔPT of .55 m/sec (VM technology).

The propulsion of the kick is determined primarily by the amount of surface area of the instep and lower leg and the speed of that surface moving backward. The breaststroke kick also has the potential to utilize the vortex or slipstream caused by the motion of the legs moving forward in preparation for the kick and the body moving forward. Because the feet and legs are fairly close together as they are drawn forward, the vortex they form is also narrow. By using a wider kicking technique, the swimmer essentially misses the vortices, losing out on the opportunity to push back against the slipstream that they created and increase the propulsion.

We will discuss the kicking and pulling motions in more detail in Chapters 18 and 19.

Using Pressure Meter technology (PM), we now have the ability to measure the pressure from the hands during the breaststroke pull, but not from the feet during the kick. However, we can get a pretty good idea of the amount of propulsion generated from the hands and feet by using Velocity Meter technology (VM). Since the two propulsive forces are acting independently, by analyzing the difference between the trough (slowest) and peak (fastest) velocities, before and after the kick and pull, which we refer to as ΔPT, we know how much each propulsion effort increases the swimmer's velocity. Since there is a considerably higher drag coefficient of the swimmer's body during the pulling motion than there is with the kicking motion, the ΔPT does not correlate exactly with the amount of propulsion generated by each motion. Rather, it is more indicative of the net difference between propulsion and drag forces during each motion.

In the data presented above from elite swimmer Josh Zuchowski, we found that the average ΔPT for his pull was about 1 m/sec and for his kick about 2 m/sec. It is not exactly precise to deduce from that information that his kick generates 2/3 or 67% of his total propulsion, but the kick propulsion is greater than the pull. With elite women, we can find the propulsion even more dominated by the kick, with up to 80% of the swimmer's velocity coming from the legs.

In either case, because of the strong contribution from the kick, we consider breaststroke to be the most kick-dependent of the four strokes. Without a strong kick in breaststroke, a swimmer doesn't have a lot going for him or her.

Before the kick, Mike Alexandrov's speed drops to 0.25 m/sec, as his legs are drawn forward (graph above). The peak drag force occurs as the legs are being drawn forward and the upper body is still out of the water (VM technology).

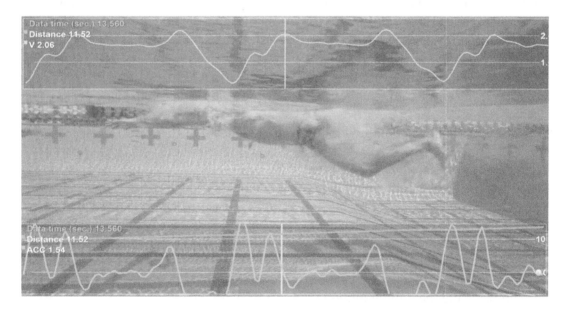

After the kick, Mike's peak velocity reaches 2.06 m/sec. The ΔPT is 1.81 m/sec (VM technology).

Inertia

With the huge variance of speed found in breaststroke, it is the least mechanically efficient stroke. It also the slowest stroke. However, the law of inertia still applies. Since the numbers of kicks and pulls are equal, if a swimmer can maintain the correct timing of the kicks and pulls, then a higher stroke rate will produce a faster swim. That is a big *if*.

The biggest challenge with increasing the stroke rate with most breaststrokers is the kicking cycle speed. The time required for Peaty and Soni and other elite breaststrokers to get from their peak acceleration (propulsion) from the pull to their peak acceleration (propulsion) from the kick is about .5 seconds or less. That not only requires the key flexibility in the hips and ankles, it also requires tremendous leg strength. Most other swimmers will take considerably longer than .5 seconds to do the same thing. In that case, they miss the coupling opportunity, and while trying to get to a faster stroke rate, the kick propulsion peaks when the hands are already separating out front for the next pull. That will result in more drag force and less distance per stroke from the kick.

In slower stroke rate breaststroke, as we find in the beginning of the 200-meter race, for example, swimmers will hold their *racing* streamline position for a much longer time. In this case, there is much less chance of swimmers kicking into a bad drag position. Even when swimmers are streamlined in front and in the back at the end of their kicks, there will be a greater percentage of velocity lost after the kick with a slower stroke rate, just on the basis of waiting and gliding longer before starting the next pull.

In breaststroke, it is far better to teach the correct technique and use of coupling motions with a slower stroke rate. Only after the swimmer is able to use a faster kicking cycle effectively, can the stroke rate increase efficiently. Getting to a faster kicking cycle is not something that can happen overnight. Developing a powerful, fast-stroke-rate breaststroke requires years of work and development.

The Breaststroke Pullout

With the breaststroke pullout, there are four propulsive events: the push off the wall or starting block, the dolphin kick, the arm pulldown and the breaststroke kick. The objective of the pullout is to average the same or higher speed as during the breaststroke swim and do so with less energy expenditure. Otherwise, there would be no advantage in using it.

Increasing the average velocity through the pullout depends on maximizing all four of the propulsion events and minimizing frontal drag. While the pullout was once done (and still is by some) with the dolphin kick and pulldown occurring simultaneously, we now know that is not the best technique. In VM testing, we found that when the dolphin kick and pulldown are separated in time, the time to 8 meters improved by as much as .5 seconds. It is more efficient and faster to take the dolphin kick, pulldown and breaststroke kick at separate times.

Whether from a dive (starting block), when the body enters the water at a downward angle, or from a push off the wall, the trajectory of the body should initially be angled down, perhaps 15-20 degrees. There are two reasons for leaving the wall with a mild downward trajectory. First, it enables the swimmer to take a longer path of the feet on the initial dolphin down kick, as the swimmer should complete the down kick in a slightly hip-flexed position. Second, it helps prevent the swimmer that is holding his or her breath from floating up and reaching the surface too soon.

The duration of the entire pullout, from feet leaving the wall or the beep of the start to head breaking the surface, is typically 4.5 seconds on a turn and about 5 to 5.5 seconds on the start. The swimmer's speed is greater off the start and he reaches a greater depth, requiring a little more time to reach the surface. The time interval between the push off the wall and the peak acceleration from the down kick, the pulldown and the breaststroke kick should all be about the same, around 1.2-1.4 seconds. There should be less than a second of time remaining between the final breaststroke kick peak propulsion and the head breaking the surface. Otherwise, the swimmer is too deep in the water for the breakout.

The first propulsion after the push off the wall is a strong dolphin kick, while the swimmer is in a *hyperstreamlined* position. The first motion of the dolphin kick is a small up kick which is minimally propulsive, as the legs are starting from a straight back, toe-pointed position. Once the knee bend starts, the swimmer decelerates more rapidly. The more the knees bend and the faster the legs are drawn forward, the greater the deceleration. Ideally, the knees should not bend excessively, more than about 75 degrees, nor the speed of the swimmer drop below 1 m/sec at the slowest point. With the bending of the knees prior to the down kick, the lower back is arched (lumbar extension) and chest and arms are elevated to gain propulsion for the down kick. The hands will raise about 8-10 inches in the water. During the forceful down kick, the upper body and arms come down again, aiming slightly downward. At the end of the down kick, the hips should be flexed slightly to enable the feet to follow through the body vortex and maximize the propulsion. The body immediately straightens out in preparation for the pulldown. We found that a tighter, more forceful down kick was 15% faster than a bigger, more undulating and knee-bending dolphin kick during the pullout.

Elite breaststroker Nikola Obrovac over bends his knees for this dolphin kick on the pullout. Notice that he elevates his chest by extending the lumbar spine and flexing the thoracic spine to increase propulsion from the dolphin kick (VM technology).

The pulldown should be done like a butterfly pulling motion, not a breaststroke pull, using less out-sweeping of the hands. The chin should remain on the chest as the hands push straight back using a powerful, high-elbow motion. At the completion of the pulldown, the hands should finish below the swimmer's thighs, not adjacent to the legs. Placing the hands below the thighs will insure that the shoulders are hunched, rather than flat. In our drag (PDM) studies, a hunched shoulder reduced frontal drag by 4% compared to squared shoulders. With the pulldown, the trajectory of the swimmer should start to climb.

Nikola pulls too widely during his pulldown. The pulldown motion should resemble the butterfly pulling motion.

After the pulldown, there is a very brief pause before the swimmer begins to draw the hands back forward as close to the body as possible. As the hands and arms move forward along the body, the direction of the squeezed fingers steadily transitions from pointing backward to pointing forward. When the hands reach the level of the chest, the legs begin to draw forward for the breaststroke kick. By the time the hands reach the face, the squeezed fingers should now be pointing forward with the hands moving toward *prayer* position, with little fingers down. The chin still remains on the chest.

Nikola draws his arms forward close to his body. The hands are now transitioning back to the prayer position.

The mechanics of the breaststroke kick on the pullout should be essentially the same as during the swim. The objective is to get as much from this last propulsion effort as possible. By the time the feet start moving backward on the breaststroke kick, the arms should be fully extended in front in the lowest drag streamline position possible. It is here that the teaching at The Race Club differs from most coaches. We believe that the swimmer should not go to *racing* streamline or have the hands separated in front, as is usually seen. We believe that the swimmer should go back to the same *hyperstreamline* position that was used pushing off the wall or on the start. That is the lowest drag position for the human body. Using Velocity Meter (VM) Technology, we found that elite breaststroker Aaron Greenberg was .16 seconds faster to 7 meters finishing the pullout in a *hyperstreamline* position, compared to *racing* streamline. From the ascent after the pulldown, and when the kick is completed with toes pointed backward, the swimmer should now be nearing the surface.

Nikola prepares to finish with a strong breaststroke kick. He doesn't draw the knees forward too far, yet his speed drops almost to zero (graph above) before he accelerates again because his feet are drawn too far forward and knees bent too much.

Nikola finishes the breaststroke kick near the surface. His arms are in *hyperstreamline*. His chin should be on his chest.

Finally, the swimmer completes the pullout by initiating a strong breaststroke pull, with wide out sweep, keeping the chin down on the chest until the elbows begin to bend near the end of the out sweep. At that time, the head and shoulders are lifted up to break the surface to complete the pullout.

These are the most common mistakes we find on the breaststroke pullout:

1. Pushing off the wall too deep, ending the pullout too deep in the water (too much downward incline to start the pullout or not initiating an incline)
2. Pushing off the wall too shallow (not initiating the push with a downward incline), reaching the surface too soon
3. Not working hard enough on any of the three propulsive efforts: dolphin kick, pull down or breaststroke kick
4. Delaying too long between the dolphin kick, pull down and breaststroke kick (taking too long for the pullout to get to the surface)
5. Not taking enough time between the dolphin kick, pull down and breaststroke kick (hurrying through the pullout)
6. Taking the dolphin kick and pulldown simultaneously, rather than separately
7. Pulling too widely on the pull down (more like a breaststroke pull), rather than using a higher-elbow, narrower pulling motion (more like a butterfly pull)
8. Not pulling the hands to the tops of the thighs (hands end up at the sides of the thighs)
9. Not bringing the hands and arms forward close enough to the body after the pull down
10. Not finishing the breaststroke kick with the legs straight and toes pointed backward
11. Not keeping the chin on the chest all the way through the pullout (including not waiting to lift the head until the hands transition into the propulsive phase on the breakout breaststroke pull)
12. Finishing the pullout in a non-streamlined position (we prefer to finish the pullout in *hyperstreamline).*

To summarize, breaststroke is a challenging stroke, particularly for those swimmers that do not have great tools to perform it well. Developing the anatomical tools for the breaststroke kick is essential to building a strong breaststroke. Without the proper tools, a swimmer simply has too many disadvantages compared to swimmers that do. A fast breaststroke kick requires key flexibility, strength and fitness.

Over the next three chapters, we will discuss how to improve your breaststroke pull, your breaststroke kick and how to utilize the three important coupling motions in breaststroke.

Chapter 18

Breaststroke Techniques

The Four Phases of the Pulling Cycle

If an athlete takes a swimming stroke to an entirely different level, the world needs to pay attention to what he or she is doing differently. Such is the case with Adam Peaty (Great Britain), and, to a lesser extent, Lilly King (USA), in sprint breaststroke technique. Each swimmer uses a pulling motion that is wider and with less length from front to back than has been traditionally taught for many years. It has been called the *loop* pull, forming a wide and fast elliptical path of the hand.

In breaststroke, there are four different phases of the pulling cycle—the lift phase, the propulsion phase, the release phase and the strike phase. As in freestyle and backstroke, each phase of the breaststroke pull has its purpose.

The pull contributes less to the total speed of the breaststroker than the kick does. Yet it is still important. A strong pull often leads to a much better pullout, so it becomes more important in short course than in long course meters. Ian Finnerty is a good example of an elite breaststroker with an extraordinarily strong pull, but not such a strong kick. He also has an amazing pullout. Because of that, he excels more in short course races than he does in long course races.

The Lift Phase

The lift phase begins with the first outsweeping motion of the hands and ends once the hands start moving backwards, causing some acceleration, indicating that more significant propulsion has begun. The duration of the lift phase will range from about .25 seconds with a narrower pull to about .30 seconds with a wider pull.

The two primary forces that are occurring during the lift phase are lift and frontal drag. The palms of the hands should not be facing directly to the sides during the lift phase, but rather pitched at about a 45-degree angle. The pitch of the hand results in lift (a force down) and some propulsion (force backward), particularly towards the end of the lift phase. The outward forces that are generated by each hand basically cancel each other out, since the hands are moving in the opposite direction. Once the hands begin pressing outward, the fingers and thumb of each hand should be separated slightly.

One would think that a wider pull would also cause a lot more frontal drag than a narrower pull, but we do not believe that it does. First of all, as the arms sweep outwards in a horizontal plane, the motion is circular, not straight out to the sides. That means that the forward velocity of the hands and arms (relative to the water) begins to slow as the hands move wider, lessening the impact of frontal drag. In addition, toward the end of the outsweeping motion, the shoulders and upper body begin to elevate in the water, which slows the forward motion of the hands and arms even further. In fact, by the end of the lift phase, as the elbows start to bend, there is very little, if any, forward motion of the arms at all. With no forward motion of the arms, there is no drag.

Toward the end of the lift phase, the shoulders, head and upper body begin to elevate out of the water. The majority of the elevation of the shoulders occurs during the propulsion phase of the pull, serving as an important coupling motion.

Olympian Mike Alexandrov initiates the lift phase with a 45-degree pitch of the hand and fingers separated (VM technology).

Propulsion Phase

The propulsion phase in the breaststroke pull does not last long, approximately .15-.20 seconds, but it provides virtually all of the propulsion from the arm pull. It starts with the bending of the elbows toward the end of the outsweep and a change in direction and position of the hand from a horizontal side motion to a vertical, quick backward motion. The hands drop deeper in the water and the fingers point down and press backward. The hands should not move backward very far nor for very long. Since the forearm and hand release and recover mostly under the water, moving the hands too far backward results in too much frontal drag on their way forward.

With the *loop* pull technique, as the hands turn the corner, drop deeper in the water and start moving backward, they should be positioned well outside the elbows. Before the hands reach the level of the shoulders (from side view) as they are moving backward, they turn inward and start moving toward each other. This is referred to as the *insweep*. At that time, the elbows begin to drop down and press backward quickly toward the chest, generating a small amount of propulsion in the process from the upper arms. Once the insweep begins and the hands, pitched to about 45 degrees, move toward each other, the propulsion is over.

For two reasons the propulsion and resultant increase in body speed generated by the arms is short-lived. First, as the arms near the out sweep and prepare for the propulsion phase, the shoulders, head and upper body begin to elevate out of the water, putting the body into a very bad drag coefficient position. Second, immediately after the pull propulsion, the legs begin to

139

draw forward in preparation for the kick, putting the body into an even worse drag position. With both of those movements happening, the swimmer's velocity drops to nearly zero, even with the Olympians.

The elevation of the shoulders high above the water is for a good reason, however. The propulsion of the pulling hands is augmented by the elevation of the shoulders, head and upper body during this phase, an important coupling motion. The faster and higher the swimmer elevates the shoulders, the more positive impact that upper body motion has on the propulsion of the hands, similar to rowing a boat. It is always better in rowing to use the back muscles along with the arms.

Mike Alexandrov during the propulsion phase of the breaststroke pull. His hands are moving backward and his acceleration and propulsion are at a peak (graph below at vertical line). His shoulders are moving upward.

It is worth mentioning that Rebecca Soni (USA) used a different technique with her pulling motion. As her hands turned the corner to press backwards, she kept her elbows higher in the water, rather than dropping them down to her chest. In doing so, she likely sacrificed some of the propulsion from the upper arms, but was able to recover with half of her forearm out of the water, reducing drag during the strike phase.

Olympian Rebecca Soni used a somewhat unique high-elbow breaststroke strike motion. By using this technique, she could get more coupling energy for her kick and reduce drag from the forearms moving forward partly out of the water.

Release Phase

While some refer to this phase as the *in sweep,* we like to call it the release phase. During the release phase, the hands rotate, turn inward, start to move toward each other and elevate. As the hands transition from propulsion to release phase, they should end up facing each other with the thumbs up, in the *prayer* hand position. Before the hands reach the surface of the water, they are now moving forward again. The *prayer* position will cause the least amount of frontal drag as the hands and arms begin to move forward under water. The duration of the release phase ranges from about .18 seconds to about .25 seconds.

Getting the hands to break the surface of the water through the release and strike phases is very important. We often find swimmers that keep their arms and hands completed submerged during those two phases. There is so much more drag caused by the water compared to air, that even getting a part of the hand over the surface will reduce frontal drag during the strike period.

During the release phase, the hands should reach the surface not by over-elevating the hands and arms, but by lifting and elevating the shoulders high enough out of the water, so that the hands break the surface with the least amount of arm elevation. Once the hands reach the surface of the water, that marks the transition point between the release and strike phases. If the hands do not reach or break the surface, the strike phase starts when the two hands begin to move forward under water. With the *fast arm recovery* breaststroke technique, it is very important for swimmers to accelerate their hands through the pulling cycle from the transition of lift into the propulsion phase, all the way through the release and strike phases back to the *racing* streamline.

Mike Alexandrov releases his hands in prayer position back to the surface of the water.

Strike Phase

The strike phase of the breaststroke pull begins when the hands either meet the surface of the water or they start moving forward. We refer to it as the strike phase, rather than recovery phase, because there is really no recovery going on—no relaxation of the wrists nor hands nor arms. With the elevation of the shoulders and the elbows dropping down at the end of the propulsion phase, the arms will typically strike forward with the upper arms completely out of the water, the hands partly or completely out of the water and the forearms under water. The hands should feel as if they are shooting almost straight forward, with a slight downward trajectory, but not upward. As the hands re-enter the water and the arms hyper-extend fully forward as far as possible, the shoulders subluxate into the *racing* streamline position. At this point, after each strike phase of the arms, the swimmer should feel as if he or she is trying to reach out and touch the wall at the other end of the pool. In *racing* streamline, the swimmer's chin should actually be touching his chest, the only stroke where this happens while swimming. No part of the back of the head (occiput) should protrude above the two upper arms. When the arms are fully hyper-extended forward, the hands should rotate from palms facing each other to palms down. During the strike phase, the fingers and thumb should remain squeezed together to minimize frontal drag and remain so until the lift phase begins. Once the palms turn down with the arms extended forward, the thumbs should move under the palms so the index fingers can press against each other, leaving no space between the hands. The strike phase shows the greatest variance in duration, because it depends on the stroke rate and the time that the hands are held out in front in *racing* streamline. For example, with a stroke rate of 33/minute, Olympian Mike Alexandrov will spend 1.0 second in the strike phase, most of which time he is in *racing* streamline. Yet, at a stroke rate of 56/minute, he is in the strike phase for .54 seconds, with very little time spent in *racing* streamline.

As Mike drives his hands forward in prayer position during the strike phase, he will quickly get back into *racing* streamline with the palms facing down. His legs, which are drawing forward now, will not reach peak propulsion until after his arms are fully hyper-extended in front (VM technology).

With a *fast arm recovery* breaststroke technique, the swimmer's arms are fully extended in the *racing* streamline position well before the kick reaches its maximum propulsion. The rationale for using this technique is that if the swimmer is streamlined well in front, then he will get the least amount of drag moving forward after the kick. This technique also puts the hands back in front sooner, so it enables a much faster stroke rate.

With a *delayed arm recovery* breaststroke technique, the swimmer will slow down the strike phase motion at some point. Rebecca Soni would pull her elbows as far back as they would go, with elbows held high, pausing a moment in that position before striking them forward. Then, when she did strike forward, she did so with her upper arms, most of her hands and half of her forearms above the water. Most of the *delayed arm recovery* breaststrokers, like Daniel Gyurta (Hungary), slow down the motion of their hands just after they break the surface, when they are under the chin, delaying the aggressive forward movement of the arms until the legs are in propulsion phase. The peak propulsion of the kick is reached as the upper body, head and arms are all moving forward and downward. The rationale for using this technique is that the swimmer is adding the mass of the arms moving forward to the mass of the upper body and head, increasing the coupling energy for the kick. The arms get into the *racing* streamline very soon after the peak propulsion occurs. With this technique there is an increase in frontal drag and an increase in kicking propulsion. Because of the slowing of the hands during the strike phase, *delayed arm recovery* technique cannot be used with a very fast stroke rate. Peaty, King and others that use the *fast arm recovery* breaststroke technique will try to make up for the loss of mass in their arms moving forward by pressing the body down and snapping the head down aggressively. If timed correctly, those two motions can augment their kicking propulsion.

Rebecca brings her arms back far with elbows high, pausing briefly before striking forward.

In summary, regardless of the breaststroke technique used, we advocate using a wider pulling motion and as much shoulder elevation as possible. The wider pull can result in greater pulling propulsion and more lift for the shoulders and upper body. The higher shoulder elevation can lead to a stronger kick and faster breaststroke, without slowing the stroke rate or causing excessive frontal drag.

The fingers and thumbs should be squeezed together and the hands in *prayer* position as they strike forward. Once the arms are fully hyper-extended in front, the fingers remain squeezed and the hands rotate to palms down, index fingers touching and thumbs underneath. To initiate the lift phase, or out sweep, the fingers and thumb spread slightly and the hand continues rotating to a pitch of about 45 degrees. The arms remain straight during the out sweep until the hands are well outside the elbows. With the bend of the elbow and the start of propulsion phase, the fingers remain spread but turn downward toward the bottom and the hand pushes straight back for a short duration and distance. The elbows then sweep downward and backward toward the chest, as the hands turn and sweep inward. With the turn of the hands, they transition from palms facing backward, to a pitched angle and then back to the *prayer* position, with palms facing toward each other. In this position, the fingers and thumbs squeeze together again. The hands and arms then release back into the strike phase, preparing for another pull.

At no point during this pulling cycle is there any relaxation or recovery time. Even in the slower stroke rate breaststroke used in the 200-meter events, where the hands and arms remain in front longer, they should be held out front fully straightened and with the shoulders hyper-extended forward and the chin touching the chest, the *racing* streamline position. There is no relaxation in that position, either.

While it may contribute less to the total swimmer's velocity than the kick, the pull is still extremely important. It should not be taken lightly. A strong pull will always make the breaststroke faster.

The inability to take a *breather* or *vacation* in breaststroke for the entire duration of the swim, for both kicking and pulling cycles, makes the stroke exhausting to perform. Great technique in breaststroke is a challenge to learn, to teach and to perform.

Helpful Drills for Breaststroke Pulling Motion:

Freestyle Kick with breaststroke pull wearing fins

Dolphin Kick with breaststroke pull wearing fins

Seated position pull drill

Chapter 19

Breaststroke Technique

Kicking

To develop a strong breaststroke, swimmers need to develop strong breaststroke kicks. Breaststroke is the most kick-dependent of the four strokes. The kick likely contributes anywhere from 60 to 80 percent of the total average breaststroke speed. The reward for developing a strong breaststroke kick goes beyond the improvement of the breaststroke races. Today, the strong breaststrokers virtually own the individual medleys (IM). At the highest level, swimmers cannot even be competitive in the IM without having a strong breaststroke. There is a lot to gain with a good breaststroke.

Tools for a Faster Breaststroke Kick

The anatomical tools required to develop a strong breaststroke kick are completely different than those required for a fast freestyle, backstroke or dolphin kick. There are three primary areas of joint flexibility which are especially important in developing a strong breaststroke kick: pronation of the ankle (dorsiflexion, eversion and abduction), internal rotation of the hip and extension of the lumbar spine. The first two abilities help increase the surface area of the instep and the inside of the leg to push backward in the water. The latter flexibility helps with shoulder and upper body elevation.

Small degrees of increased pronation and/or internal rotation of the hip, with resultant increases in surface area of the instep and leg pressing backward, can have a profound effect on the propulsive force that is generated with breaststroke kick. We estimate that for each degree of additional internal rotation in the hip, for example, swimmers would add at least 5% more propulsive force.

The ankle joint is a modified hinge joint. That means besides just moving in two directions, plantar flexion (pointing toes) and dorsiflexion (drawing toes upward), the foot also has the ability below the joint to rotate inwards and outwards (adduction/abduction) or swing inward and outward (inversion/eversion). Pronation is dorsiflexing, abducting and everting the ankle, all of the movements required for breaststroke kick. Some swimmers can pronate their ankles better than others.

Internal rotation of the hip is perhaps the most important anatomical tool for breaststroke. To point the toes outward in breaststroke kick, with the knees and hips flexed, the femur in the upper leg must rotate internally in the hip joint. The farther the hip internally rotates, the more the toes can point out and the more surface area the swimmer has to push with. The causes for restricted internal rotation of the hip can be many, such as tightness in the quadriceps muscle, a large head of the femur, the angle of the neck of the femur or tightness in the many muscles, tendons and ligaments surrounding the hip joint.

Swimmers who do not have much internal rotation flexibility in the hip gain instep surface area for their breaststroke kicks by spreading the knees wider (hip adduction) as they draw their legs forward. While this motion enables them to get more propulsion from their kicks, the widening of the knees creates three problems

- It causes more frontal drag as the legs are drawn forward in that wider position.
- It slows the cycle time, making it impossible to have an extremely fast kicking cycle time.
- It causes the swimmer to have to push the instep back outside of the vortex or slip stream, losing more propulsion opportunity.

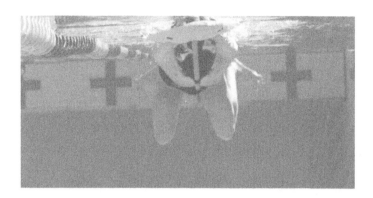

Breaststroke kick with knees at the ideal width—hip or shoulder distance apart.

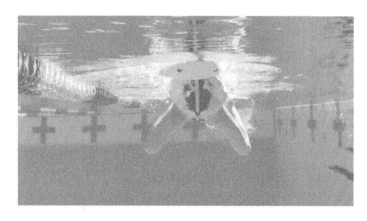

Breaststroke kick with knees spread too widely causes more drag and a longer kicking cycle time.

Breaststroke kick with wide knees. The insteps push back so widely they miss the slipstream.

Swimming is a sport of millimeters, hundredths of seconds and degrees. When it comes to improving breaststroke kick, swimmers that have not been blessed genetically with great flexibility in the two specific areas of the hip and ankle need to work hard to improve them. They need those few more degrees of range of motion. That involves dryland and stretching exercises.

The third anatomical tool, lumbar extension, is important for the swimmers' ability to elevate their shoulders high above the water during the pulling propulsion, while still maintaining their legs in a straight back position. Effectively, breaststrokers need to bend on the short axis, not rotate on the short axis. The more that they can extend or arch the lumbar spine and bend their bodies toward a 90-degree angle, resulting in higher elevation of the shoulders, the better. Flexibility in the lumbar spine is quite variable and usually diminishes with age, but like the other two anatomical tools, it can be improved with dryland stretching and exercises.

Olympian Rebecca Soni bends her lumbar spine to almost 90 degrees before her kick.

The higher elevation of the shoulders provides two benefits to the swimmers' breaststroke kicks. First, it enables them to generate more kinetic energy from the upper body and head coming down and striking the water. The higher the swimmers climb, the harder they fall. If timed

148

correctly with the kick, the upper body energy at impact will couple with the kick and increase its propulsion. Second, by elevating the shoulders higher, swimmers essentially buy more time before their bodies strike the water on the way down. That extra time becomes crucial, as most swimmers cannot get their legs into the propulsion phase fast enough to synchronize with the moment that the upper body kinetic energy peaks. By the time their legs are moving backwards generating propulsion, the upper body is already in the water and relatively motionless, with its kinetic energy having dropped to nearly zero. They missed the opportunity for coupling. It is like arriving at the train station 5 minutes late. The train has already left the station. That is precisely the technique that breaststrokers used with the old *drop-and-shoot (or shoot-kick-glide)* breaststroke, but it is not the technique that fast breaststrokers use today.

There is a fourth tool that can also help with the propulsion of the breaststroke kick, but this one is largely genetic. I am not sure it can be changed. That is the laxity in the knee joint. Even more so than the ankle, the knee joint is primarily a hinge joint, offering flexion and extension only. However, there are some swimmers that have some ability to externally rotate at the knee joint, aiding their quest to increase the surface instep area pressing backward. Decades ago, a world record holding breaststroker, Brian Job, had such laxity in his knees, when he would cross his legs while sitting with the ankle of one leg resting just above the knee of the other leg, his foot of the crossed leg would hang almost straight down. Fortunately for him, he never played football.

Kicking Cycle Speed

For several reasons, developing a fast kicking cycle time is extremely important. First, if the legs are drawn forward quickly, they cause a bigger vortex to form behind them. That vortex creates a slip stream that they can potentially use to kick back against, if the kicking motion is not too wide.

Second, if they want to take advantage of all of that energy from the upper body and head crashing downward toward the water, they don't have a lot of time to get their legs into propulsion mode. In most of the breaststrokers we have tested, the time between the peak acceleration (propulsion) from the pull and the peak acceleration (propulsion) from the kick is .54 seconds or longer. Adam Peaty, Rebecca Soni and Lilly King are able to shorten that time to .5 seconds or less, which is a huge advantage. In that shorter time period, they have a better chance of harnessing the upper body kinetic energy coming down and add more propulsion to their kick. Furthermore, since drawing the legs forward for the kick puts swimmers into about the worst drag position imaginable, spending less time in that position is always a good thing.

Third, if they are able to move the instep of their feet backwards faster, then they will generate more propulsion with the kick, particularly if they are pushing back against part of the vortex or slipstream. As with the pull, the propulsion happens very quickly with the kick and it is over. The magnitude of propulsion is not so much determined by how far the legs press backwards. It is more about the amount of the surface area available to press backwards and the acceleration of that surface area moving backward.

As I mentioned in the last chapter, Adam, Rebecca and Lilly have such great flexibility in the three key breaststroke areas that they can get their insteps into a high surface area position without drawing the thighs and feet forward quite as far and by keeping their knees much closer together. By decreasing the flexion angle of their hips and knees by 10 degrees or so, compared to most other swimmers, they are able to move through the kicking cycle and hit peak propulsion in that very fast .5 second interval or less from their peak pulling force. And with great propulsion!

Of course, there is one other important matter involved in their ability to shorten their kicking cycle time, strength. Swimmers simply cannot get their legs through a complete kicking cycle quickly without having great leg strength. Specifically, the quadriceps femoris and hamstring muscles must be extremely strong to flex and extend the hips and knees very quickly. Kicking fast over and over again also requires tremendous stamina.

Finishing the Breaststroke kick

There is a very common tendency for breaststrokers to not finish the ends of their kicks well. After all the effort to draw the legs up and press the insteps back as quickly as they can, they often relax the legs and feet at the end of the kick. The legs and feet then hang down, even more so with hyperextended knees. This is their brief vacation time, their moment to recover before the next kicking cycle. If they want to kick and swim breaststroke fast, there is no vacation time for the legs, either.

From our Propulsion/Drag Meter studies done in Florida, where we tested three different swimmers independently, we found the increase in frontal drag at race speed from allowing the feet to hang down was 31% at the lowest and 41% at the highest. We don't know how much more frontal drag will be added to that from the legs also hanging down some, but we are certain it is a significant amount. Unfortunately, both of these bad drag positions come right on the heels (no pun intended) of the most powerful propulsive moment in the stroke, the kick. The frontal drag of a swimmer is proportional to the square of the swimmer's velocity. Right after this powerful kick, when the swimmer's speed usually reaches its highest level, is not a good time to put himself into a bad drag position. A huge penalty will be paid for that—deceleration. In fact, more deceleration is likely caused by poor technique at the end of the kick than is caused by poor streamlining in front. We often see breaststrokers not doing either one very well.

Elite swimmer Josh Zuchowski allows his hyperextended legs and feet to hang at the end of his kick, causing him to lose 46% of his velocity after the peak from his kick.

Rather than relax the feet and legs at the end of the propulsion in the kick, the swimmer must elevate the legs and point the toes backward immediately, while the two legs are moving closer towards one another. If the swimmer waits until the two feet and legs are together, before elevating and pointing the toes, it is too late. The drag damage has already been done. There is also a little bit of propulsion that is generated by the upward movement of the legs at that time. If the movement upward is done sooner with the toes pointed, there is an opportunity for more propulsion to be gained by this upward motion of the legs and feet.

By finishing her kick with legs straight back and toes pointed, Rebecca Soni reduces frontal drag from her previous kick and during the next pull.

Testing for and building Better Breaststroke Tools

Years ago, Gary Sr. wrote this about his coach at Indiana University, Doc Counsilman:

Doc was a brilliant coach and a pioneer in understanding the science of swimming. He tried valiantly to improve my breaststroke kick. I was a pretty good swimmer with a bad breaststroke kick. Doc built me some alligator shoes, which were a pair of high-top Converse All-Stars, nailed to a piece of wood that was mounted on another piece of wood, angled at 45 degrees. When I wore them clumsily up and down the dormitory hallway with my toes up in the air, hoping to stretch my gastrocnemius muscle and/or my Achilles tendon, we thought it would improve my ankle dorsiflexion.

While Doc's focus was on increasing my ankle pronation, the bigger problem of my breaststroke was actually in my hip. I had extremely poor internal rotation of the hip. The extension of the lumbar spine was not important in those days, because swimmers weren't allowed to put their heads under water in breaststroke. The breaststroke technique was entirely different, very flat and not very fast. Anyway, after a few months of wearing alligator shoes, I didn't improve my breaststroke time by very much.

Today, at The Race Club, we test all swimmers for all three anatomical breaststroke tools, plus the tools for the other three strokes. For breaststroke evaluation, we score swimmers for each of three important categories of ankle pronation, hip internal rotation and lumbar extension from 0-10, with 10 being the best.

It is important for swimmers to know where they stand with all three anatomical breaststroke tools. It is even more important for them to understand how to improve their breaststroke tools. Without developing the right tools for breaststroke, all of the training in the world will not help much. Here is how we evaluate swimmers for breaststroke:

Ankle Pronation

Mostly a test for dorsiflexion, the swimmers should get in the downward dog position and press their heels into the ground. The farther they can move their hands away from their feet, while still keeping the heels on the ground, the more dorsiflexion they have.

Rebecca Soni is in the *downward dog* yoga position, improving her ankle pronation.

Another test for ankle pronation, which includes eversion and abduction, is to have the swimmers stand on one leg and bend over at the waist, holding on to something in front of them. Then have them draw one knee forward toward the chest with the knee at the width of the hip, similar to what they would do in a breaststroke kick. Holding the knee in that position, have them pronate the foot by pointing the toes directly out to the side. While this test also involves internal rotation of the hips, it will give you an idea of how well they pronate the foot and how much instep surface area they have to push with.

Hip Internal Rotation

A good test for internal rotation of the hip is the W squat position. Have the swimmers squat down with their lower legs on the cushioned mat with the feet pointed directly to the sides. The knees should be no wider than the hips. The insteps of the feet should be resting on the mat. Then have the swimmers move their bums backward toward the mat, hoping to reach the mat with their bums. If they are able to do so comfortably, they have good hip internal rotation. If not, they don't. The swimmers may feel tightness or pain in the hips, knees or insertion of the quadriceps. If they have pain in the knees, abandon the test, knowing that they do not internally rotate at the hips well. If the discomfort is in the quadriceps insertion, you know that they are tight there. If the discomfort is in the hip, then they need to work on the hip restriction.

By sitting in the W squat position, with the feet pronated outwards, a swimmer can test their internal hip rotation. Michaela Sceli (Canada) sits with her bum on the mat very comfortably, demonstrating she has excellent hip flexibility.

Lumbar Extension

The best test for lumbar spinal flexibility is the back bridge. Lying on their backs with hands and feet placed on the padded mat, fingers pointed toward the feet, have the swimmers push up into a back bridge. Once up, have them walk their hands and feet as closely together as possible. The closer that they can get them together, the more lumbar flexibility they have.

Elite swimmer Sabir Muhammed demonstrates the back bridge for lumbar extension flexibility.

If they are unable to do a back bridge, which requires some strength, have them lie face down on the mat. With their palms down on the mat around the shoulders, have them press down with their arms on the mat, lifting their shoulders as high as possible off the mat (upward dog position), while also pressing their pelvis into the mat. The higher they can reach with the shoulders, the more lumbar flexibility they have.

153

In *upward dog* position, Rebecca Soni demonstrates amazing flexibility in her lumbar spine

Here are some of our favorite stretches to improve each of these three key areas of flexibility:

Ankle Pronation

1. Downward dog static stretch. The swimmer gets into the downward dog position and hold for 2 minutes, pressing the heels firmly toward the mat.
2. Incline board dynamic stretch. Place both feet of the swimmer on an incline board. Bend one knee forward, then the other, pressing the heels down firmly to the ground each time.

Hip Internal Rotation

1. Dynamic hip stretch. Place one knee on the mat and one foot on the mat in front. Bring the entire upper body as far forward as possible, then as far backward as possible, until the bum reaches the heel of the back leg. Repeat 10 times. Then move the front foot over 30 degrees to the opposite side, while keeping the back leg in the same straight position. Bring the upper body forward and to the side as far as possible, following the path of the front thigh, then all the way back until the bum touches the heel. Repeat 10 times. Then move the front foot over 30 more degrees (60 degrees) and do the same thing 10 times. As the front leg gets farther over, it will become more difficult to move forward as far. Also, be sure that the back leg remains straight for all 30 reps. Otherwise, the hip internal rotation will not be reached. Repeat the same exercises with the other leg, moving to the other side. This stretch is working on the internal rotation of the hip of the back leg, not the front leg. The following photos illustrate the hip internal rotation dynamic stretch for the left hip:

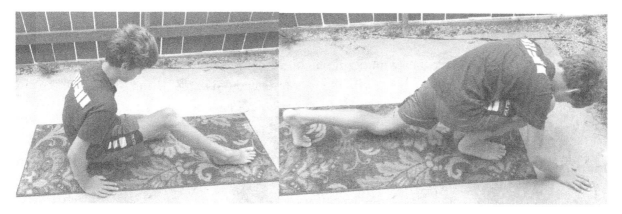

Dynamic hip stretch begins with 10 repeats of full flexion (left) and full extension (right) of the left hip.

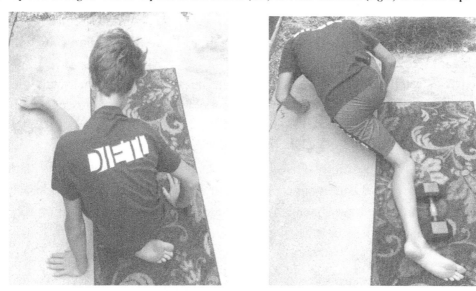

Next, the right foot is moved 30 degrees to the left, repeating 10 full flexions and extensions, following the path of the front leg. Notice the internal rotation of the hip of the back leg occurring on the stretch forward.

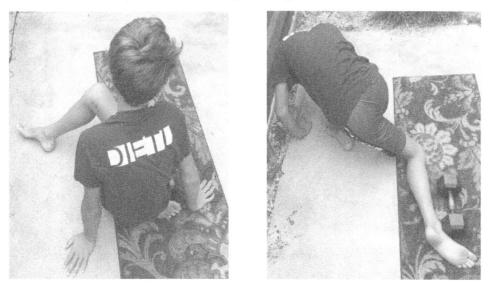

The final 10 dynamic left hip stretches are done with the right leg at 60 degrees. The dumbbell keeps the back leg straight.

2. Static hip stretch. Have the swimmer lie on his or her back on the mat with one leg straight and the other knee bent, with the foot pronated outwards. Bring the heel of the foot of the bent knee as close to the body as possible. Press the bent knee to the mat, while trying to keep the bum flat on the mat. Hold for 2 minutes and repeat on the other side.

Lumbar Extension

1. Dynamic back stretch (*upward dog* or *cobra position*). The swimmer lies prone (face down) on the mat and presses the shoulders upward into upward dog position, using the arms with the palms down at around the shoulders. Then the swimmer returns to the prone position on the mat. Repeat 10 times, pressing the pelvis into the mat and extending the neck backward (cervical extension) each time.
2. Dynamic back stretch (back bridge). The swimmer lies on his or her back with knees bent and palms on the mat, fingers pointed toward the feet. The swimmer presses with hands and feet to lift the body into a back bridge and then returns back to the mat. Repeat 5-10 times.
3. Static back stretch (bow position). The swimmer lies prone on the stomach. With the knees bent, the swimmer reaches back with each hand, grabbing each leg at the ankle, with the palms facing inward. The lower back is fully extended and held in the position for 30 seconds to 1 minute.

Rebecca holds a static *bow position* for one minute, increasing her lumbar flexibility.

Building a Faster Kicking Cycle

Developing strong propulsion with a fast kicking cycle time and finishing the kick with a low drag coefficient are the two primary components of a great breaststroke kick. Here are five of our favorite training sets to help you develop faster breaststroke leg speed and strength:

1. 10 x 50 meters with an alignment board and snorkel. 25 meters piston kick (kicking breaststroke one leg at a time horizontally) and 25 meters fast breaststroke kick.

2. 10 x 50 meters with an alignment board and snorkel while using a tempo trainer set on mode 3 at 75 beeps per minute. Alternate one dolphin kick and one breaststroke kick with each beep, trying to get the breast kick completed as fast as the dolphin kick.

3. 5 x 45 second wall breaststroke kicks with snorkel on. 15 seconds rest. Get in as many kicks as possible in 45 seconds, take 15 seconds rest and go again. 50 kicks in each 45 seconds is considered average. 60 kicks are in the top 25%. 70 kicks are in the top 10% of all our swimmers tested.

4. 10 x 50 meters breaststroke on 60 seconds. Set the tempo trainer to a 46/minute stroke rate for the swims. Alternate 50 breaststroke and 45 seconds of vertical eggbeater breaststroke kick (one breaststroke leg kick at a time in vertical position) with arms in the streamline position over head. Try to keep the chin above the water for the entire 45 seconds of eggbeater. If you want to make the set even tougher, try doing a double pullout at the turn for the 50-meter swim at a 46/minute stroke rate.

5. 10 x 50 meters with alignment board and snorkel using yellow Finis ankle strap to ensure the kick is staying narrow and finishing all the way through, holding a kicking stroke rate of 75/minute.

In summary, as with the pull, to kick correctly with a fast cycle time and a streamlined end to the propulsion, there is no vacation time. The legs are either drawing forward quickly, pushing back quickly, or lifting and pointing toes. There is no opportunity to relax or to recover. The legs must be working at all times. In breaststroke, the recovery period for the arms and legs begins when both hands touch the wall at the end of the race.

To improve your breaststroke kick, build better anatomical tools, increase your leg strength and stamina. To do all of that requires stretching, strength training and kicking—lots of kicking.

Chapter 20

Breaststroke Techniques

Coupling Motions

In other chapters we have defined and described coupling motions as they exist in all four strokes. There are three important and powerful coupling motions in breaststroke, one for the pull and two for the kick. The coupling motion for the pull is easier to understand than the two for the kick. It is also easier to accomplish.

The Pull

As the hands outsweep and near the end of the lift phase, and before the hands turn and press backward to generate propulsion, the swimmer should begin to lift his chin off of the chest and elevate the shoulders out of the water. Through the propulsion phase of the pull, the shoulders continue to elevate to the highest level possible, extending or arching the lumbar spine. At that point, the swimmer should be looking straight forward, not downward, with the chin well off of the chest. The lift generated by the out sweeping hands helps the swimmer elevate the shoulders high out of the water.

The angular velocity of the shoulders and upper body moving upward and backward has a profound influence on the propulsion of the pulling hands. One can compare this breaststroke pulling motion to using a rowing machine in the gym. If one were to just pull with the arms only on the rowing device, and not use the back muscles, not nearly as much weight could be lifted or power generated using the machine. The muscles in the back are strong and if the swimmer is lifting and moving the upper body backward, simultaneously with the hands moving backward, he or she will generate much more propulsion from the pull. The faster the swimmer elevates the upper body, the stronger the pull becomes. The speed of elevation of the shoulders is a powerful coupling motion for the pull.

The peak propulsion of the pull coincides with the peak acceleration (graph below at vertical line). How fast the shoulders elevate from the water affects the force of the pulling hands and the body's acceleration (VM technology).

The Kick

The two major coupling motions for the kick propulsion are the upper body coming down and the head snapping down. The reason that we separate the two motions is because they are connected by a neck that allows the head to move at a much faster angular velocity than the upper body. In Martial Arts, advanced students are taught to use their heads as a weapon. Weighing about 12 pounds and protected by a thick skull, the head can be snapped quickly toward a foe and inflict some serious damage. It is like swinging a bowling ball against someone.

Using the head for coupling energy is a relatively new phenomenon. In the past, swimmers have been taught to act as if the neck was stiff and the head was just an extension of the upper body. Some may recall or still use the *tennis ball* drill, where swimmers compress a tennis ball against their chests with their chins at all times in the breaststroke, not allowing the tennis ball to fall out. The purpose of this drill is to get the chin tucked down more under water, lowering frontal drag. Meghan Quann (USA), who won an Olympic gold medal in the 100-meter breaststroke in 2000, used this chin-down technique. Some swimmers are still being taught to keep their chins down all of the time in breaststroke.

In either case, stiff neck or chin down, the technique does not encourage or allow the swimmers to move their heads, eliminating an important coupling motion. Adam Peaty lifts his chin well off his chest during the elevation of his shoulders, so that he is looking straight forward at the height of the body elevation. He then snaps his head down aggressively as he is coming down, like he is trying to break a board in Tai Kwan Do class with his head. Once underwater, the chin goes all the way down to his chest, as his arms are already back into *racing* streamline position.

Besides the head moving quickly, the downward motion of the upper body is also an important coupling motion for the kick. It is natural for the gravitational force to bring the upper body down to the water again, without any assistance from the swimmer, but that is not what Adam does. He presses the body downward toward the water forcefully, using core muscles assisted by gravity, and reaches the water with more velocity and kinetic energy than he would have by simply falling down. Once in the water, he continues the downward motion of the upper body past the horizontal alignment position, into a small flexion of the hips, or a slightly pike position. By moving his body past alignment, he pushes the hips upward, reduces frontal drag and continues the kinetic energy of the moving body a little longer.

There is really only one purpose for snapping the head down and pressing the upper body aggressively toward the water, and that is to increase the power of the kicking propulsion. If those two events don't happen simultaneously, then all of that extra effort and energy from the upper body and head coming down is wasted. Getting those two events to happen at the same time is one of the greatest challenges of the modern power breaststroke. For it to happen, the kicking cycle has to be lightning fast.

Gary Sr. once asked Indiana University Head Coach, Ray Looze, what made Lilly King so great in breaststroke. He answered with three words, "lightning-fast-legs".

Olympian Mike Alexandrov reaches his peak acceleration or kick propulsion (graph below at vertical line) precisely as his upper body crashes into the water. The kinetic energy from his body and head coming down increase the propulsion from his kick, as the two actions occur simultaneously (VM technology).

The swimmers that use a *delayed arm recovery* breaststroke technique use a different strategy for coupling with their kicks. By slowing the arms down somewhere during the strike phase, they end up moving the arms forward along with the head and upper body coming down during the propulsion phase of the kick. In effect, by moving the arms forward during kick propulsion, they are adding more mass to their head and upper body, resulting in even more kinetic energy coupling at the right time. The downside of using this technique is that by having the arms moving forward during kick propulsion, they are adding some frontal drag at the same time.

A *delayed arm recovery* breaststroke technique should be used primarily in the longer 200-meter event, as it causes a slower stroke rate. The *fast arm recovery* breaststroke technique can be used at any distance, from 50 to 200 meters, and with a wide range of stroke rates, depending on the kicking cycle time and how long the swimmer chooses to remain in *racing* streamline out front. In the former technique, the swimmer is trying to maximize the coupling energy, while in the latter technique, the swimmer is trying to minimize the frontal drag during peak kick propulsion.

Because of the uniqueness of her technique, it is also worth mentioning that Rebecca Soni, using a *delayed arm recovery* technique, reduced the frontal drag from her arms moving forward during kick propulsion by elevating half of the forearm out of the water. (It is illegal to bring the arms completely out of the water in breaststroke during the strike phase). However, she kept her head in alignment with her body (stiff neck) which potentially reduced some of the coupling energy from her head.

Rebecca Soni strikes forward with elevated forearms half out of the water. Her head stays in alignment with her body.

In teaching breaststroke technique to swimmers of all ages and abilities, the real question is this: If very few swimmers have the ability to get through the kicking cycle fast enough to take advantage of all of that coupling energy coming down, is it worth teaching them to do the power breaststroke technique?

Here is what we think are important techniques for all breaststrokers to learn at any age:

1. To streamline both ends of the body after the kick, using *racing* streamline position in front and lifting the legs and pointing the toes back toward the end of the kick (immediately after the propulsion is finished) in back.
2. To use a wider *loop* pulling motion, with maximum shoulder elevation. Even if the swimmers can't take advantage of the kinetic energy on the way down, they can take advantage of it on the way up, strengthening their pulling propulsion.
3. Use dryland and swimming techniques to help improve the three anatomical breaststroke tools: ankle pronation, hip internal rotation and lumbar extension
4. As the breaststroke tools improve, narrow the knees to hip or shoulder width apart, enabling them to develop a faster kicking cycle.
5. Dryland and swimming exercises to help build strength in the quadriceps and hamstrings and drills that focus on kicking cycle speed.

It is a mistake to try to get young swimmers to use too high of a breaststroke stroke-rate early in their careers. If they do try, it usually doesn't end well. Through bad timing or technique, more frontal drag is often caused than additional propulsion is gained. The young swimmers end up slower and more exhausted. More than any other stroke, breaststroke must be nurtured along patiently, while developing the proper tools and strength.

When Katie Ledecky was a young age-grouper, she used a fast (100/minute stroke rate) freestyle with a 2-beat kick. By the time she was 15, at the Olympic Games of London in 2012, she had transitioned into a hybrid freestyle (86/minute stroke rate) with a strong 6-beat kick. As she grew older and her kick developed, she adopted a different technique that enabled her to swim faster. Actually, her technique is still evolving, even as a collegiate post-graduate, to become more pulling dominated.

161

The same is true with breaststroke. The power, fast-stroke-rate breaststroke technique must evolve over time. Ultimately, with a fast kicking cycle, it makes sense and has worked wonders for Adam Peaty, Lilly King, Rebecca Soni, Cameron Vanderburgh and many others. Getting there is a process that takes time.

With Masters swimmers, much of their ability to get faster in breaststroke depends on developing the above-discussed anatomical tools. Fortunately, the tools can be improved at any age, with work. The fundamentals of good streamlining and increasing propulsion in breaststroke also apply at any age.

In conclusion, the decision to use *delayed arm recovery* or *fast arm recovery* breaststroke technique is a personal one and must be evaluated with each swimmer and for each event. Either way, the powerful coupling motion of shoulder elevation should be used by all breaststrokers. Developing the ability to use the coupling motions for the kick takes time and work. Knowing that a powerful tool is out there for those that earn it is pretty enticing. In the last chapter we shared four of our favorite Race Club sets to improve your kicking cycle time. Here are two of our favorite drills to improve your breaststroke coupling motions:

1. <u>2 kick-1 pull dolphin kick breaststroke with fins</u>. We love to use this drill to bring awareness to the swimmer of the power of coupling energy. It is relatively easy to time the crashing of the upper body into the water with the quick snap down of the dolphin kick. The fins just add more propulsion. The swimmers need to think about the timing of their bodies hitting the water with that snap down of the fins. It is precisely the same, and the result is a surge forward in speed.

2. <u>Flutter kick breaststroke with fins.</u> In this drill, we really focus on three things: wide pulling motion, maximum elevation of the shoulders with head lift and pressing the upper body and head down forcefully into *racing* streamline. They are all part of the coupling effort.

Chapter 21

Butterfly Techniques

Fundamentals

Butterfly is a challenging stroke, requiring great strength and stamina to do and to sustain for very long. Like breaststroke, butterfly is mechanically inefficient, with tremendous variations in speed during the stroke cycle. The arm propulsion comes with both hands pressing backward, followed by a relatively long period of recovery without any arm propulsion.

Butterfly is also a very kick-dependent stroke. Without a strong kick, the butterfly does not function well. There are potentially four individual dolphin kicks that can be utilized during a single stroke cycle, two down kicks and two up kicks. Rarely do swimmers take advantage of all four of them by working them hard.

Butterfly is considered to be one of the two *short-axis* strokes, along with breaststroke. The short axis is a line going latitudinally through the human body at the midline, around the hip area. Freestyle and backstroke are considered *long-axis* strokes, as the body rotates around the longitudinal body axis.

While body rotation in the long axis of freestyle and backstroke is desirable, too much short axis rotation in butterfly is undesirable. The more vertical the swimmer's body becomes in the water, the greater the frontal drag. One of the major objectives in butterfly is to minimize the frontal drag forces, while still managing to achieve great propulsion. To gain propulsion from the legs for both the down and up kicks, the hips must flex on the down kick. To gain propulsion from the arms during the pull, the lumbar spine must extend (arch) and the shoulders must elevate, with or without a breath. In butterfly, it is more accurate to consider that the body bends on the short axis, rather than rotates on the short axis. It just can't bend too much.

In perhaps what some people may consider to be an over-simplification, we classify butterfly into two techniques—*side breath* and *front breath*. In the *front breath* category, we also place two sub-categories—*early breath* and *late breath*. Within the *front breath* category, there are also two variants of that technique that can be used with either an early or late breath. Those are the *second-down-kick* technique, that has been used by two of the greatest 400 individual medley swimmers in history, and the *dolphin-dive* technique, that is commonly used by Masters swimmers. Since the *front breath* butterfly technique is by far the most common one used, let's start with that one.

Early Front Breath Butterfly Technique

Most of the front breathers in butterfly will use an early breath technique. With *early breath* butterfly technique, the chin should be tucked down very close to the chest just prior to the hands entering the water on the recovery. Simultaneously with the hands striking the water, the chin begins to lift off of the chest. The maximum hip flexion of about 25-30 degrees should occur shortly after the hands enter the water (about .12 seconds later), when the swimmer's chest is pressed downward. At this moment, the swimmer's shoulders are at the deepest point in the water throughout the entire cycle.

During the lift phase of the pull, as the hands move downward and slightly outward, the shoulders begin to elevate and the chin continues to lift forward. The back of the head will break the surface with *early breath* butterfly technique, with or without a breath, when the hands just begin their propulsive phase (moving backward) and they are about 1.5 feet in front of the shoulders. When the front breath is taken, however, the chin continues lifting forward and the shoulders and head elevate until the head is completely out of the water. Without taking a breath, only a part of the head breaks the surface. With the breath, by the time the pulling hands are around the shoulders moving backward, the head is completely out of the water.

After the front breath, the face re-enters the water when the arms are moving forward near the shoulders during the recovery. On a breath stroke, with *early breath* technique, the head is partially or completely out of the water for about .64 -.68 seconds.

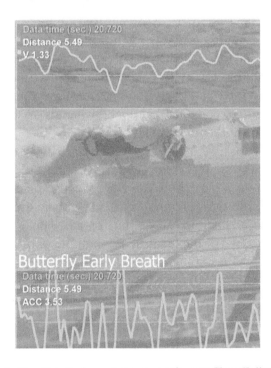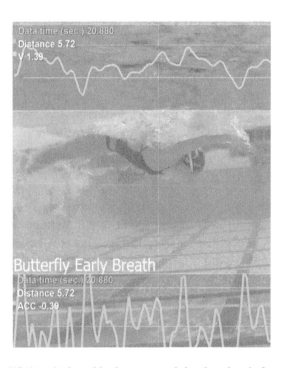

Early Breath technique. Age group swimmer Ciera Fujiwara (USA) tucks her chin down toward the chest just before hand entry (left). The chin is already lifting forward. As she presses down with chest and arms, she reaches maximum hip flexion of about 25 degrees (right). The chin keeps moving forward and head elevating (VM technology).

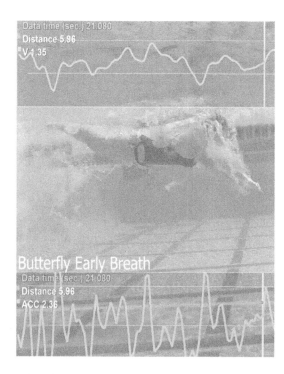
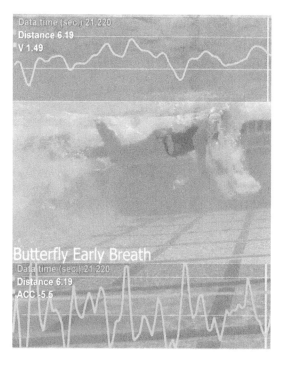

Early Breath technique. Ciera's head first breaks the surface when her hands are about 1.5 feet in front of the shoulders (left), starting her propulsion phase. By the time her hands are at her shoulders moving backward, her head is completely out of the water. Her head remains out (at least partially) of the water for about .66 seconds (VM technology).

Late Front Breath Butterfly Technique

There are very few elite butterfliers who use a late breath technique. That does not mean that it is a bad technique. We just don't think many coaches know about it or understand it. We first became aware of the *late breath* technique after watching Joseph Schooling win the gold medal in the 100-meter butterfly in the 2016 Olympic Games. It looked different, and we didn't understand why until we began to study it.

With the *late breath* butterfly technique, the chin should be tucked down toward the chest just prior to the hands entering the water, the same as with the *early breath* technique. From this point on, the *late breath* technique changes, compared to the *early breath* technique. Rather than start to lift the chin forward when the hands strike the water, the swimmer keeps the chin tucked down, more like a breaststroke pullout, as the hands begin to press outward and backward.

Even though the shoulders begin to elevate with extension of the lumbar spine at the start of the propulsion phase, by keeping the chin tucked down, the back of the head will not break the surface until the hands are past the shoulders moving backward. That is considerably later than with the *early breath* technique. The head does not become completely out of the water until the pulling hands are near the belly button moving backward. That means the head is partially or completely out of the water for about .56-.60 seconds, .08 -.10 seconds less than with the *early breath* technique.

165

Now, eight one hundredths to one tenth of a second may not seem like much time, but with the amount of drag caused by the head being out of the water and the energy required to move the swimmer's body forward in that position, that is significant.

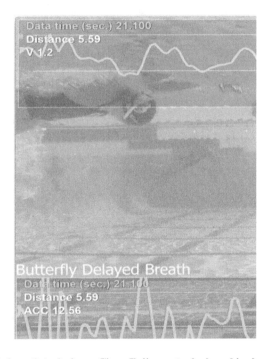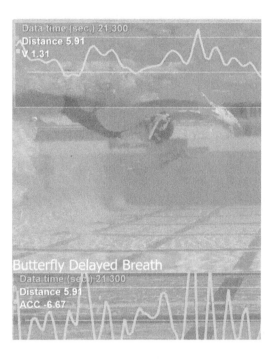

Late breath technique. Ciera Fujiwara tucks her chin down nicely before her hand entry (left), the same as with the early breath technique. As she presses down with her chest and hands reaching maximum hip flexion, she keeps her chin tucked down (right) and her head under water (VM technology).

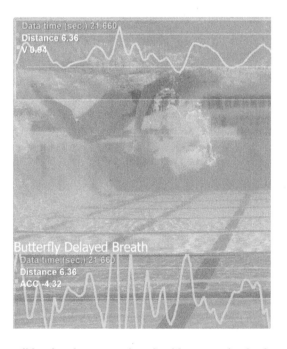

Late Breath technique. Ciera's head doesn't break the surface until her hands are near her shoulders, pressing backward (left). Her head isn't completely out of the water until her hands are back near her belly button (right). The total time her head is at least partially out of the water is about .58 seconds (VM technology).

Second-down-kick Butterfly Technique

While this is not a technique that is widely practiced, it is worth mentioning because two of the fastest butterfliers and individual medley swimmers in the world, Laszlo Cseh (Hungary) and Chase Kalisz (USA), use it, among others. We call it the *second-down-kick* technique, because they maximize the propulsion from the second down kick on their stroke cycle, but almost forego the first down kick of the cycle.

Of the two dolphin down-kicks that normally occur during a butterfly stroke cycle, the peak propulsion from the first down kick usually occurs when the pulling hands are near the belly button, on their way backward. The second peak propulsion from the down kick occurs precisely as the recovering arms hit the water. Both of those peak acceleration points are closely followed by the two peak velocities during the cycle.

With the *second-down-kick* technique, the swimmer almost foregoes generating propulsion during the first down kick. Instead of pressing the tops of the feet down through the body's vortex and flexing the hips, the swimmer stops the legs at the horizontal position, with toes pointed straight back, so the swimmer gets little or no propulsion from the shortened down kick. It would be similar to taking a *check swing* of the bat in baseball. One can't get much power that way. Instead, the swimmer chooses to leave the legs in the back in a straightened, low-drag position, muscling the pull through with as much propulsion as they can from the arms.

When it comes time for the second down kick, however, it is a different story. They put all of their eggs in that basket. Both Laszlo and Chase elevate their shoulders higher on the breath than one would think advisable. They both use a very vertical arm recovery with the hands well above the elbows. Then, they come down extremely hard with the head, shoulders and straightened, vertical arms, coupling with a perfectly timed and forceful second down kick. The result is a tremendous propulsion from that second kick that surges them forward.

While they may lose a little ground on the first down kick, compared to the other more conventional butterfly techniques, they gain on the second down kick. In the process, they save a little bit of energy in their legs, hopefully to finish the race well. In particular, we think that this technique may have greater purpose and merit in the 400 IM, where the legs are badly needed after the fly leg. It is also worth mentioning that Laszlo won the silver medal in the 100-meter fly in the Olympic Games, and swam a personal best time of 50.8 using this *second-down-kick* technique. Butterfliers that master this technique can go very fast using it.

Dolphin-Dive Butterfly Technique

This is another technique that is rarely used by elite butterfliers, and if so, only in the 200-meter event, not the 100 or 50-meter fly. It is commonly used by Masters swimmers and makes great sense for many of them.

With the *dolphin-dive* technique, both of the down kicks of the dolphin kick are taken when the hands are held out in front. One down kick occurs as the hands strike the water (what I refer to as the second down kick above) and another just before the hand start their outsweep for the pull.

By holding the hands out in front so long, the stroke rate is slowed way down and the swimmer gets a little vacation time. To work well, both kicks need to be extremely propulsive. Similar to the *second-down-kick* technique used by Cseh and Kalisz, a higher elevation of the shoulders, vertical arm recovery and aggressive downward motion helps strengthen that kick. Once the hands are in the water, the arms need to be held in a relatively streamlined, straight position until the next kick is taken.

Butterfly is such a difficult stroke to do well and requires so much strength, fitness and flexibility, something that Masters may not have a lot of, the *dolphin-dive* butterfly is a very useful technique for them. For elite swimmers, we would not have thought it possible to swim 200 meters using this technique with a stroke rate of 33 per minute (conventional 200 fly stroke rates are 46-48 per minute) and go 1:55.7. That is precisely what Japanese swimmer Yuya Yajima (lane 2 closest to camera) did in the 2015 World University Games using this technique. So, with a strong enough kick, the *dolphin-dive* butterfly may be a viable 200-meter technique at any age.

Side Breath Butterfly Technique

Side breath butterfly, where the swimmer breathes to the side rather than to the front, is a technique that is still used by some butterfliers. In the past, great butterfliers have used the side breathing technique successfully, including Olympians Ross Wales (USA 1968), Melvin Stewart (USA 1992) and Denis Pankratov (Russia 1996).

While we once taught each Race Club swimmer to use *side breath* butterfly technique, we no longer do so. Today, we feel the advantages of the *front breath* technique outweigh the advantages of *side breath* technique, except in a few swimmers that have trouble with excessive shoulder elevation for the front breath.

One advantage of *side breath* technique is that it will enable some swimmers to maintain a lower drag profile during the breath. It also may enable swimmers to use a faster stroke rate, while taking a breath with each cycle. One can get the breath in less time with the side breath, compared to the front breath. The three disadvantages of side breathing are, first, that swimmers cannot see ahead and anticipate the wall for either a turn or the finish. Second, there is greater risk of taking in water and choking during the side breath. When that happens, it can ruin a swimmer's day. Third, swimmers will not get as much coupling energy from the head rotating as they will with the head snapping downward, using the front breath.

When using a *side breath* butterfly technique, it is important to breathe back and to the side, trying not to elevate the head any more than is necessary for the breath. We usually have the swimmer focus on keeping the lower ear on the water while taking the breath when using the *side breath* butterfly technique. Often, we find swimmers elevate their heads too high when taking a side breath, which defeats the purpose of using that technique.

Olympian Roland Schoeman (South Africa) uses a low-profile, side-breath butterfly technique here. He keeps his left ear on the water while breathing to the right, causing the least amount of frontal drag possible.

Fundamentals of Butterfly

Reducing Frontal Drag

The primary causes of excessive frontal drag in butterfly are from over-elevation of the shoulders and upper body, particularly during the breath stroke, and over-bending the knees and hanging of the feet during the kicking cycles.

While there are coaches who still teach swimmers to keep their heads in alignment with their upper bodies in butterfly (stiff neck), for two reasons, we believe that is not good technique. One reason has to do with frontal drag. The other has to do with propulsion.

During the stroke cycle in butterfly, we feel that the head and neck should go from extreme flexion (almost touching the chest), just prior to the hand entry, to extreme extension (during the breath). Both of these extremes of the head position will help reduce drag. Michael Phelps was particularly good at using the full range of motion of flexion and extension of his neck in butterfly. When the chin is tucked down, the drag is lower than when the head is in alignment. With our Propulsion/Drag Meter (PDM) technology, we found a 4% reduction in drag at race speed (2.3 m/sec) with the chin tucked down compared to having the head in alignment with the body. With the head fully extended forward for the breath, the swimmer can keep the shoulders closer to the water, reducing the upper body angle with the surface and with it, the frontal drag. We call this butterfly breathing position with the head extended forward a *low-profile* breath. For many swimmers, it becomes more difficult to extend their necks fully forward as their muscles fatigue.

The dolphin kicking motion is another common cause of excessive frontal drag. We discuss dolphin kick in great detail in Chapter 22, but the mechanics of the dolphin kick should not differ much during the swim. Once the knees bend past 60 - 70 degrees of flexion, the frontal drag forces increase quickly and dramatically. We often find excessive knee bend before the first down kick, the second down kick or both. After the down kick, the feet should hang for the least amount of time possible. The feet will always hang some after the swimmer snaps them down through the body vortex, which is necessary to gain propulsion. However, some swimmers leave their feet hanging way too long. After completing the down kick, the toes need to be pointed backward quickly. The soles of the feet are then added to the surface area of the leg pulling upward, potentially generating more propulsion from the up kick.

The pulling motion of the butterfly can also be problematic for frontal drag, particularly if the outsweep is too wide or the pull is too deep. The pulling motion for each arm in butterfly should be very similar to the high-elbow freestyle pulling motion, except for the initial small outsweep. The hands should enter the water slightly inside the shoulders, perhaps 8-10 inches apart, preferably with the thumbs down. Michael Phelps entered his hands pitched with the thumbs down slightly, which causes less drag than with the palms down. That pitched hand also enabled him to begin a short out sweep immediately. He was careful to not allow the hands to enter the water until his arms were fully extended in front. In fact, his upper arms entered the water before his hands did. He lifted the hands slightly at the end to gain more coupling energy from his second down kick. At hand entry, the fingers should be directed forward, not downward, and squeezed together.

Once in the water, there is a very brief and short outsweeping motion of both hands for a few inches. The hands are pitched some during the short out sweep, but not as much as with the breaststroke pull. This brief outsweep is followed by a pressing downward of the palms then a backward motion with the fingers pointing down. The hands initially start the downward motion just outside the elbows, but as the hands begin moving backward, they swing back inside the elbows. During the pressing backward of the hands, Phelps would allow his hands to move pretty far under his body, once they passed his shoulders. Milorad Cavic (Serbia), who was second to Phelps in the 100-meter butterfly in the Olympic Games in Beijing in 2008, pressed his hands backward in more of a straight line, using a higher elbow pulling motion. They both maintained high-elbow positions through the early pulling motion to reduce frontal drag.

Increasing Propulsion in Butterfly

Nearly all of the propulsion in butterfly is derived from the hands and feet during the pull and kick. The pulling motion in butterfly is very similar to the motion of freestyle with the same six phases of the pulling cycle. Two differences with the butterfly pulling motion are in the very small out sweep that occurs during the brief lift phase and in the more inward motion of the hands under the body during the back-quadrant propulsion phase. Since both hands are pressing simultaneously, any outward or inward forces will cancel each other out, so no zig-zagging will occur. There is no longitudinal rotation in butterfly, so there is usually more lateral motion of the hands during the propulsion phases when compared to the freestyle pull.

During the pulling propulsion phase, the fingers and thumb should be separated, the palm held close to perpendicular to the swimmer's line of motion, pressing backward as firmly as possible. Neither the outsweep nor the insweep of the hands should be excessive. The key to improving the pulling propulsion is to apply backward pressure to the hands early and maintain that pressure on the hands all the way back to the full extension of the elbows.

Olympic butterflier Milorad Cavic used a very small outsweep and pulled with an extremely high elbow with his hands inside his elbows to help reduce frontal drag.

Roland Schoeman uses a little wider outsweep of the hands, with more outward and inward motion of the hands during the pulling cycle, compared to Cavic.

Using Pressure Meter technology (PM), we usually find two pressure peaks during the butterfly pull. The first peak occurs when the hands are moving backward just past the shoulders, and is synchronized with the peak angular velocity of the shoulders moving upward. The second pressure peak of the hands usually occurs as they are releasing from the water, starting to recover. The latter peak pressure has no relevance to propulsion, since the direction of the force on the hands is upwards, not backwards, by then.

The first peak pressure on the pulling hands (graphs above) is timed perfectly with the peak angular velocity of the shoulders moving upward (graph below using PM technology).

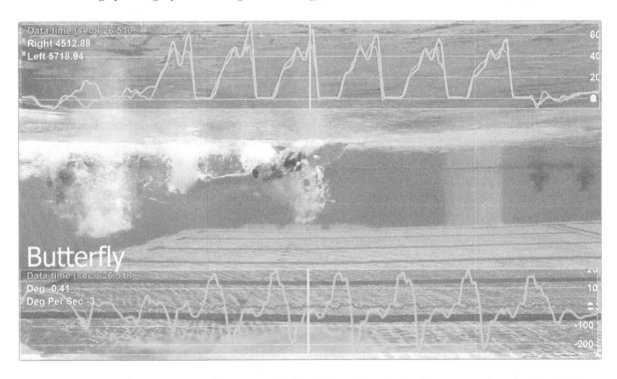

The second peak in pressure on the hands occurs as the hands leave the water for the recovery (graphs above). The direction of the force is upward and will not increase propulsion by this point.

Acceleration caused by the propulsion from the dolphin kick can potentially occur in four different places during a single kicking cycle: First, at the initiation of the down kick. Second, as the feet pass downward through the body vortex. Third, at the initiation of the up kick and fourth, as the feet pass through the body vortex on the way up. The amount of propulsion that is generated from the kick is quite variable among swimmers, ranging from very little to a lot. The amount of propulsion and acceleration depends on the plantar ankle flexibility and inversion ability of the ankle, the size of the feet surface, and the speed at which the feet and legs are moved against or through the vortices in both directions.

Of all the factors that determine a good butterfly technique, regardless of which fly technique is being used, the kicking propulsion is the most important. In Chapter 22, we will discuss how a swimmer can get more propulsion from the dolphin kick.

Coupling Motions of Butterfly

There are two important and major coupling motions that will augment the propulsion of the second down kick in butterfly—the end of the arm recovery and the head and shoulders coming down. To a smaller degree, the elevation of the shoulders couples with the pulling motion and the first down kick. Since the shoulders don't elevate very far or fast, there is not as much coupling energy happening for the pull and first down kick as there is with the second down kick.

There are two techniques of recovering the arms in butterfly, horizontal and vertical. With the horizontal recovery, the objective is to have the arms just high enough to clear the water on their way forward. With the vertical recovery, the arms are positioned more vertically, with the hands higher than the elbows. With either technique, the most important aspect of it is the speed of the recovering arms and hands when the hands enter the water. That is when the second down kick will pass through the body vortex, generating the most propulsion. The ability to do a vertical recovery technique in butterfly depends on the swimmer having extraordinary extension flexibility in the shoulders. Those swimmers that are not highly flexible in their shoulders, that do not have the ability to extend their arms backwards very far, will not be able to use a vertical arm recovery technique in butterfly.

The vertical recovery requires more work to accomplish than the horizontal recovery. The advantage of it, like with the vertical freestyle arm recovery, is that gravity is of more assistance on the way down. The vertical arm recovery makes it harder to go up and easier to come down with more kinetic energy in the arms. Some notable elite butterfliers of today using the vertical arm recovery include Rikako Ikee (Japan), Laszlo Cseh (Hungary), Emma McKeon (Australia) and Chase Kalisz (USA).

The horizontal recovery offers the advantage of being easier to accomplish. As in freestyle, the release and early recovery phases of the butterfly recovery offer a better opportunity for the arms to rest some than when using the vertical recovery. Many swimmers who use this horizontal recovery technique have found a trick to use to help increase the kinetic energy of the arms just before entry. They may not have the ability or choose not to elevate the hands during the early recovery in butterfly, but once the hands are in front of them, they can lift them and often do at the last moment, just before they drop them into the water. The coupling energy may not be as much as with the vertical recovery technique, but it helps. This is a technique that Phelps and World Champion Maggie MacNeil (Canada) use.

Vertical arm recovery in butterfly. Butterflier Ciera Fujiwara has extraordinary shoulder flexibility, enabling her to elevate her arms higher during the recovery. Gravity helps to bring her arms and hands down toward the water with more kinetic energy.

World record holding butterflier Roland Schoeman, using a horizontal recovery with an early breath technique

Similar to freestyle, the speed at which the arms and hands approach the water is directly linked to the speed of the shoulders coming down. The speed of the head coming down is different. As in breaststroke, a swimmer can snap the head down with more energy or lay it down with less energy. By snapping the head down in butterfly, along with an aggressive arm entry, the swimmer will increase the propulsion from the second down kick.

When we tested elite butterflier Amanda Kendall (USA), using VM technology, we compared her average velocity, average peak acceleration and average change in velocity (ΔPT) during her second down kick over 10 meters using two different techniques of head position. In the first test, she kept her head in alignment with her upper body. In the second test, she extended her neck forward for the breath and snapped her head down quickly to nearly full flexion at the hand entry. By snapping her head down hard, her second down kick resulted in the following improvements: increase in average peak acceleration by 41%, increase in her average speed by 28% and increase in average peak velocity of 6%.

One month later, after learning this technique, Amanda won the USA National Championships in the 100-meter butterfly with a personal best time by snapping her head down after the breath. For Amanda, using her head turned out to be her secret weapon.

Using Velocity Meter technology, we measure the speed, acceleration and deceleration of Amanda Kendall using a stiff neck technique in butterfly (graphs above and below).

By snapping her head down more aggressively and tucking her chin in tighter, Amanda increases her speed and acceleration significantly (graph below at vertical line).

Inertia

Butterfliers are hindered by the law of inertia. As in breaststroke, there is not enough continuity or frequency of propulsive moments to be able to sustain a very constant speed. Nevertheless, the law of inertia still applies to every stroke. The best ways to avoid such wide fluctuations in speed in butterfly is by avoiding any of the major drag-causing technical errors we discussed above, working a tighter kick in both directions and by increasing the stroke rate. It is the mechanical inefficiency of butterfly and the additional drag caused by holding the head above water for so long that makes this stroke so hard to do for any prolonged period of time.

These are the typical stroke rates that we commonly see among men and women in the three butterfly races.

50-meter sprint: 62-70 strokes per minute

100-meter event: 52-56 strokes per minute

200-meter event: 46-48 strokes per minute

Breathing Rate in Butterfly

The act of lifting the head or turning it to the side will always increase frontal drag in butterfly. Yet the breath provides the most important nutrient the body needs to sustain the enormous energy requirements of a fast butterfly stroke—oxygen. The fastest way to swim butterfly for a short distance is without breathing.

In the 50-meter sprint, where 95% of the energy is coming from the anaerobic system, the best strategy is to breathe as little as possible. That amount of breathing can range from 4-6 breaths for a young age group swimmer to no breaths at all for an elite butterflier. One of the most impressive swims in history was Sarah Sjostrom swimming 24.4 in the 50-meter butterfly in 2014 in Sweden. She maintained a stroke rate of 62 per minute, took no breaths and nailed her finish. She is the only female swimmer to date who has swum the event under 25 seconds.

In the 100-meter butterfly, where about half of the energy requirement comes from the aerobic and half from the anaerobic energy systems, we see a different breathing pattern between the elite men and women. Most of the elite men will breathe every cycle, often holding the breath on the first stroke off the start and turn. Many will finish the last several strokes into the wall without a breath. By holding the breath and increasing the stroke rate, the swimmer's speed will increase for a better finish.

The elite women will breathe less than the men in the 100-meter butterfly race, similarly to the 100 freestyle. The majority of elite women breathe one up and one down or two up and one down. Very few women breathe every cycle in butterfly in this race. Since most of the energy demands of the first 50 meters is provided by the anaerobic system and most of the energy of the second 50 meters is provided by the aerobic system, it can also make sense to change breathing patterns and breathe more on the second 50 meters of the race. Much of the breathing pattern will also depend on the individual fitness level and efficiency of delivering oxygen to the muscles (VO2 Max) for each athlete. Whatever the breathing pattern is, make sure that it is established before the beginning of the race and implemented correctly. Breath holding for the first several strokes of a 100-meter butterfly race is always a bad idea.

In the 200-meter butterfly event, elite men will continue breathing every cycle. Some elite women will breathe every cycle in the 200-meter race, but the majority of women in the 200-meter fly are breathing two up and one down or three up and one down.

In summary, picking the right butterfly technique depends on many factors, such as the age, the kicking speed, the event, flexibility and level of fitness of each swimmer. As with other strokes, the butterfly technique will sometimes need to change as the swimmer grows older or perhaps stronger and fitter. Whatever butterfly technique the swimmer chooses, make sure that the dolphin kick develops along with it. A strong kick is a vital part of a successful butterfly.

With our Race Club swimmers, we never know for certain which butterfly technique will work the best. Often, our swimmers haven't even tried or are unaware of the different techniques. For example, in testing early breath versus late breath butterfly technique, we find about half of the swimmers like one technique and the other half like the other. We never know which half will choose which technique until we test them.

When comparing these two techniques, or other butterfly techniques, we usually look at three parameters during a short butterfly set, which is long enough to get the swimmers fatigued. Often, we will do 8 x 25 meters butterfly on 30 second intervals. We compare average time (speed), heart rate at completion of the set and the subjective opinion as to which technique is harder or easier. All three parameters are important.

What is also important is that swimmers pick the right butterfly technique that works well for them and that they practice using it. Usually, when a swimmer tries a new technique for the first time, it will feel strange and uncomfortable. Here are some of our favorite Race Club butterfly drills to work on specific techniques:

Drills for Early Breath to Front with Low Profile Technique

Left/Right/Front drill **with fins on**. One arm butterfly with the left arm, breathing to the left side. One arm butterfly with right arm, breathing to the right side. Both arms pulling butterfly, breathing to the front while extending the neck forward with shoulders low to the water.

Butterfly skate drill **with early breath and fins on.** The skate drill is used for two different techniques, early and late breath. In this drill the swimmer takes a low-profile breath to the front with neck fully extended, while pulling through the water with both arms in a butterfly pull. The idea is to skate over the surface of the water. Stop the hands at the end of the pull with them by your waist. Then drop the head down into the water and recover the arms over the water. Two down kicks are taken, the first while pulling under water and the second when the hands strike the water.

Drills for Late Breath to Front with Low Profile Technique

Butterfly skate drill with early breath **and fins on.** In this drill, the swimmer pulls through the water under water, with both hands using a butterfly pull, with the chin remaining on the chest. This motion is almost identical to a breaststroke pullout. Once the hands are at the swimmer's side, pause them there for a moment. Breathe to the front with a low-profile breath during the arm recovery. Two down kicks are taken, the first while pulling under water and the second when the hands strike the water.

Left/Right/Front drill with fins on. One arm butterfly with the left arm, breathing to the left side. One arm butterfly with right arm, breathing to the right side. Both arms pulling butterfly, breathing to the front. With the front breath, keep the chin on the chest until the arms reach the belly button on the way back. When the hands reach that point, the head is lifted to the front with a low-profile and comes right back down. There is just enough time to get the breath in with the head out of the water and get it back down.

Drills for Coupling Motions Technique

<u>Freestyle kick butterfly</u> **with fins on.** Do butterfly with a freestyle kick, focusing on coming down hard with the recovering arms and snapping the head down almost to the chest. Try to time the head snap so it doesn't happen too early. It should be held forward and come down at the same time as the hands enter the water.

Drills for Vertical Arm Recovery Technique with Early or Late Breath

<u>Left/Right/Front drill</u> **with fins on.** One arm butterfly with the left arm, breathing to the left side. One arm butterfly with right arm, breathing to the right side. Both arms pulling butterfly, breathing to the front extending the neck forward with shoulders low to the water, with either early or late breath, whichever the swimmer prefers. The difference in this drill from the others above is that the single arm recovers vertically, straight over the top. With both arms recovering, the swimmer tries to get the hands as high as possible, working on a vertical arm recovery.

Drills for Stroke Rate Technique

Freestyle kick butterfly with fins on. Do butterfly with a freestyle kick, focusing on coming down hard with the recovering arms and snapping the head down almost to the chest. Try to time the head snap so it doesn't happen too early. It should be held forward and come down at the same time as the hands enter the water. With this drill, using the <u>Tempo Trainer</u>, we gradually increase the stroke rate with a breath in front to reach the maximum rate for each swimmer.

Chapter 22

Dolphin Kick

Fundamentals of the Fifth Stroke

The dolphin kick has become so important in the sport of swimming, that it has earned the title as *The Fifth Stroke*. Dolphin kicking is now used in every stroke, in nearly every race, and on nearly every start and turn. In the short course 100-meter backstroke event, for example, elite swimmers spend more time underwater dolphin kicking than they do swimming on the surface. The bottom line is that if you want to become a fast swimmer, you had better become a fast dolphin kicker. The question is, how?

Developing a better dolphin kick starts with an understanding of how it works. When we began teaching swimming technique at The Race Club in 2008, we really didn't understand the dolphin kick, or any kick for that matter. Since then, we have learned more about kicking from the Velocity Meter (VM) technology than from any other source. VM measures the swimmer's velocity, acceleration and deceleration, synchronized to a video, at each .02 seconds. Using this technology, we are able to determine for each swimmer their average speed; where in the kicking cycle the peak propulsion occurs (corresponding to peak acceleration); where in the cycle the peak drag forces occur (corresponding to peak deceleration); how much of an average increase in velocity results from the down kick (ΔPT) and the up kick (ΔPT), correlating to the amount of propulsion generated from each motion; and the average percentage of velocity lost during both the up kicks and down kicks, as a result of the motions causing deceleration.

All of those metrics are important in understanding the swimmer's dolphin kick. The velocity curves of each swimmer during a VM study with many dolphin kicks are nearly identical, indicating that the swimmer is performing the same biomechanical movements over and over again. Yet, surprisingly, the velocity curves for the dolphin kicks among the several hundred swimmers we have tested are quite different. In fact, no two curves are exactly the same, almost like snowflakes or fingerprints. Even among the elite swimmers, there are always findings in the VM study that can be improved. No swimmer we have studied has had a perfect dolphin kick.

Through this technology and measuring hundreds of swimmers, we have begun to understand how the dolphin kick really works. Some of this information has been explained earlier in Chapter 1, in the physics discussion, and again in Chapter 8, in the discussion of freestyle kick. It is worth mentioning again. The propulsion of a swimmer is mostly derived from the movements of the hands and feet. In a fluid medium, such as water, to generate propulsion to move the swimmer forward, there must be some backward movement of the object generating the propulsion, the hand or the foot, relative to the position of the non-moving water, or a fixed object in the pool.

The mechanics of the pulling motion and kick are very different because of the difference in fluid dynamics in front and behind the swimmer. While the hands must move backward in the pool to generate propulsion, because the water in front of the water is still. Behind the swimmer, the feet do not need to move backward to generate propulsion, because they are utilizing the vortices created by the swimmer.

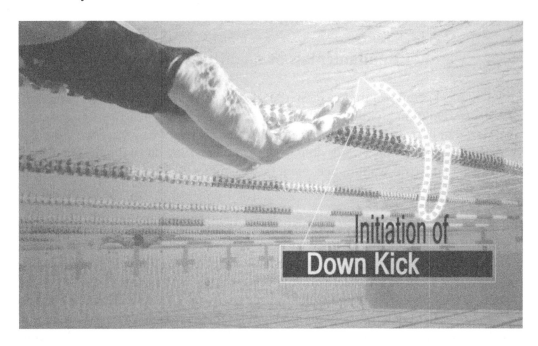

The path of the feet is downward, upward and forward, but almost never backward.

There are two primary vortices behind the swimmer kicking dolphin. The first is caused by the non-streamlined body itself moving forward, resulting in a slipstream of water following the swimmer. The second is caused by the movement of the foot and leg in dolphin kick, which is almost entirely upward, forward and downward, resulting in a smaller vortex or slipstream behind the feet.

In one complete dolphin kicking cycle, there are four potential places where the feet can generate propulsion and cause the swimmer to accelerate. Starting at the top of the kicking cycle, here are the four potential locations that the swimmer can accelerate through one cycle:

1. The initiation of the down kick, kicking down into the foot vortex.
2. As the feet pass through the body's slipstream on the way down.
3. The initiation of the up kick, kicking upwards into the foot vortex.
4. As the feet (and back of the swimmer's legs) pass through the body's slipstream on the way back up.

The amount of propulsion, if there is any at all, generated from each of these four places in the dolphin kick varies for every swimmer. Propulsion at each of the four points depends on their anatomical tools for kicking, strength, biomechanics and where he or she decides to put the effort.

Many refer to the up kick as the *recovery* phase of the dolphin kick. That is a misnomer for anyone that wants to kick fast, as a significant amount of propulsion can be generated from the up kick. The fastest dolphin kickers are using the surface of their feet and legs by pressing hard in both directions.

In addition to those four places for possible acceleration (propulsion), there are also four places where deceleration occurs. Only two of those four will usually cause significant deceleration, however. The other two happen so quickly that there is not much time for any appreciable change in the swimmer's speed.

Most of the deceleration on the way up occurs from the amount of knee bend, the speed at which the lower legs are brought forward, the position of the lower legs as they are brought forward and the amount of time that lapses before the initiation of the next down kick. While the amount of knee bend may be important, we have seen VM studies where the knees were bent a lot, but because the knees dropped and the feet were kept closer to the body's streamline, less deceleration occurred. In other cases, where the feet end up higher, well out of the body's streamline, with the same amount of knee bend, the swimmer's deceleration is much greater.

The second major place for deceleration to occur is during the down kick, after the feet pass through the body's slipstream, as a result of the hip flexing and the feet hanging. The amount of deceleration is determined by the degree of hip flexion, but more importantly by the amount and duration of the feet hanging.

Between the initiation of the down and up kicks, where there is an opportunity to generate propulsion (although that doesn't always happen), there is a very brief period of time when the feet pass through that smaller vortex and before they reach the body's vortex, where some deceleration also occurs. It is usually not a significant amount, because the feet are moving quickly and not much time is spent in that small place between the two vortices.

Using VM technology, the following photos of Olympian Kelsi Dahlia, who has an excellent dolphin kick, illustrate the four potential points for acceleration through the complete kicking cycle. They also show the two points of major deceleration and the resulting loss of velocity that occur in the cycle.

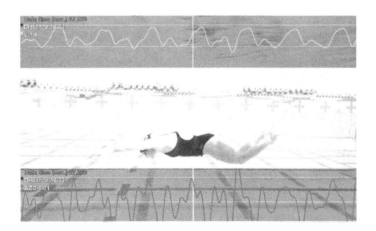

Olympian Kelsi Dahlia accelerates at the initiation of her down kick (graph below at vertical line).

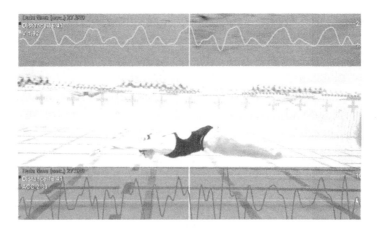

Kelsi gets a second boost of speed as she accelerates down through the body's vortex (graph below), reaching her peak velocity (graph above).

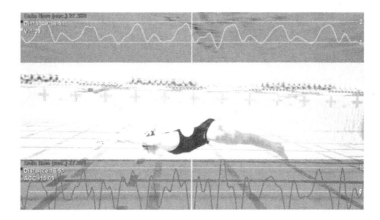

From her hip flexion and feet hanging, Kelsi decelerates (graph below) and loses an average of 37% of her velocity after the down kick, which is too high (graph above).

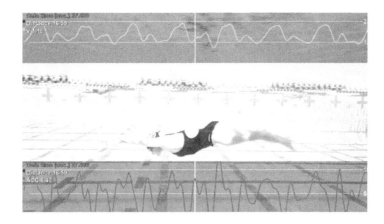

Kelsi begins to accelerate again from the initiation of her up kick (graph below), causing her velocity to start to climb again (graph above).

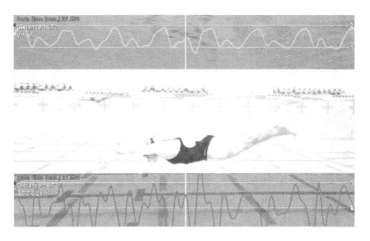

Kelsi get a fourth acceleration as her feet move upward through the body's vortex (graph below), resulting in another uptick in her velocity (graph above).

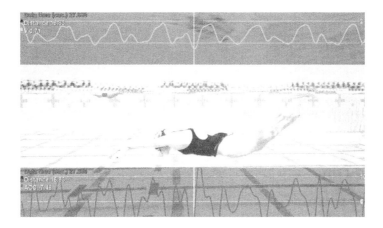

Once Kelsi's knees start to bend and her legs draw forward, another major deceleration occurs (graph below). Since Kelsi bends her knees an average of 58 degrees before the down kick (which is very low), she loses only 30% of her speed from her knee bend (also very low).

We have also learned that each swimmer is capable of changing their VM curves substantially by putting the emphasis on different aspects of the dolphin kick. When we did a VM study on National Champion butterflier, Amanda Kendall, after doing her normal kick, we asked her to do a second study placing more emphasis on her up kick than usual. With her normal kick, she achieved her peak velocity on the down kick, as her feet passed through her body's slipstream. This was, by far, her greatest propulsive moment in the cycle. When she placed more emphasis on her up kick, just a few minutes later, her peak velocity in the cycle came after the up kick, not the down kick. The two velocity curves from her VM study below are very different.

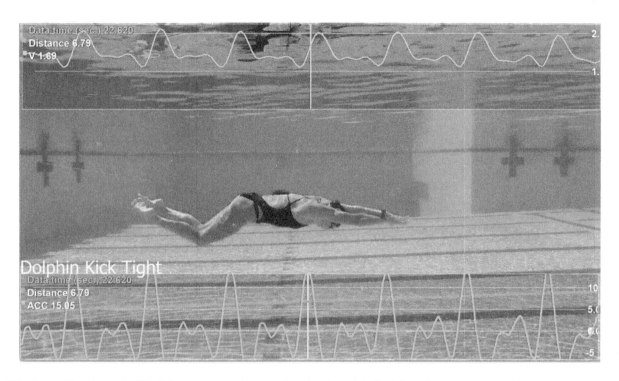

Elite butterflier, Amanda Kendall, gets tremendous acceleration (graph below) from her strong down kick, resulting in a huge climb in velocity (graph above, using VM technology).

When Amanda puts more emphasis on her up kick, pointing her toes backward, her peak velocity now occurs during the up kick, through the body slipstream, not the down kick (graph above). Notice the big differences in this velocity meter curve compared to the one above (VM technology).

From the data of each of her studies, this is what we learned. With her normal dolphin kick, her average peak down kick velocity was 2 m/sec and her average peak up kick velocity was 1.4 m/sec. Her average change from her trough (slowest) velocity to peak (fastest) velocity for the down kick (ΔPT) was .92 m/sec and her ΔPT for her up kick was .15 m/sec. Her average loss of velocity at the end of the down kick was 38% and her average loss of velocity at the end of the up kick was 23% with a 55-degree knee bend. Her average speed using this technique was 1.67 m/sec.

Dolphin Kick Tight				1.67 m/sec	55 degrees					
Time	DT	Time	DP	Difference		Time	UT	Time	UP	Difference
21.7	1.12	21.8	2.13	1.01		21.9	1.35	22.06	1.44	0.09
22.14	1.11	22.24	2.06	0.95		22.34	1.32	22.48	1.39	0.07
22.56	1.1	22.66	2.02	0.92		22.78	1.31	22.92	1.37	0.06
22.98	1.14	23.08	2.04	0.9		23.28	1.28	23.34	1.43	0.15
23.42	1.12	23.52	2.03	0.91		23.7	1.25	23.78	1.43	0.18
23.86	1.13	23.94	1.96	0.83		24.14	1.23	24.22	1.42	0.19
24.28	1.03	24.38	2.03	1		24.5	1.23	24.66	1.44	0.21
24.74	1.05	24.84	2.01	0.96		25.02	1.19	25.1	1.47	0.28
25.18	0.98	25.28	1.93	0.95		25.46	1.17	25.52	1.28	0.11
25.6	1.07	25.72	1.82	0.75		25.92	1.11	26	1.28	0.17
AVG	1.09		2	0.92		AVG	1.24		1.4	0.15

Dolphin Kick Tight II										
Time	DP	Time	UT	Difference		Time	UP	Time	DT	Difference
21.8	2.13	21.9	1.35	-0.78		22.06	1.44	22.14	1.11	-0.33
22.24	2.06	22.34	1.32	-0.74		22.48	1.39	22.56	1.1	-0.29
22.66	2.02	22.78	1.31	-0.71		22.92	1.37	22.98	1.14	-0.23
23.08	2.04	23.28	1.28	-0.76		23.34	1.43	23.42	1.12	-0.31
23.52	2.03	23.7	1.25	-0.78		23.78	1.43	23.86	1.13	-0.3
23.94	1.96	24.14	1.23	-0.73		24.22	1.42	24.28	1.03	-0.39
24.38	2.03	24.5	1.23	-0.8		24.66	1.44	24.74	1.05	-0.39
24.84	2.01	25.02	1.19	-0.82		25.1	1.47	25.18	0.98	-0.49
25.28	1.93	25.46	1.17	-0.76		25.52	1.28	25.6	1.07	-0.21
25.72	1.82	25.92	1.11	-0.71						
AVG	2		1.24	-0.76		AVG	1.41		1.08	-0.33
Vel loss	38%						23%			

Data taken from the VM study of Amanda Kendall's dolphin kick study with her normal technique. DT and DP refer the lowest and highest velocities achieved during the down kick. UT and UP refer the lowest and highest velocities achieved with the up kick. The difference between the two is the ΔPT for each kick. Averages are at the bottom of each column.

Dolphin Kick w/ Undulation				1.51 m/sec	73 degrees					
Time	DT	Time	DP	Difference		Time	UT	Time	UP	Difference
21.4	0.91	21.52	1.75	0.84		21.62	1.56	21.72	1.96	0.4
21.86	0.96	22.02	1.64	0.68		22.1	1.53	22.2	1.94	0.41
22.32	0.91	22.46	1.64	0.73		22.56	1.48	22.68	1.89	0.41
22.8	0.96	22.98	1.58	0.62		23.04	1.5	23.14	1.92	0.42
23.26	1.01	23.44	1.58	0.57		23.54	1.41	23.64	1.84	0.43
23.76	0.98	23.96	1.55	0.57		24	1.53	24.12	1.77	0.24
24.24	0.99	24.4	1.63	0.64		24.48	1.49	24.58	1.81	0.32
24.7	0.97	24.86	1.51	0.54		24.92	1.43	25.04	1.8	0.37
25.18	0.84	25.28	1.52	0.68		25.4	1.45	25.54	1.72	0.27
25.66	0.92	25.74	1.41	0.49		25.9	1.42	26.02	1.7	0.28
AVG	0.95		1.58	0.64		AVG	1.48		1.84	0.36

Dolphin Kick w/ Undulation II										
Time	DP	Time	UT	Difference		Time	UP	Time	DT	Difference
21.52	1.75	21.62	1.56	-0.19		21.72	1.96	21.86	0.96	-1
22.02	1.64	22.1	1.53	-0.11		22.2	1.94	22.32	0.91	-1.03
22.46	1.64	22.56	1.48	-0.16		22.68	1.89	22.8	0.96	-0.93
22.98	1.58	23.04	1.5	-0.08		23.14	1.92	23.26	1.01	-0.91
23.44	1.58	23.54	1.41	-0.17		23.64	1.84	23.76	0.98	-0.86
23.96	1.55	24	1.53	-0.02		24.12	1.77	24.24	0.99	-0.78
24.4	1.63	24.48	1.49	-0.14		24.58	1.81	24.7	0.97	-0.84
24.86	1.51	24.92	1.43	-0.08		25.04	1.8	25.18	0.84	-0.96
25.28	1.52	25.4	1.45	-0.07		25.54	1.72	25.66	0.92	-0.8
25.74	1.41	25.9	1.42	0.01						
AVG	1.58		1.48	-0.1		AVG	1.85		0.95	-0.9
Vel loss	6%						49%			

Data taken from VM study of Amanda Kendall's dolphin kick with emphasis on the up kick.

With the emphasis on her up kick, her average down kick peak velocity was 1.58 m/sec. Her average up kick peak velocity was 1.84 m/sec. The average ΔPT for the down kick was .64 m/sec and the average ΔPT for up kick was .36 m/sec. Using this technique, she lost 6% of her velocity at the end of the down kick and lost 49% of her velocity at the end of the up kick with a 73-degree knee bend. Her average speed with this technique was 1.51 m/sec.

What did we learn from this comparative study? First, Amanda is considerably faster with her normal technique than she is with her strong up kick technique. Is that true for everyone? No.

Second, using such a strong up kick led to a 73-degree knee flexion and a 49% loss of velocity from the excessive knee bend. Yet, by pointing her toes back more on the up kick and not letting the feet hang, her loss of velocity on the down kick dropped from 38%, which is high, to just 6%.

By taking some of the benefit of the second technique and adding it to the first technique, she could possibly improve her average speed to greater than 1.67 m/sec. Can she do that? We think she can. Without the study, and knowing the data, she wouldn't know what to do to improve her speed, nor would we.

Here are two examples of studies where the up kick was unusually strong and led to a faster kicking speed overall than with a less powerful up kick technique.

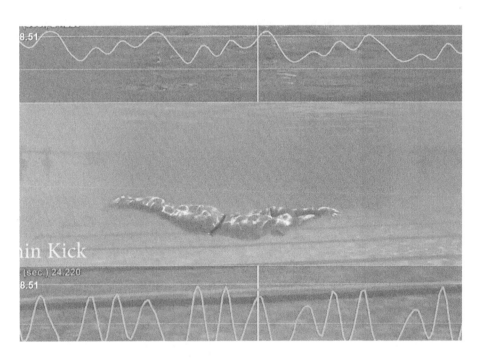

Butterflier Olivia Jubin reaches her peak velocity on her powerful up kick. Her peak acceleration on the way up (graph below) leads to her peak velocity over 2 m/sec (graph above). Olivia's technique can improve by not delaying so long before initiating her down kick, as she loses over 50% of her speed in the process.

Elite backstroker Holden Raffin uses a strong down kick and up kick. While his peak velocity occurs on the down kick (graph above), his powerful up kick leads to an average ΔPT of .96 m/sec, the highest we have ever measured. He also loses 44% of his speed after the down kick and 49% of his speed after the up kick, both too high. He needs to tighten his kick more to keep his velocity from fluctuating so much.

One question that is commonly asked in dolphin kick is *how much is the right amount of undulation, or hip flexion?* To find out, we did a comparative VM study with elite butterflier Marcus Schlesinger (Israel), using three different dolphin kick techniques. The first was with his normal kick, producing about 4-6 inches of hand movement in the streamline. The second test was with a big undulation of the hip (flexion), producing about 12-14 inches of hand movement in the streamline. The third test was holding his upper body as rigid as possible, producing about 1-2 inches of hand movement in the streamline.

Elite butterflier Marcus Schlesinger tests his normal dolphin kick with VM technology. He shows an unusually efficient technique, with very little fluctuation in his velocity (graph above).

VM testing on Marcus, using an over-undulating dolphin technique. Hip flexion reached 45 degrees (excessive). There is much more fluctuation in the velocity (graph above) and acceleration/deceleration curves (graph below).

VM testing on Marcus, using a rigid, almost fixed, upper body position in dolphin kick. This technique produces very little propulsion from the up kick, resulting in a needed strong down kick. Knee flexion goes to 78 degrees, which is excessive.

Technique	ΔPT Down (m/sec)	ΔPT Up (m/sec)	Knee Flexion (degrees)	Hip Flexion (degrees)	% Vel loss Up kick	% Vel loss Down kick	Average Velocity (m/sec)
Normal	0.38	0.14	71	32	4	24	1.74
Undulating	1.22	0.05	85	45	30	51	1.38
Rigid arms	0.88	0.07	78	28	21	33	1.62

Comparison of metrics used to evaluate three different dolphin kick techniques with Marcus Schlesinger.

Marcus was much more efficient and faster using his normal dolphin kicking technique. By either over-undulating or by keeping his upper body rigid, his average velocity dropped. Over-undulating was the worst technique. With his normal dolphin technique, Marcus had the most efficient dolphin kick that we have tested to date. His 4% loss of velocity from his knee bend is incredibly low. I believe that he is able to sustain his speed better during the knee bend for the down kick by dropping his knees lower and keeping his lower leg and feet more in the slipstream. Marcus had very little acceleration and deceleration on both up kicks and down kicks with his normal technique. We have seen very few swimmers using this technique.

After performing hundreds of VM tests on dolphin kick, we have a better idea of the range and what the expected desirable outcome is for each metric. Of course, the values are also age dependent. For hip flexion, the right amount seems to be in the range of 25-35 degrees. The ideal knee bend seems to be in the range of 55-70 degrees.

	ΔPT Down (m/sec)	ΔPT Up (m/sec)	Knee Flexion (degrees)	Hip Flexion (degrees)	% Vel loss Up kick	% Vel loss Down kick	Average Velocity (m/sec)
Range of values seen	0.25 - 1.5	0 - .96	55 - 100	0 - 45	4 – 95	5 - 75	.5 – 1.9
Desired	.75 or higher	.25 or higher	55 - 70	25 -35	30 - 40	20 - 30	1.6 or higher

Range of measured values and desired values for dolphin kick metrics using Velocity Meter technology on all Race Club testing.

The velocity curves of a dolphin kick on the stomach and on the back are different. Typically, the dolphin kick on the back produces a more consistent (flatter) curve than dolphin kicking on the swimmer's stomach. Often, the peak velocity on the back occurs during the down kick, which is biomechanically the weaker side, rather than during the up kick. There are two reasons for the higher velocity being attained during the weaker side kick. First, with the big vortex moving upward from the stronger up kick, the vortex will tend to mushroom out and stay around, as gravity is resisting its upward flow. The swimmer then has a greater opportunity to press down against the vortex. Second, the feet are moving downward with the help of gravity, which makes it easier to place more force on the weaker down kick. On a swimmer's stomach, gravity helps the vortex caused by the more forceful down kick continue in its downward path, making it more difficult for the feet to catch it during the up kick.

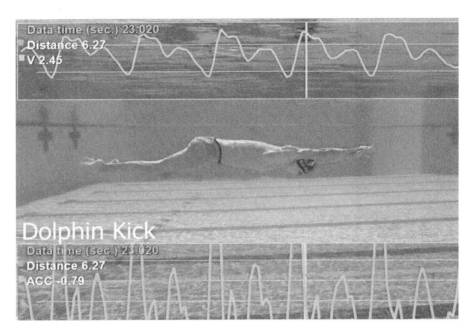

Data time (sec.) 23.020
Distance 6.27
V 2.45

Dolphin Kick
Data time (sec.) 23.020
Distance 6.27
ACC -0.79

VM study of elite swimmer Josh Zuchowski, showing wide variation of speed from dolphin kick on his stomach. The peak velocities achieved on the down kicks are much greater than those achieved on the up kicks (graph above).

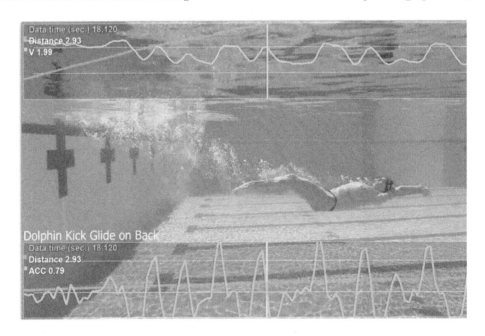

Data time (sec.) 18.120
Distance 2.93
V 1.99

Dolphin Kick Glide on Back
Data time (sec.) 18.120
Distance 2.93
ACC 0.79

VM study of Josh Zuchowski, showing less change of speed while dolphin kicking on his back. The peak velocities achieved on the down kicks are slightly greater than those achieved on the up kicks (graph above). Dolphin kicking on the back is more efficient and faster than dolphin kicking on the stomach.

Using VM technology, dolphin kicking on the back has proven to be more mechanically efficient (less fluctuation in speed) and faster than dolphin kicking on the stomach. What about dolphin kicking on the side? It seems to be in between the two others. When we compared the three different techniques of dolphin kicking with elite butterflier Kelsi Dahlia, here is what we found:

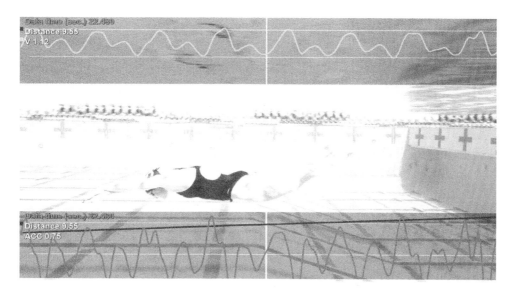

Olympian Kelsi Dahlia shows a typical fluctuation of her velocity during her dolphin kick on stomach. Her peak velocity was achieved during her down kicks (graph above). Her average velocity was 1.56 m/sec (VM technology).

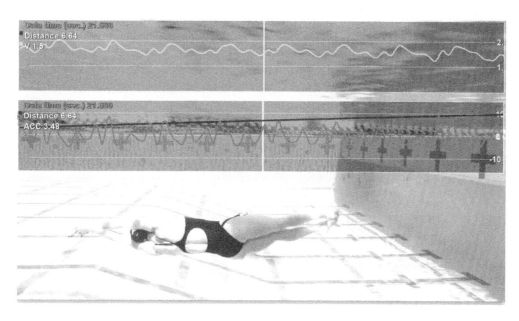

Kelsi's velocity curve flattens more while kicking on her side (graph on top). Her peak velocity now occurs during the weaker side kick. Her average velocity was 1.64 m/sec (VM technology).

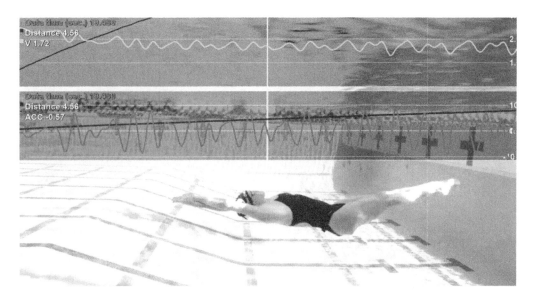

On her back, Kelsi's velocity curve is more balanced between up and down kicks (graph on top). Her velocity peaks from the up kick are still slightly less than with the down kick, but higher than when she is on her side. Her average speed was 1.70 m/sec, fastest of all three positions (VM technology).

We believe that the results of Kelsi's study are typical of most swimmers, with the dolphin kick speed slowest on the swimmer's stomach, better on the side and fastest on the back. In this test, Kelsi's velocity on her stomach was 1.56 m/sec. On her side, it was 1.64 m/sec. On her back, it was 1.70 m/sec. Bob Gillette, coach of Olympic gold medal butterflier Misty Hyman, came to this conclusion years before others did. On the start and every butterfly turn, he had Misty remain on her side for as long as possible before turning over onto her stomach before breakout.

Improving Your Dolphin Kick Speed

The anatomical tools for a fast dolphin kick are similar to those used for freestyle kick. A prerequisite for a fast dolphin kick is having extreme ankle plantar flexibility and extreme ankle inversion (pigeon-toeing). In Chapter 8, we described some dryland stretches that will help swimmers achieve more of that.

Kelsi Dahlia demonstrates the extreme ankle plantar flexibility and inversion (pigeon-toe) required to get strong propulsion with the down kick. The more transverse to the slipstream the feet can be passing through it, the greater the propulsion.

Hyper-extension of the knee joints is also desirable as it increases the strong-side kick stroke excursion (volume) and also positions the swimmer for a stronger weak-side kick. Other than genetically, or through years of kicking, we know of no other way of developing hyper-extension of the knees. It likely serves no other good purpose in life and, in fact, is likely bad for human erect posture and running. Hyper-extension of the knees definitely helps swimmer's kicking.

Flexibility in the lumbar and thoracic spine are also needed in dolphin kick, though not as much as is required in breaststroke.

The biomechanics of the swimmer during the dolphin kick involve ankle plantar flexion and inversion, knee flexion and extension, hip flexion with some extension, extension of the lumbar spine and flexion of the thoracic spine, all of which occur while the swimmer's head and arms are held in a tightened *hyperstreamline* position. Very small deviations from the normal or acceptable range of motion in all of these movements can have drastic consequences on the swimmer's kicking speed.

One of the great dilemmas of kicking dolphin kick fast is that if a swimmer does not have enough ankle plantar flexibility, then it becomes necessary to flex or bend the knees more to get any meaningful propulsion. Unfortunately, that knee bend causes such a huge deceleration that it is not possible to go very fast using that technique. That is why ankle flexibility is essential to fast dolphin kicking.

Without having VM technology, a coach is best able to evaluate the biomechanics of the dolphin kicking motion by having the swimmer dolphin kick on his or her side underwater. While standing on the deck at one end of the pool, with the swimmer kicking toward the coach, separately observe two different motions. First, how far are the hands (being held in a tight *hyperstreamline*) moving back and forth. The hand motion reflects the amount of the hip flexion before the weak-side kick is taken. It seems that 6-8 inches of motion of the hands from side to side is about the right amount. To evaluate the amount of knee bend, observe how far the feet extend out from the body line. The farther the feet move away from the body and outside of the slipstream, the more the swimmer is bending his knees. That means more deceleration. Finally, make sure that the kicking cycle time is not too slow. Fast cadence kicking cycles are necessary to go fast.

Strength in dolphin kicking on a swimmer's stomach during the down kick comes mostly from the ankle plantar flexors and the knee and hip extensors, which includes the gastrocnemius and quadriceps muscles. During the up kick, it is mostly the ankle plantar flexors, hip extensors and lumbar extensors that are working. Those include the gastrocnemius, hamstrings, gluteus and lower back muscles. Thoracic flexion occurs during the up kick in preparation for a more forceful down kick and to help maintain the arms more in the line of the swimmer's motion.

Of course, the core muscles never stop working during the dolphin kick motion and are extremely important in gaining propulsion and maintaining the tight, streamlined position.

To develop a fast dolphin kick you will need to develop the key anatomical tools, tremendous leg strength and stamina. That involves stretches, strength training and lots of kicking. There are hundreds of great dolphin kick workout sets. Eddie Reese, Head Coach at the University of Texas men's team, does a dolphin kick set every day in his practices. Here are a few of our favorite dolphin kick sets to help get you started:

Sets to Improve the Up Kick

1. 10 x 100 meters dolphin kicks descending each set of 5. Take no more than 20 seconds rest between each one. Focus on pulling the straight legs up firmly on each kick.
2. 20 x 25 meters dolphin kicks on your back under water with fins (use a nose clip). Take 10 -15 seconds rest. Focus on pressing down hard against the vortex with the bottom of your fins.
3. 5 x 45 second vertical kicks with fins and arms above the water with 15 seconds rest between each one. If you are a strong kicker, keep the arms in streamline position and your chin above water. In vertical kicking, both forward and backward kicking motions must be strong, if you want to breathe. Try to keep the kick tight and from the hips.

General Sets to Improve Dolphin Kick

1. 10 x 100 meters dolphin kicks with drag socks on. Take no more than 20 seconds of rest between each one. We like using the alignment board and snorkel, but a regular kick board will do.

2. 10 x 100 meters dolphin kicks with fins and small parachute behind. Take no more than 20 seconds of rest between each one. The parachute will add tremendous drag so plan on this one taking a while.

3. 20 x 25 meters dolphin kicks with 5-10 pounds of weights clutched in both hands against the chest. 15 seconds rest between each one. Use a snorkel and kick hard with the head down to stay on the surface.

4. 20 x 25 meters dolphin kicks with fins, hands at sides and snorkel. 15 seconds rest between each one. We call this the Sea World set, because you want to be like a seal skipping over the surface of the water with tight fast dolphin kicks.

5. 10 x 100 meters dolphin kick with fins. 15 seconds of rest after each one. The first 25 is on the right side, the second 25 is on the left side, the third 25 is on the stomach and the last 25 is on the back. Stay under water as long as possible for each 25.

6. 10 x 50 meters dolphin kicks with kick trainer (Stretch Cordz) on 60 seconds. The kick trainer is an excellent tool to improve the biomechanics of your dolphin kick by not enabling you to over-bend the knees. It also does a great job of building the stronger down kick.

Chapter 23

Starts

Fundamentals of a Great Start

Since the early 2000s, when the last of the *two-feet-forward* starters among the elite swimmers retired, virtually all of the world's elite swimmers of today use a track start. The only swimmers remaining that we are aware of using a *two-feet-forward* start are the older Masters swimmers that have stability problems while standing on the block with the track start. They are safer with both feet forward. Otherwise, everyone else today in the sport of swimming should be using the track start, with one foot placed forward, with toes over the front edge of the block, and the other placed behind. It has proven to be the superior starting technique.

There are two techniques used in the track start, *weight forward* and *weight back*. The numbers of swimmers using each technique seem to be pretty even overall, with more elite women using a *weight forward* start and more elite men using a *weight back* start. While the differences between the two techniques may appear to be subtle to the observer, they are actually not. Let us explain the differences.

With the *weight forward* start, the predominant weight of the swimmer is placed on the front foot. The swimmer's center of mass is centered more toward the front edge of the block, with the shoulders located directly over the front edge of the block and the arms directed down from the shoulders. The head above protrudes out over the front of edge of the starting block. The swimmer is not leaning forward, but rather balanced at the furthest point forward on the block that he or she can possibly be.

At the take-your-mark command, using the *weight forward* start technique, the swimmer pulls upward with the hands on the front of the block or the bars located on the top sides of the block, either with straightened or bent arms. At the sound of the beep, the front foot, where most of the weight is distributed, produces nearly all of the propulsion for the start. Neither the arms, which are not in a good mechanical position to push or pull backwards on the block, nor the back foot, which carries very little weight, can generate much propulsion for the start.

With the *weight back* start, the swimmer starts out with the weight predominantly on the front foot, in the same balanced position as the *weight forward* starter. At the take-your-mark command, the *weight back* starter will grab the front of the block or the bars on the top sides of the block with the hands and shift the weight to be predominantly placed on the back foot. In so doing, the entire body moves backward just a few degrees from vertical, perhaps only 5-10 degrees. In that position, the swimmer's center of mass is now behind the swimmer's hands on the front of the blocks, with a slight backward angle of the arms from the vertical position.

From that set position, the *weight back* starter has the potential to generate significant propulsion from three different sources: arms, back foot and front foot. Potential is an important word here, because not every swimmer uses all three sources of propulsion well with the *weight back* technique.

Olympic sprinter Brad Tandy demonstrates the weight forward position (top) and the weight back position (bottom). There are only a few degrees of movement backwards, but that changes all of the dynamics of the start.

There are advantages and disadvantages to using each start technique. That is probably why we see a fairly even distribution of swimmers using them. These are the major advantages and disadvantages of each technique:

Weight Forward Technique

Advantages

- Usually shorter time required to leave the starting block
- May be beneficial to swimmers that depend on fast dolphin kicking

Disadvantage

- Not as much propulsion leaving the block

Weight Back Technique

Advantages

- Greater propulsion leaving the starting block
- May enable swimmers to use more powerful coupling motions

Disadvantage

- May take longer to leave the block

In our opinion, among the male elite swimmers of today, the two best starters in the world are Caeleb Dressel (USA) and Brad Tandy (South Africa). Both use a similar *weight back* start technique. They also have incredible vertical leaping ability, an indication of strong, fast twitch muscle composition. Caeleb allegedly has a 42-inch vertical leap, similar to LeBron James.

Among the elite women, two of the best starters are Sarah Sjostrom (Sweden) and Ranomi Kromowidjojo (Netherlands). Both use a *weight forward* start technique. They also have incredibly fast dolphin kicking speed.

There are several reasons why a swimmer would choose a *weight forward* start over a *weight back* start, besides having a fast dolphin kick. Having a slow reaction time, a poor vertical leap or not being able to implement the advantages of the *weight back* technique might also be reasons to choose a *weight forward* start.

In 2000, at the Sydney Olympic Games, Anthony Ervin (USA) tied Gary Jr. for the gold medal in the 50-meter freestyle using a *weight forward* start. In 2012, at the London Olympic Games, Anthony switched to a *weight back* start technique. In the finals of the 50-meter freestyle, he was the last swimmer to leave the blocks and never had a chance to win. Four years later, at the Olympic Games in Rio de Janeiro, he went back to the *weight forward* start and won again. He still didn't have a great start. He doesn't have a high vertical leap. His reaction time isn't the fastest and his dolphin kick speed is not the greatest. But he is the fastest swimmer on the surface. His strategy was to get into the water as quickly as possible, take as few kicks as necessary to break out and start swimming down the pool. It worked.

Not everyone has great leaping ability, like Caeleb or Brad, or dolphin kicking speed like Sarah or Ronomi. In addition to those two factors, there are eight other important techniques that can help the start, which we will describe in detail. Of the ten points to a great start, **by far** the two most important factors are the vertical leaping ability (muscle composition) and the underwater dolphin kicking speed. If a swimmer is fortunate enough to have both of those abilities, he or she can do all other eight techniques poorly and still end up ahead. That makes the understanding and appreciation for those eight other techniques more challenging. Nonetheless, they need to be understood. Many swimmers need all of the help they can get on the start.

We like to divide the ten points to a great start into three categories of 3 techniques each, with the last point being the breakout. The first category is what we call the *challenging techniques*, because they are the most difficult to improve. They include the vertical leap height (muscle composition), the reaction time and the dolphin kick speed.

The second category is called the *clean entry techniques* and includes the techniques of hyper-streamlining, the hip lift and pointing the toes. All three of these techniques help the swimmer enter the water with the least amount of splash, resulting in less frontal drag.

The third category is called the *coupling motions techniques,* which can augment the propulsion forces coming from the two hands and feet. They include the head lift, the arm motion and the back-leg kick. All three can be very powerful techniques, if used correctly.

Finally, we will discuss the breakout and the common mistakes that are made there.

Ready Position

Before swimmers takes their mark for the start, which is called the *set* position, let's first explain how they should set themselves up in the *ready* position. The *ready* position is the position the swimmers assume on the starting block after the starter has blown the whistle and before the take-your-mark command. Here is the strategy that Brad Tandy uses in preparation for his starts. If there is a back wedge on the starting block, be certain that it is placed at the right distance back from the front. This is something that needs to be determined in warm up, well before the start of the race. Swimmers do not want to be guessing or be unsure of where that back-foot wedge should be placed.

With the sound of the starter's whistle, signaling permission to climb up on the starting block, the swimmer climbs up on the block and places the front foot, with toes barely over the edge, in the middle of the front of the starting block, not off to one side. It is controversial which foot should be in front, the dominant or non-dominant foot. We have seen it done both ways. The most important factor is which way the swimmer feels the most comfortable. This should be tested in practices or warm up before the race starts. Usually, if swimmers are not sure which foot should be placed in front, they can try it both ways and then they will know.

Once the swimmer finds the position for the front foot in the middle of the starting block, he or she needs to position the back foot on the back wedge, slightly offset from the front foot, but with the back heel well above the top of the wedge. If there is no back wedge, then the swimmer should place the back foot where it feels the most comfortable, on the ball of the foot, with the back heel elevated off the block. The precise placement of the back foot is less important in the *weight forward* technique, but nonetheless, it should be in a comfortable position, so that the swimmer feels balanced. In the *ready* position, Brad likes to keep the front and back feet separated laterally about hip distance apart for balance. Later in the *set* position, as we will explain, he will line the two feet up in almost the same line, one behind the other.

There is some controversy about how far back the back foot should be placed on the block or the wedge. Using VM technology, we tested elite sprinter Margo Geer (USA) with her back foot in her normal comfortable position. Then we tested her with her back foot closer to her front foot than her normal position. Then we tested her a third time with her back foot farther back than her normal position. She performed a start in each position twice and we averaged her results for comparison. She was the fastest to 12 meters with her back foot in her normal (middle) position. She was .06 seconds slower to 12 meters with her back foot farther back and .1 seconds slower to 12 meters with her back foot closer to her front foot. Usually, by positioning the back foot where the swimmers are most comfortable, they will perform the start better.

Once the swimmer finds the right placement for both feet and feels balanced in that position, the predominant weight should be distributed on the front foot with that knee bent slightly. The next technique that Brad uses is different than what most swimmers do. Most swimmers will bend down and grab the front of the block or the bars loosely with their hands, often with the thumbs on the top of the block, waiting for the *take-your-mark* command from the starter.

Brad bends down, but stops his hands when they get just above his ankles. Both arms are loosely hanging straight down from his shoulders. He wiggles his fingers at this moment, preparing his hands for the forthcoming grip on the block. At the starter's command, he then reaches down and grabs the front of the block with his fingers and thumb on the front of the block, pulls upward very firmly on the block with his hands, lifts the back foot off of the wedge and moves it over to line up almost directly with the front foot. In this process, which happens quickly, he leans backward slightly, shifting the weight to the back foot.

He has a rationale for doing using this technique of stopping his hands a little above the front of the block in the *ready* position. One of the worst things that can happen on a start is having the beep go off before the swimmer is in the *set* position. The other is being held in the *set* position for too long. The longer swimmers remain in the coiled position, with the muscles contracted and ready to spring forward, the less effective they become. The ideal timing is to have the beep go off as soon after the swimmer reaches the *set* position as possible.

If the swimmer starts from the standing position before the starter's command, there is too much risk that by the time the swimmer bends all the way down, grabs the front of the block and shifts his weight back, the beep will have gone off. Many swimmers have been left standing on the block that way, including Gary Jr in the men's 100-meter freestyle finals at the 2004 Olympic Trials in Long Beach.

On the other hand, if there is a slow starter, a swimmer who has the hands already down on the front and pulls back right away can be left in that position for a long time, potentially weakening the start. That may be the safest starting technique, but it is likely not the fastest.

Set Position

Brad starts his descent at the starter's command from a higher position, with his hands just above his ankles. It takes him a short time to get into the set position, after bending down and grabbing the front of the block, but he doesn't want to be the first swimmer in the *set* position. Usually with that technique, he is not held in the *set* position for very long.

Olympian Brad Tandy in the ready position before the start. His weight is predominantly on the front foot, back heel well off the top of the wedge, arms and hands relaxed and hanging at a level just above his ankles. His head is in alignment with his upper body and his sight is down toward the front foot.

When the swimmer reaches down to grab either the front of the block or the bars above the block on the sides, we see many variations in how that is done. Some, like Brad, keep their arms straight, locked in from the shoulders, with their fingers and thumb on the front side of the block. Others bend the elbows to the side. Still others bend their elbows backwards. Caeleb grabs the front corner of the block with his thumb on the front and his fingers on the side. He bends his elbows backward slightly. We also see many swimmers place their thumbs on top of the block. What is the best way?

First of all, with the *weight back* start, when there is a small angle of force pulling the swimmer forward, a considerable amount of acceleration can be gained by pulling upward aggressively on the blocks. With velocity meter technology, we are able to measure three distinct acceleration points on the start, correlating to the amount of propulsion generated from each one. The first one comes from the arms pulling upward on the block. The second acceleration peak comes from the back foot pushing off of the wedge. The third acceleration peak comes from the front foot as the swimmer leaves the block.

Watching a slow-motion video of elite swimmers, like Brad or Caeleb, using the *weight back* technique, they pull upwards so aggressively on the block that the front of the block actually lifts upward. Even though the direction of the force of the arms pulling is mostly upward, since their center of mass is behind their hands, there is a small vector of force that also moves them forward. Therefore, whatever the grip on the block and the position of the arms is, with *weight back* start technique, the swimmer needs to be in the position that will generate the strongest pulling force from the arms moving him or her in the forward direction.

The rationale for bending the elbows backward is that the swimmer is increasing the vector of the force from the arms in the forward direction. The rationale for using the straight arm is that the swimmer is lifting from the shoulder and using more of the back than while bending the elbows, thus getting a stronger pull.

When we tested elite swimmer Zane Grothe, in Islamorada with VM technology, we compared two starts using the straight arm *weight back* technique with two starts using the bent elbow technique. We measured the peak acceleration (from the arms), peak velocity leaving the block, distance to hand entry in the water, time to hand entry in the water and the time and average speed to 12 meters. We then averaged the results of the two starts for comparison. Here is what we found:

Start Technique	Peak Acceleration (m/sec2)	Peak Velocity (m/sec)	Time to hand entry (seconds)	Distance to hand entry (meters)	Time to 12 meters (seconds)	Average speed to 12 meters (m/sec)
Bent Arms	16.63	5.29	.89	2.97	4.87	2.47
Straight Arms	16.74	5.38	.87	2.91	4.77	2.52

Comparison of results of start using a straight arm versus a bent arm during the *set* position with Zane Grothe.

The most important metric above is the peak acceleration derived from the arms pulling upward on the block after the beep. In the averages taken from two starts, using each technique, we found that the peak accelerations were almost identical. All of the other metrics, while important, could have been influenced by other factors, such as the propulsion of the back foot, front foot, angle of trajectory and entry and the dolphin kick speed.

From this small study, it appears that, at least for Zane, it doesn't really make a lot of difference whether he keeps his arms straight or bends them for the start. It may be the best advice for each swimmer to use whichever technique feels more powerful, and then practice using it.

However, with respect to holding on to the block, regardless of where the swimmer grabs it and which technique is being used, we believe that the thumb should be down, not on top of the block. In theory, the swimmer should be able to pull with more force using all of the fingers and thumb, not just the fingers.

Elite freestyler Zane Grothe is tested with VM technology comparing bent arms with straight arms on the weight back start. His front and back foot are lined up in almost a straight line.

Elite swimmer Zach Hayden uses a weight back start, holding on to the bars on top of the block with bent elbows. If the bars are too wide, the swimmer can lose power using them.

With the command of take-your-mark, Brad leans down and grabs the front of the block firmly with all fingers, thumb in front, lifting upward. After grabbing the block and while shifting his weight to the back foot, he lifts the back foot off of the plate and moves it over a few inches to line up more directly behind the front foot. He doesn't place it there to begin with because he needs more separation of the feet for balance. Once he has ahold of the block with his hands, there is no more concern for balance. He lines the two feet up because he wants to get the propulsion from his back foot and front foot directed in the same line forward.

As he reaches down, grabs the front of the block, pulls upward and leans back, he keeps his back rounded and his bum as high as possible. Many swimmers flatten their backs after the starter's command, with either the *weight back* or *weight forward* technique. Some of those same swimmers will also tilt their head forward. With VM technology, to test which back position, rounded or flattened, is better, we asked elite swimmer Isabella Arcila (Colombia) to use each technique twice. Isabella was accustomed to flattening her back for the start, so we had her try both techniques and averaged her results. Here is what we found.

Testing flat back versus a rounded back on the freestyle start with elite swimmer Isabella Arcila.

Start Technique	Peak Acceleration (m/sec2)	Peak Velocity (m/sec)	Distance to hand entry (meters)	Time to hand entry (seconds)	Time to 12 meters (seconds)	Average speed to 12 meters (m/sec)
Flat Back	22.48	5.22	2.75	.83	5.34	2.25
Rounded Back	23.46	5.44	2.89	.80	5.24	2.29

Comparison of results from using a rounded versus flattened back during the *set* position with Isabella Arcila.

By rounding her back on the start, Isabella enters the water .14 meters farther (5% improvement) and reaches 12 meters .1 seconds sooner (2% improvement) than the start with the flattened back. With a rounded back, Isabella improved in every category. For Isabella, the rounded back is clearly a superior technique.

We also believe that the head should be in alignment with the upper body in the *set* position. It should not be extended forward, nor looking backward behind the swimmer. As you will soon learn, the head lift is one of the three important coupling motions on the start. A swimmer cannot lift the head on the start if it is already extended forward.

Brad is now in the *set* position. He is pulling up firmly with his hands on the front of the block. His weight has shifted backward (minimally) to be predominantly distributed on his back foot. The feet are lined up in nearly the same line, with the back heel well off the wedge. His bum is high, his back rounded and his head in alignment with his upper body. His body is now cocked and ready to explode forward.

Let's discuss the ten points that enable Brad to be one of the best starters in the world.

Ten Points to a Great Start

All ten of these important points are relevant to both the *weight forward* and *weight back* start techniques.

Three Challenging Techniques

The first challenging technique, arguably the most important one for a good start, is the **vertical leaping ability**. Essentially this is a test for muscle composition of the athlete, the percentage of fast twitch versus slow twitch muscle fibers, and muscle mass. Although the vertical leap tests the leg muscles, according to exercise physiologist, Dr. David Costill, the percentage of fast twitch and slow twitch muscle fiber is the same throughout all of the skeletal muscles of the same body, with the exception of those involved in holding our posture erect. Those are predominantly slow twitch muscles, since they need to be working most of the time.

Expensive equipment is not needed to measure a vertical jump. By placing black marks on a tall pole or wall, spaced at every foot or .25 meter, anyone can test the vertical jump. Simply have the swimmer (wearing shoes), stand next to the pole or wall and extend the arm upward from a standing position. Make a note of that height. Then have the swimmer bend down and jump up as high as possible, noting how high the fingertips get on the wall or pole. Repeat it a couple of times to be sure. While not perfectly accurate, this test will give you a pretty good idea of the swimmer's vertical leaping ability and what you might expect on the start.

Swimmers can improve their vertical leaping ability by doing ballistic type leg exercises, such as plyometric jumps, fast leg presses and squats. In younger swimmers, the vertical leap will increase with age and increasing muscle mass. The muscle composition doesn't change dramatically, but the muscle mass can.

Whatever the propulsion that occurs from the feet and hands on the start, the trajectory of the swimmer off of the blocks needs to be horizontal, not upward. Since the blocks are situated a couple of feet higher than the surface of the water, there is no need for an upward trajectory of the swimmer. That will delay the time for the swimmer to reach the water and often causes too steep of an entry angle. The speed of the swimmer is high enough without jumping up. The swimmer needs to jump straight out or forward, not upward.

The swimmer's **reaction time** is the time it takes from the time he hears the beep until there is a neuromotor response to the beep and the swimmer begins moving. The time that is indicated on the electronic scoreboards at major competition, which measures the time from the sound of the beep to the time the swimmer leaves the block, is somewhat representative of the reaction time, with one understanding. The swimmers using *weight forward* technique will have the advantage of getting off of the block sooner, since they are positioned farther forward. That time does not determine the quality of the entire start, since it is just one factor of many. The quality of the start should be judged by the swimmer's time to 15 meters, or where the swimmer breaks out in relationship to the other swimmers in the race.

Science has shown that reaction times can improve, when trained. The best way to improve one's reaction time to the sound of the starter's beep is by practicing starts and reacting to the same beep sound used in competition. The brain can be trained to react sooner to that sound with practice.

In Chapter 22, we discussed the **dolphin kick** mechanics and how to develop more speed. We consider it to be one of the two most important techniques of a great start. To improve your start, improve your dolphin kick speed.

On the start, the first down kick of the dolphin kick occurs as the feet enter the water. Because of the angle that the body enters the water and the immediate change of direction, the feet and legs move downward in the water and generate some propulsion in the process. It is really only a matter of when the following up kick is taken. We recommend taking the up kick as soon as possible. Similar to what we have found on the turns, the longer the glide after the entry, the longer it will take to get to 15 meters. Because of the extraordinary speed of the swimmer, the kicks need to be tight and fast, with very little knee bend, hip flexion or drop of the feet.

Three Clean Entry Techniques

If a swimmer's trajectory from the starting block is horizontal, as it should be, then all swimmers that leave the block in such a manner at the same time, regardless of their mass and the propulsive force leaving the block, will reach the water at exactly the same time and with the same vertical speed. It doesn't matter whether the swimmer weighs 200 pounds or 50 pounds, whether he or she falls off of the starting block or has a 42-inch vertical jump, like Caeleb. From the time swimmers start moving forward to the time their fingers touch the water will take just under one second and at that moment, they will be travelling at somewhere between 5 and 6 m/sec., which is around 13 mph. That is nearly three times faster than the world record speed for the men's 50-meter freestyle sprint. The difference will be in the horizontal component of their speed, where they strike the water, the angle of their entry and how well they carry their speed, once they are in the water. Most of the elite swimmers that we have tested first touch the water at just less than 3 meters distance from the wall. Brad reaches the water at 3.44 meters in the same time, which is a big advantage.

How well a swimmer carries his speed in the water depends on two main factors, frontal drag and the swimmer's mass. The momentum of the swimmer is determined by the swimmer's mass times the velocity (M x V). Of two swimmers that enter the water at the same angle, with the same amount of drag and at the same distance from the wall, the bigger swimmer will move forward farther and faster than the smaller swimmer. With greater momentum, it takes longer for the water to slow the bigger swimmer down.

We don't have the ability to change our mass very easily, but we can change the angle of our entry and the amount of frontal drag we cause at the entry and beyond, once we are in the water. A clean entry implies that we are entering the water with minimal frontal drag. That is somewhat correlated to the amount of splash that the body causes at the entry. Usually, the bigger the splash, the greater the frontal drag caused by the entry. The swimmer's start is not a cannon ball contest.

The hyperstreamline position is the lowest drag-coefficient position for the front end of the human body. The chin is placed on or very near the swimmer's chest. The arms are placed behind the swimmer's head with the elbows squeezed as closely together as possible. The arms are straightened and pulled forward, sub-luxating or hyperextending from the shoulder joints. By pulling the shoulders forward, the entire shape of the upper body changes. The abdominal cavity excavates, and the skin overlying the chest and abdomen tightens considerably. The hands are wrapped together, wrist over wrist, with the fingers and thumbs pointing forward and squeezed together. The lumbar spine is arched or extended in this position. All of these positional changes lead to a lowering of the drag coefficient of the human body.

Hyperstreamlining is both unnatural and uncomfortable. Not everyone can do it well. Only about one out of twenty swimmers we evaluate for their streamline position can actually touch the two elbows together behind their head, essentially turning two arms into one. We call those swimmers that can do that, who have hyperextended elbows, *unicorns.* Their two arms look like a horn coming off the top of their head.

We find it interesting that nearly every competitive swimmer, regardless of the type of streamline that they use off the walls on turns, will use the *hyperstreamline* position during the start. Perhaps it is because the drag forces are proportional to the square of the swimmer's speed that they recognize that any streamline position other than *hyperstreamline* will cause more deceleration at such a high speed. In the *hyperstreamlining* attempt, the costliest mistake we find is not getting the hands wrapped back together in time, after going through the arm motion. This can have disastrous consequences if the force of the water at impact either moves one arm out to the swimmer's side, or causes the two arms to cross.

The **hip lift** is a subtle but important technique for attaining a clean entry on the start. At some point before entry, the swimmer should flex the hips to about 15 degrees, while he or she is still in the air. This usually occurs right as the two hands are wrapping together for the *hyperstreamline.* The hip lift causes the legs to be approximately horizontal to the water, while the upper body angles downward at around 15 degrees. The hip lift enables the swimmer to enter the water cleanly, without needing to overbend the knees and without going too deep.

If the swimmer fails to lift the hip, either one of two problems will usually occur. The body will enter the water straight, cleanly (if the toes are pointed) and at an angle. From a maintained straight body line, the swimmer cannot change direction forward soon enough, so the body ends up too deep in the water. More commonly with a straight body entry, we see the swimmer bend the knees excessively, just before the legs enter the water, in an attempt to change the swimmer's direction. The excessive knee bend will cause more frontal drag during the entry.

At the other end of the spectrum, if a swimmer lifts the hips too far (over flexes the hip), the swimmer will also go too deep after the entry. We typically see more hip-flexion on the breaststroke start, compared to a freestyle or butterfly start, as the swimmer needs to go a little deeper for the pullout. The right amount of hip flexion appears to be from about 10-20 degrees for freestyle and butterfly, and perhaps 20 - 30 degrees for breaststroke. Any more than that will lead to an entry depth that will require too much time and too much distance to get back to the surface.

For those swimmers that are trying to learn the hip-lift technique, we have found that the running dive is the best drill to learn it. When a swimmer takes 8-10 running steps up to the edge of the pool and jumps out for a dive, the additional speed of the swimmer nearly always leads to lifting the hip before entry. At that speed, the water is less forgiving of the incorrect angle of entry, so it also teaches the swimmer to enter at the correct 15-degree angle.

Olympian Brad Tandy demonstrates a nice *hyperstreamline* position and hip-lift technique before entry.

The failure to **point the toes** well (plantar flexion) before the feet enter the water may be the most common mistake over all that we find on the start. If the feet are relaxed on the start, then they will be hanging straight down while the swimmer is in the air. Swimmers don't need to point the toes until just before they enter the water, but if they fail to do that, it is like throwing a parachute out the back. More drag is caused by the feet hanging than even a poor streamline in front.

In our Propulsion/Drag Meter (PDM) testing in Florida, we found that the feet hanging down can increase frontal drag by as much as 41% more than when the feet are pointed backwards. That test was done at swimming race speed (2.3 m/sec) which is slower than the speed of the feet entering the water on the dive. The actual drag caused by the hanging feet on the start could easily be more than the 41% increase that we measured compared with the toes being pointed.

To help the feet slip into the water more cleanly, causing even less drag, we often see the elite swimmers bend their knees very slightly at entry. The small knee bend helps the swimmer point the toes even more upward or vertically at entry. A slight knee bend is helpful. A large knee bend is harmful.

Brad Tandy bends his knees very slightly and points his toes straight backward and upward, just before they enter the water. That way, the feet are following the body line and path of the legs into the water, causing the least amount of frontal drag.

Coupling Motions Techniques

Lifting the head or not lifting the head on the start is another controversial technique. Many swimmers are taught to look down on the start and keep their heads down in the forward trajectory. We don't agree. We believe that the kinetic energy from a quick head lift can help increase the propulsion off of the starting block. We also believe that the body tends to follow in the direction of where the swimmer is looking. In other words, a swimmer looking down will tend to follow a more direct line down to the water. A swimmer that is looking forward will tend to stay in a more horizontal trajectory longer. There is no swimmer's dolphin kick speed that can even approach the speed of the swimmer moving through the air, so the farther distance from the wall the swimmer enters the water, the better.

What is so unusual about the head lift that Brad Tandy uses on his start is not just that he snaps the head forward quickly. Nearly all of the elite swimmers will lift their heads abruptly on the start. It is how long he keeps it up, looking forward, that is unusual. If the head is tucked down too soon after being lifted, that can cause a problem of overbending the hip, leading to a steep entry angle and too deep of a start. The head should snap upward on the start, looking directly forward, and should remain looking forward for as long as possible. Brad keeps his head looking forward until his arms pass his shoulders during the circular motion forward. Weighing about 11 or 12 pounds, the head can become a powerful coupling tool, if used correctly.

Brad lifts the head quickly on his start, but keeps looking forward even after his arms have passed his shoulders in their big swing forward toward the streamline. Only at the last second does he tuck his chin down for the entry.

Using VM technology, we compared the starts of elite butterflier Amanda Kendall using the head down and head lift techniques. We compared the averaged data from two starts, using each technique and here is what we found:

Amanda Kendall keeps the head down during the entire start during this VM test.

For this test, Amanda lifts her head for the start, though she does not lift it far, nor hold it up for very long.

Start Technique	Peak Acceleration (m/sec2)	Peak Velocity (m/sec)	Distance to hand entry (meters)	Time to hand entry (seconds)	Time to 12 meters (seconds)	Average speed to 12 meters (m/sec)
Head down	14.37	4.96	2.64	.84	5.56	2.16
Head lifted	14.96	4.91	2.96	.86	5.41	2.22

Comparison of results of lifting the head versus keeping the head down on the start with Amanda Kendall.

By lifting her head, Amanda reaches the water .32 meters farther than with her head down (11% increase), supporting our theory that keeping the head down results in a more direct path to the water. She also reached 12 meters .12 seconds sooner, which is an improvement of 3% over keeping her head down. For Amanda, lifting the head on the start was a better technique.

The **arm motion technique** on the start can also be a very powerful coupling motion. We categorize the arm motion on the start into four different types in the order of increasing kinetic energy or effectiveness: **swing forward, stop-and-reverse, small circle** and **big circle**.

With the **swing forward** technique, the swimmer does exactly that. There is no lifting or pulling on the front of the block with the arms. The arms simply release from their hold on the block and swing forward into a streamline. The arm motion is slow and deliberate, without producing much kinetic energy, so there is very little coupling going on.

The **stop-and-reverse** technique is what we see many young swimmers use, for some reason. As they leave the block, they move the arms abruptly to their sides, but then stop the motion. From that point, they swing the arms forward underneath their bodies back into the streamline. In effect, they have just added a little short energy motion to the swing forward technique. There is more coupling than with the swing forward technique, but the energy and motion are short-lived.

The **small circle** arm motion technique is what most of the American swimmers use, even at the elite level. Some refer to this technique as the *quick draw* or the *attacking cat* start. With this technique, once the hands leave the block, whether with a straight arm or bent arm technique, the arms immediately bend and move upward and then forward, forming a small circle. The size of the circular motion of the arms depends on the amount of bend in the elbows and the shoulder motion, ranging from small, where the hands pass by the swimmer's head on the way forward, to large, where they pass above the swimmer's head on the way forward. Caeleb, for example, bends the elbows slightly in this motion, creating a pretty big circular motion with his hands. His arms move forward in a circular motion well above his head and body.

The **big circle** technique is used when the arms remain straight throughout the entire circular motion. Brad uses this technique. The kinetic energy in the circular arm motion is proportional to the square of the length of the swimmer's arms and the square of the angular velocity of the arms around the circle. Lengthening the arms and the speed of them coming around will increase the coupling energy dramatically.

While the big circular arm motion does not require having extreme shoulder flexibility, it doesn't hurt to have that flexibility when using this technique. Swimmers with very tight shoulders may have a difficult time making a full circular arm motion with this technique. Often, they end up with a half circle, but that may be more coupling energy than they get by bending the elbows.

Using the big circular arm motion technique is not without risk. If the hands do not get wrapped together before the entry, or if they should overshoot each other (not uncommon), the result can be far worse than using a smaller energy, yet safer technique.

Depending on the level of risk the swimmer is willing to take, we think the big circle with a straight arm is the best arm motion technique to use. Like anything else, it takes a lot of practice to perfect this start technique. Brad started using this start technique at the age of seven, taught to him by his mother.

Elite breaststroker Nikola Obrovac being tested with VM technology, comparing small circle and big circle arm motion techniques. Here he is using the small circle, bending the elbows as the arms come around.

Niko is tested with VM technology using the straight arm, big circular arm motion start technique.

Using VM technology, we compared the small circle and big circle arm motion techniques on the start, using world class breaststroker, Nikolas Obrovac, from Croatia. Here is what we found by averaging the data from his two starts using each technique.

Start Technique	Peak Acceleration (m/sec2)	Peak Velocity (m/sec)	Distance to hand entry (meters)	Time to hand entry (seconds)	Time to 12 meters (seconds)	Average speed to 12 meters (m/sec)
Small circle (bent elbows)	19.09	5.39	2.90	.83	5.66	2.12
Big circle (straight arms)	30.14	5.34	2.92	.79	5.54	2.17

Comparison of results of using a straight circular arm motion versus a bent-arm motion on the start with Niko Obrovac.

By using the circular straight arm motion on his start, Niko improved his peak acceleration off the blocks by 37%. His time and average velocity to 12 meters improved by 2% over the bent arm technique. For Niko, the straight arm circular arm motion technique, similar to what Brad Tandy uses, is better.

Brad Tandy uses a big, circular and powerful straight arm motion on his start, helping to augment his propulsion.

Of the three coupling motions on the start, the back-leg kick may be the most important one. Depending on the age and size of the swimmer, the back leg can weigh between 20 and 40 pounds. As with the arm swing, if the back-leg motion is used aggressively and correctly, it can produce a tremendous amount of coupling energy on the start.

Brad may get more boost of propulsion from his back-leg kick than either from his arms or head lift. He does all three extremely well. Brad kicks his back right leg up so high that he needs to extend or arch his lower back at the same time to keep from toppling over. The lower back extension tends to balance the forward motion of the back leg. The back-leg kick starts with the leg straight and ends with foot pointing almost vertically with a slight knee bend. The leg ends up so high that even the front leg reaches a position above the horizontal plane.

Most swimmers are not aware of what they are doing with their back legs, nor do they recognize how powerful the motion can be. Consequently, they don't do much at all with their back legs.

We have found the most effective ways of teaching the back-leg kick is by first having swimmers hold on to the back of the starting block with one leg on the ground, knee bent slightly, and the other leg held straight back with the toes pointed. The swimmer then practices kicking the back leg up into the air aggressively and as high as possible. If they are unable to get much height with the back leg, then we allow them to jump off the ground with the front foot, while kicking up with the back leg, the so-called *donkey kicks.*

Next, we have them do their start on the block, holding a beach ball, just over their back, about half way up. The object for them is to kick the beach ball up with their back foot as high as possible. It is amazing how well this drill works. With a few tries, the swimmers have usually vastly improved their back leg kicking technique.

Swimmers practicing the back-leg kick drill using the backs of the starting blocks.

Elite sprinter Aaron Greenberg struggled with the back-leg kick until he did these drills.

World class butterflier Marcus Schlesinger sends the beach ball flying with a ferocious back leg kick on his start.

Brad Tandy's back leg is almost vertical with the toe pointing straight up. The knee bends slightly at the end of the upward motion.

The Breakout

The tenth and final point to a great start is the swimmer's breakout. Much time can be gained or lost during the swimmer's breakout. In Chapter 17 we discussed the breaststroke pullout techniques and in Chapter 13, we discussed the options for the backstroke breakout. Now we will discuss the freestyle breakout, which is relevant to both the start and the turns. Many technical mistakes are often made on the freestyle breakout.

The number of dolphin kicks that should be taken on the start (and the turns) depends on several factors. In Chapter 25 on freestyle turns, we will discuss how we determine the optimal number of dolphin kicks, or if any dolphin kicks should be taken at all (mostly Masters swimmers), for starts and turns.

Here are the key techniques that are recommended for an explosive freestyle breakout from your start:

1. Initiate the first pull simultaneously with the final dolphin down kick, not during the freestyle kick after the transition.
2. After the final dolphin kick, transition to a strong freestyle kick.
3. Hold the *hyperstreamline* position until the first pull is initiated. Don't separate the arms or break the streamline early.
4. Initiate the first pull forcefully with the pulling hand inside the elbow. Do not allow the hand to outsweep on the first pull.
5. While pulling with one arm, push the lead arm forward with the fingers and thumb squeezed together. Don't relax the lead arm or allow the elbow to bend.
6. Keep the chin on or near the chest throughout the entire breakout. Refrain from looking forward. Learn to trust your instincts on your depth. Looking up will cost you a lot of time.

7. Don't take a breath on your first stroke. Even though on every freestyle event from 200 meters up, a breath should be taken on the first stroke off each turn, swimmers can hold their breath on the first stroke of every start, no matter what the distance.

This swimmer lifts her head right at the breakout, causing her to slow considerably.

This swimmer keeps her head down at breakout, reducing frontal drag and gaining speed.

In summary, the best way to improve the start is by practicing starts. There is no substitute for doing starts to get better. Understand your strengths and your weaknesses. Understand each of the ten points to improve your start and work on each of them, but only one at a time.

The starts are most important in the 50-meter sprints and diminish in importance as each event becomes longer. Nonetheless, at whatever race distance, it is always nice to start out in the lead. However, there is only one start, and, in most races, there are several turns or more. Work hard on your start but spend even more time learning how to do fast turns. We will discuss how to do that in Chapter 25.

Chapter 24

Starts

Fundamentals of the Backstroke Start

A great backstroke start is a thing of beauty. When watching a really good backstroke start, one should see almost no splash and hear almost no splash. It is like watching the dolphins jump through hoops at Sea World. Yet, a great backstroke start is not easy to perform well.

The objectives of the backstroke start are the following:

1. Get the body completely airborne on the start, using the greatest amount of propulsion possible from the legs.
2. Use the lowest body trajectory path possible, while still getting airborne with the entire body.
3. Maximize the energy of the three coupling motions: head motion, arm motion and leg kick.
4. Enter the water as cleanly as possible at the correct body angle, using *hyperstreamline*, lumbar extension, and the correct feet position.
5. Initiate and sustain the fastest underwater dolphin kick possible to breakout, holding the *hyperstreamline* position.
6. Explode out of the breakout with the least amount of frontal drag and into a fast stroke rate, appropriate for the event.

Getting Airborne

The same laws of physics apply to the backstroke start as with all strokes and turns. In some respects, they are even more important on the backstroke start because of the profound difference in density between air and water.

One of the most common mistakes made on the backstroke start is not getting the body airborne. If any part of the human body, most commonly the legs, drags through the water on their way out from the wall, that will surely cause the swimmer to slow down more than if the body can get completely out of the water.

Getting the body to be airborne on the backstroke start is easier said than done. Unlike the freestyle start, where the swimmer begins from a height of a few feet above the water level, with the backstroke start, the swimmer must begin from sea level, or at the surface of the water. Technically, on a flat walled surface, the toes can be above the water level and with a gutter wall, the toes are supposed to be below the water level. Either way, the feet should be close to the surface of the water for the backstroke start.

From underwater, the toes are placed as high up on the touch pad as possible.

To get the body airborne on the backstroke start, the trajectory needs to go up and out, not just straight forward, as in the freestyle start. The two feet are the only source of propulsion in a backstroke start. The arms are used at first to lift the swimmer into the correct *set* position, but cannot provide any propulsion. To drive the body upward and away from the wall, there needs to be a downward vector of force by the feet against the wall. If the wall does not provide enough friction, or if there is not a backstroke wedge, providing some protruding surface to push down against, the risk of the feet slipping down on the wall is pretty high. The wedge helps tremendously in providing a surface to push down against, preventing slipping on the wall.

There are at least four reasons why the backstroker cannot get airborne on the start, assuming the feet do not slip on the wall. The first, and perhaps the most common one, is not pulling the body high enough for the *set* position.

At the starter's command to *take-your-mark*, swimmers need to use the bars on the starting block above, whether situated vertically or horizontally (personal preference), to pull themselves upward until the bum is very close to the surface of the water. The bum can be slightly above, right at or slightly below the surface, but it must be close. If the bum is too low in the water in the set position, swimmers will not be able to clear the water when they launch on the start.

World Champion Junya Koga raises his bum well above the surface of the water in the *set* position.

To help younger swimmers who may not have the strength to pull themselves up to that height, they can bring their entire bodies in closer to the wall. From that position, it requires less strength to get the bum up to the surface. From that more vertical angle, however, without using a wedge, they may be at more risk for slipping on the wall during the start.

World class backstroker Luca Spinazzola leaves his bum below the surface in the *set* position and pulls his body closer to the wall. Luca prefers to use a lower trajectory on his backstroke start from this position, but he doesn't quite get airborne from starting that low in the water.

Other reasons for swimmers not getting airborne on the backstroke start include not having the vertical leaping height to be able to clear the water. Sometimes the mass/strength ratio is not favorable to get the swimmer airborne, either. We have seen swimmers able to get airborne at any age, if they start from a high enough launching position and they have the right mass/strength ratio.

To maximize the lift and propulsion on the backstroke start, the feet need to be spaced the correct distance apart. The feet should be placed about hip width apart. Placing the feet too close together or too far apart will lead to a loss of propulsive force. We also advocate that the feet be placed at the same height, rather than at two different levels, for even distribution of the swimmer's weight.

Junya demonstrates the feet placement too close together on the wall.

Junya demonstrates the feet placement too wide apart on the wall.

Junya demonstrates the ideal placement of the feet on the wall, hip width apart.

When the swimmer reaches the set position, the back should be straight and the bum should be farther away from the wall than the shoulders. The angle of the back will vary some depending on the personal preference of each swimmer.

Junya sets up for the start with a straight back and his bum fairly far away from the wall. The head is either held in alignment with the upper body or extended backward slightly.

Luca prefers to keep his bum closer to the wall with a very slight angle from vertical with a straight upper back. The head is in alignment with his upper body, or very slightly extended back.

In the set position, the head should be in alignment with the upper body or slightly extended. The swimmer should be looking straight back behind the block, not down or up.

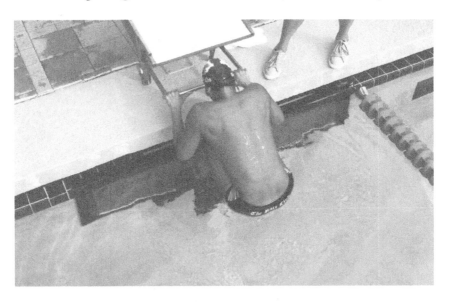

Avoid pulling the head in toward the block too far and looking down for the start.

Avoid having the shoulders farther away from the wall than the bum and looking upward.

The Low Trajectory

Getting airborne with the body is important, but doing so with the lowest trajectory is also important. There should be just one very brief moment, when the toes leave the wall and just before the swimmer's hands touch the water, with the lumbar spine extended back at the correct angle, when the body is completely out of the water. If the swimmer elevates too high, jumping upward more than outward, it can delay the entry and result in too steep of an entry angle, causing the swimmer to go too deep.

Comparing the two backstroke start techniques of Junya Koga and Luca Spinazzola, each swimmer ends up with a different trajectory and entry angle. Junya starts from a higher position, gets airborne with less drag and enters at a steeper angle. Luca uses a lower trajectory, starting from a lower position, and his legs don't quite clear the water, but his angle of entry is less than Junya's and more favorable.

Junya launches himself over the surface, getting his entire body completely out of the water prior to entry.

Luca's trajectory is lower with less lumbar extension and smaller entry angle. His legs never completely get airborne.

Coupling Motions

Moving the **head** correctly can add propulsion to the backstroke start. The head should be in alignment with the upper body in the *set* position for the start and it should end up in alignment with the body at the entry into the water. During the trajectory, some swimmers, like Junya, will throw the head back aggressively, increasing the coupling energy, but then will bring it back in alignment with the upper body in time for the entry. Other swimmers, like Luca, prefer to keep the head in alignment for the entire duration of the start.

If the head is snapped backward, it will tend to cause the lumbar spine to extend more (arch). If the head is left in that position the angle entry will assuredly be too steep and the swimmer will end up too deep in the water. Swimmers who snap their heads all the way back must bring their heads back in alignment with the upper body by the time of hand entry.

Junya snaps the head back quickly on the start, but gets it back in alignment with his upper body at entry.

Luca prefers to keep his head in alignment through the start. With his low trajectory, he does not want to over extend his lumbar spine at entry.

The **arm motion** is also an important coupling motion for the backstroke start. The kinetic energy of the arms will increase by keeping the arms straight, as Junya uses, rather than bent, as Luca uses in the above photo. With either technique, the hands need to get wrapped together by the time they reach the water. Otherwise, arms that separate under water at the entry can lead to a significant increase in frontal drag on the start.

The **leg kick**, which occurs before the entry of the legs into the water, is the third important coupling motion. As with the freestyle start, the leg kick happens after the peak propulsion is over (feet pushing off the wall), but while the force is still acting.

The leg kick on the backstroke start can be compared to the long jumper, who, after running down the track and leaping off one foot, continues running and swinging the arms in the air during the upward trajectory. The peak propulsion of the foot pushing off the ground is over, yet, when the legs and arms are moving in mid-air, the force is still acting. The coupling still works. The jumper goes farther with the arms and legs moving quickly in the air than without moving them.

With Junya's start, he generates more coupling energy than Luca with his head and arm motion, but Luca wins the leg kick energy contest. We have never seen such a ferocious leg kick as we did with Luca's start. He not only kicks up hard with both legs, he also comes down hard with the feet, hoping for more propulsion as the soles press downward into the water at entry.

Luca delivers a powerful up kick just before his legs are about to enter the water. He then comes down hard with the feet starting a strong down kick.

Junya's leg kick is much softer and less energetic than Luca's. His feet and legs enter the water more cleanly, but with less propulsion.

The Clean Entry

The backstroke start should produce a cleaner entry than the freestyle start. The swimmer's angle of entry should be similar, 15-20 degrees, but the swimmer's speed will be considerably less. We often see backstrokers on a good start cause very little splash at all, which also means causing very little drag.

The arms and hands must get wrapped together in the *hyperstreamline* position before entry, to enter cleanly. The position of the feet is far less important on the entry, compared to the freestyle start. Whether they are pointed back (plantar flexion) or the toes are up, with the feet in more of their natural position, the feet seem to slide into the water without much disturbance.

The entry not only needs to be clean, but also at the right angle. Swimmers who arch their backs too much (lumbar extension) will enter too steeply and go to deep. This is often caused by keeping the head and neck in full extension too long.

At the other extreme, swimmers who do not arch their backs enough will usually make a crash landing on the water. That crash not only slows the swimmer down, it hurts. This mishap happens frequently when swimmers first start to learn the backstroke start. They are often afraid of crashing into the water, fearful of the pain, so they stiffen up their bodies and brace for a crash. Usually, when swimmers brace for the crash, they will crash. To do the backstroke start well, the swimmer needs to learn to arch the back and then straighten it some, with the head in alignment, just before entry. It takes practice to do it right and they cannot have fear.

Dolphin Kick

The speed of the dolphin kick is an even bigger difference-maker on the backstroke start than it is on the freestyle start. Once the feet drop into the water, they are producing the first down kick, which is the weaker side of the kick. The next up kick (strong side) should happen quickly, without much delay or glide. It should be a tight kick without excessive knee bend to prevent too much loss of speed. The *hyperstreamline* position should be held until the breakout. All of the kicks should be done with the right amount of knee bend and hip flexion and worked in both directions, up and down.

As we discussed in Chapter 22, the dolphin kick should be faster on the swimmer's back than it is on the swimmer's stomach. The weaker side (down kick) is more propulsive than it is on the swimmer's stomach, so the down kicks should really be emphasized on the backstroke start. Since backstroke is slower than freestyle and a swimmer typically goes a little deeper on the backstroke start than on the freestyle start, more underwater dolphin kicks should be taken on the backstroke start than the same swimmer would take on a freestyle start.

The minimal number of dolphin kicks usually required to reach the surface at the breakout of the backstroke start is 5-6. The total number of dolphin kicks to be taken by each swimmer on the start depends on the dolphin kick speed on the swimmer's back compared to the backstroke speed, and is determined by doing the same test we use in freestyle. The time for a 25-yard backstroke sprint with no dolphin kicks taken is compared to the time for a 25-yard underwater dolphin kick on the back. If the times are within 1 second of each other, swimmers should stay underwater for the full 15 meters, or as long as they are able to with their aerobic capacity. If the time difference is between 1 and 2 seconds, we usually add 2-3 kicks on to the minimum, making the total 7-9 kicks on the start. If the kicking speed is over 2 seconds slower than the swim speed, swimmers should use the minimum number of dolphin kicks required to get back to the surface.

One technique that is very important on the backstroke start is to not allow any air to leave the lungs through the nose or mouth. When swimmers are on their backs, dolphin kicking, the air released from the lungs goes right to the surface. Those bubbles will not reduce frontal drag, as they do when swimmers release the air while on their stomachs. When the air remains in the swimmers' lungs, they are weightless. They float. When the air is released completely from the lungs, the in-water body weight will increase to around 8-9 pounds for an adult. Without much air in the lungs, swimmers sink. If swimmers stay under water very long on the backstroke start and are releasing air from the lungs, most of the air will be gone by the time they are ready for the breakout. Having 8-9 pounds of extra weight at the breakout is not desirable. Furthermore, some swimmers will panic, fearing they will run out of air in their lungs before they reach the surface.

Another reason why swimmers shouldn't release all of the air in the lungs on the backstroke start is that it results in the first breath after the breakout becoming a *mega-breath*—a deep, long inhalation. That long breath can cause the stroke rate to be slower for the first few strokes. It is much better to have an explosive, fast stroke rate coming out of the breakout, with a burst exhale and a quick inhale, similar to the other breaths taken during the swim. To do that, the air must be kept in the swimmer's lungs until the breakout.

There are only two ways we know of to keep the air in the lungs under water during the backstroke start. The first is by wearing a nose clip. The second is by using the upper lip to compress against the nostrils to keep the air in or the water out. Not everyone has the right nose or lip to do that. If swimmers can keep the water out of their nostrils with their upper lips, then they don't need to wear a nose-clip. They just have to remember to do it. If swimmers cannot keep the air in their lungs with their lip, they should wear a nose clip. It will help make them faster.

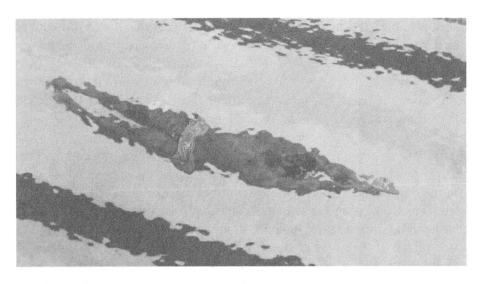

Junya holds a very tight *hyperstreamline* with his tight fast dolphin kicks. No air is leaving his lungs until breakout.

Luca holds a *hyperstreamline* position on the start, holding the air in his lungs. We'd like to see his fingers squeezed tighter together. Otherwise, he holds a perfect *hyperstreamline*.

Explosive Breakout

Besides keeping the air in the lungs, the techniques for an explosive backstroke breakout are virtually the same as for the freestyle breakout:

1. Initiate the first pull (from the streamline position) with the final dolphin up kick, not during the backstroke kick after the dolphin kick transition.
2. Transition from a strong dolphin kick into a strong backstroke kick. Don't back off the intensity of the backstroke kick.
3. Hold on to the *hyperstreamline* position as long as possible and initiate the first pull from that position. Don't break the streamline early.
4. Make the biomechanics of the first pull with the same motion as you do on the others, bending the elbow immediately and pushing the water forcefully backward in close to a straight line.
5. Push the lead arm forward hard. Keep it straight. Don't relax it or allow it to bend.
6. Keep the head in alignment with your upper body. You don't want the head to come way out of the water during the breakout. Break out forward, not upward.
7. Make the first breath a quick exhale and inhale, just like you would use on all of the other strokes. Explode forward into a fast stroke rate appropriate for the event.

Luca initiates his first pull on the breakout during the final dolphin up kick. The leading right arm is straight with fingers pointed and squeezed. His left arm pulls just like all of the other pulls, by bending the elbow initially and pushing the water straight backwards. He begins the first pull on the final dolphin up kick.

The majority of backstrokers break out on their backs, without changing their body positions. However, there are two other breakout techniques we are aware of that are worth mentioning. One is called the *rotation breakout* and the other is referred to as the *Tennessee breakout*, as it was invented by the University of Tennessee Head Coach, Matt Kredich.

With the *rotation breakout*, the swimmer will rotate the body to the same side as the initial pulling arm, while remaining in the *hyperstreamline* position, about half way to being on the swimmer's side (45 degrees). When the initial breakout pull is taken, the swimmer then rotates the body back toward the other side. The theory is that the rotation on the breakout pull will increase the propulsion from that pull.

With the *Tennessee breakout*, the swimmer rotates the body to the opposite side of the pulling arm, while remaining in the *hyperstreamline* position. The initial pull is taken with the top arm, but now, by being on the swimmer's side, the first pull is more of a freestyle type of pull than a backstroke pull. In theory, the freestyle pull should be stronger than the backstroke pull.

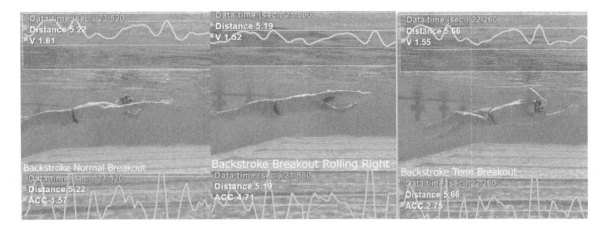

Elite backstroke swimmer Josh Zuchowski demonstrates three different backstroke breakout techniques.

Using VM technology, we compared the average speed on the breakout stroke of two elite backstroke swimmers, Josh Zuchowski and Amy Bilquist, using all three techniques. While each of them was faster using their conventional breakout on their back, they each admitted that they were uncomfortable using the other two techniques. It was the first time they had ever tried using them. Whichever breakout technique you use, practice using it often.

In summary, the fundamentals of the backstroke start are common to all swimmers. Some will excel in certain aspects of the start and vary the technique some, while others may do it slightly differently. Junya and Luca are two good examples of that. By far, the dolphin kicking speed is the greatest variable and most important factor in the backstroke start. Practice lots of backstroke starts, concentrating on one of the six major objectives at a time. Always continue working on your dolphin kicking speed to help you develop a great backstroke start.

Helpful Drills for Backstroke Starts

Ladder starts – Have the swimmer begin with the feet on the lowest rung on the ladder and the hands on the ladder handles above the pool deck. Perform a few starts in this position. Once the swimmer is comfortable with those, move the swimmer's feet up one rung at a time and repeat the process. Soon, the swimmer will be at the top rung, just below the surface of the water. The swimmer's feet should remain there until he or she is comfortable with the position before moving to the starting block.

Leg kick flops – To help develop a stronger leg kick before entry. Have the swimmer place his feet in the correct starting position. During the launch, the swimmer kicks the legs high into the air so that the bum enters the water first, rather than the hands.

Beach ball leg kicks – Hold a beach ball out over the water a couple of feet away from the wall and above the swimmer's head. After the launch, time the drop of the beach ball so that the swimmer can kick it up into the air just before the feet enter the water. It takes a little practice to get the timing right, but this is a great way to bring more awareness to the swimmer's leg kick.

Chapter 25

Turns and Transitions

The Freestyle and Backstroke Flip Turns

There are two ways of considering turns in swimming. They can be a nuisance, where the swimmer has to go to the trouble of turning around and start swimming in the opposite direction. In such cases, the turns often become a bit of a rest station, a chance to take a breather. Those types of turns are always slow.

Or a swimmer can consider the turn as a work station, an opportunity to gain on his competitors. If so, every part of the turn must be finessed in practice. Like all other strokes and aspects of swimming, there are many details involved in a great turn. They all need to be practiced and performed well.

Don't think that by doing *lazy* turns in practice, a swimmer will be able to do great turns in competition. That doesn't work. The swimmer might do the first few turns well, but after that, not so well. To do all the turns well, swimmers needs to be in *turn shape*. Turns require a different strength, different motions and a different kind of fitness than swimming. Without working turns in practice, swimmers will never attain the ability or skill to do great turns in competition.

On his final turn of his 200-meter freestyle races, or when coming off the last wall of his 400 IM, Michael Phelps would demoralize his competitors by doing an all-out, seven-dolphin-kick sprint to breakout, taking his first kick immediately off the wall. With that strategy and his kicking speed, he would gain a body length on his competitors. That amazing last turn didn't just happen coincidentally. That final turn required tremendous aerobic fitness. Michael practiced that technique directed by his coach, Bob Bowman, over and over again.

There are four important segments to the freestyle flip turn: **the approach, the flip, the underwater and the breakout**. Often, mistakes are being made by many swimmers during all four segments. It is incredible to me how much time can be gained or lost during the freestyle flip turn, yet most swimmers do not spend a lot of time working on their freestyle flip turn technique. Here are the most common mistakes we see in each segment of the turn:

The Approach

1. Slowing of the stroke rate (and swimmer's speed)
2. Gliding into the wall (not continuing the strokes long enough)
3. Overlooking the wall (lifting the head too much before the flip or rearing back)
4. Not looking at the wall (attempting to judge the wall from the T on the bottom)
5. Not increasing the kicking speed and intensity
6. Not lengthening the final stroke (and neck) into the wall
7. Over-swimming the wall (jamming the turn)

The Flip

1. Not initiating the flip with hip flexion (tucking the knees in too early)
2. Not tucking the knees tight enough or flexing the hip enough toward the chest (too long of a turning radius)
3. Rotating the body and legs on the way in toward the wall (feet not planted vertically)
4. Not pulling the arms straight back over head (bending the elbows during the flip)
5. Getting *stuck* on the wall (hesitating before the push off the wall)
6. Planting the feet too high or too low on the wall

The Underwater

1. Not initiating the dolphin kick soon enough (gliding off the wall)
2. Flipping over on to the stomach too quickly
3. Not holding a tight *hyperstreamline* position
4. Poor dolphin kicking technique (over undulation, too rigid, or not working hard in both directions)
5. Incorrect numbers of dolphin kicks (too many or too few)
6. Too deep or too shallow a trajectory off the wall

The Breakout

1. Initiating the first pull too late (after the final down dolphin kick, or during the freestyle kick)
2. Breaking the streamline position too early (separating the arms and hands)
3. Lifting the head, or lifting the chin off the chest
4. Initiating the first pull incorrectly (usually with an out sweeping motion)
5. Relaxing the lead arm during the first pull (bending the lead elbow)
6. Initiating the first pull too early (too deep) or too late (on the surface)
7. Taking a breath on the first stroke on the breakout (in sprints)

Correcting the Mistakes

With our Race Club swimmers, we typically start working on the second half of the freestyle flip turn first—the underwater and breakout. Then we proceed to the first half of the turn—the approach and the flip. Finally, we put the two halves together to complete the fast freestyle turn.

First, we will describe how we correct the mistakes on the second half of the freestyle turn. Coming off the wall on the freestyle flip turn, during the **underwater** segment, there are two widely held misconceptions about the dolphin kicks. The first is that the swimmer should glide off the wall for some period before initiating the first dolphin kick. The thought here is that with the speed of the swimmer leaving the wall at between 2-3 m/sec, initiating the dolphin kick too soon will slow the swimmer more than the glide will. It turns out, that is not the case with the four elite swimmers we tested.

Using Velocity Meter (VM) technology, we found that with all four swimmers, the fastest time to 5 meters off the wall is when the dolphin kick is initiated immediately off the wall. When the dolphin kick was delayed with a short glide, the time to 5 meters was slower by about .1 second. With a long glide, the time to 5 meters was slower by about .2 second. In the images below, one can see that the trough (slowest) velocity off the wall gets lower as the swimmer initiates the first dolphin kick later. One can also see that the amount of knee bend becomes greater on the first dolphin kick when it is delayed longer. We found similar results with doing dolphin kicks on the back, as well. As a result, the fastest technique to 5 meters is by initiation of the dolphin kick (using the weak side motion) immediately off the wall.

Elite freestyler Aaron Greenberg takes an immediate kick off the wall, using minimal knee bend. At this moment, he reaches his trough (slowest) velocity (graph above at vertical line using VM technology).

Aaron takes a short glide off the wall before initiating his first dolphin kick. He bends his knees more on this kick than he does on his immediate kick off the wall, and his trough (slowest) velocity (graph above at vertical line) is lower.

With a longer glide off the wall, Aaron bends his knees even farther on the first dolphin kick and the trough (slowest) velocity (graph above at vertical line) drops even lower.

Dolphin Technique	Time to 5 meters (seconds)	Average speed to 5 meters (m/sec)	Trough (slowest) Velocity (m/sec)
Immediate kick off wall	2.70	1.85	1.25
Short glide off wall	2.80	1.79	.95
Long glide off wall	2.88	1.74	.33

Velocity Meter data from Aaron Greenberg doing dolphin kicks off the wall on stomach.

Dolphin Technique	Time to 5 meters (seconds)	Average speed to 5 meters (m/sec)	Trough (slowest) Velocity (m/sec)
Immediate kick off wall	2.72	1.84	1.61
Short glide off wall	2.80	1.80	1.09
Long glide off wall	3.04	1.65	0.77

Velocity Meter data from elite butterflier Marcus Schlesinger doing dolphin kicks off the wall on stomach.

Dolphin Technique	Time to 5 meters (seconds)	Average speed to 5 meters (m/sec)	Trough (slowest) Velocity (m/sec)
Immediate kick off wall	2.68	1.87	1.72
Short glide off wall	2.78	1.80	1.45
Long glide off wall	2.84	1.76	.47

Velocity Meter data from elite swimmer Amy Bilquist doing dolphin kicks off the wall on her back.

Dolphin Technique	Time to 5 meters (seconds)	Average speed to 5 meters (m/sec)	Trough (slowest) Velocity (m/sec)
Immediate kick off wall	2.66	1.88	1.31
Short glide off wall	2.78	1.80	.81

Velocity Meter data from elite swimmer Josh Zuchowski doing dolphin kicks off the wall on stomach.

Dolphin Technique	Time to 5 meters (seconds)	Average speed to 5 meters (m/sec)	Trough (slowest) Velocity (m/sec)
Immediate kicks off wall	2.72	1.85	2.43
Short glide off wall	2.92	1.72	1.50

Velocity Meter data from Josh Zuchowski doing dolphin kicks off the wall on back.

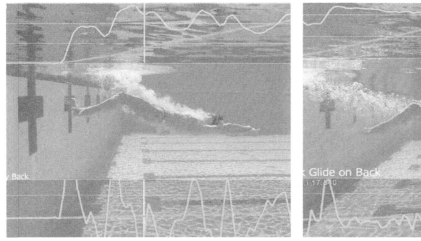

With the immediate kick off the wall on his back, Josh Zuchowski bends his knees before the first up kick considerably less (left photo) than with the short glide (right photo).

The second misconception about dolphin kicking off the wall on a freestyle turn is that the swimmers should stay underwater longer and take more kicks than they usually do. More kicks are not always better. The appropriate number of dolphin kicks for a swimmer to take on a freestyle flip turn depends on the dolphin kick speed under water compared to the freestyle speed on the surface, the aerobic capacity of the swimmer, and the event being swum. Each swimmer should be tested to determine the ideal numbers of dolphin kicks for freestyle, backstroke and butterfly events. They are all different.

For freestyle turns, we test the speed of the swimmer's dolphin kick for 25 yards underwater on his stomach and compare that time to the swimmer's freestyle speed for 25 yards, with no dolphin kicks off the wall. If the dolphin kicking speed is more than 2 seconds slower than the swimming speed, we recommend that the swimmer take the minimum of two dolphin kicks under water to breakout. If the time is between 1-2 seconds in difference, we recommend that the swimmer take 3-4 kicks to breakout. If the difference is less than a second, then the swimmer should stay under water as long as possible for the event, given their aerobic capacity, up to the full 15 meters allowed.

The advantage of dolphin kicking over swimming freestyle is that it requires much less energy to kick than it does to swim. The disadvantage of kicking under water is that there is no oxygen available down there. That is why it is important to know the relative speed of the dolphin kick compared to the swimming speed and the aerobic capacity of the swimmer.

In freestyle events, for those swimmers with sufficient dolphin kick speed and the aerobic capacity to stay under water for the full allowable 15 meters, a good argument can be made for them to remain on their back or side for as long as the rules allow. In VM testing, we have found that the average speed of the swimmer doing dolphin kicking under water is slightly greater on the side than on the stomach, and slightly greater on the back than on the side. However, we believe the transition from either back to stomach or side to stomach for the breakout should not be too done too quickly.

For the **breakout** on the freestyle turn, we covered the seven important techniques in Chapter 22 on freestyle starts. We will not repeat them here. The techniques for breakout used on the freestyle turn should be the same as for the start, with one exception. For events of 200 meters or longer, a breath should be taken on the first stroke. In the longer events that depend on using the aerobic system, it is important to keep the flow of oxygen coming and rid the body of carbon dioxide. In the events of 400 meters or longer, it is not uncommon for elite swimmers to take consecutive breaths (two or more breaths in a row to opposite sides) going into the turn, or coming out of the turn, or both.

To help correct the common mistakes listed above on the underwater segment and the breakout, we do a drill at The Race Club that we love. We turn this drill into a little contest. It can be done with or without fins, but we usually start with fins on.

The swimmer holds one hand on the wall with both feet (fins) planted on the wall, ready to push off on his side. It is important for the swimmer to push off on the same side as when he or she pushes off the wall on a freestyle flip turn. On the coach's whistle, the swimmer pushes hard off the wall underwater and on his side, taking three fast dolphin kicks. The first kick should be taken immediately as the feet leave the wall. On the third down kick, the swimmer transitions into the breakout, initiated by using three fast freestyle strokes without taking a breath. After the third stroke, the swimmer completes the drill by doing a fast flip turn in the middle of the pool, tucking the knees in tight to the chest. The drill ends when the feet hit the water on the flip.

After a few tries at this drill, where we correct any major mistakes in technique, we start the contest. The contest is who can get the fastest time from the feet leaving the wall until the feet hit the water after the flip. Three underwater dolphin kicks and three freestyle strokes must be taken before the flip is taken. We disqualify the swimmers if they make any of the mistakes we listed above, or if they take more or less than 3 kicks and 3 strokes. The world record time at The Race Club is 2.9 seconds to get all of that done legally. For all swimmers, getting under 3.5 seconds is considered good.

This drill quickly teaches the swimmers several excellent techniques for the freestyle turn. Get the dolphin kicks started quickly off the wall. Keep the dolphin kick motion tight and fast. Use a great streamline. Do not delay in the breakout transition. Explode into three fast freestyle strokes.

Tuck the knees in tight to the chest on the flip. If all of those things do not happen, they will not complete the drill in less than 3.5 seconds. Once they understand the second half of the freestyle flip turn, we go to the first half.

We begin teaching the first half of the flip turn by starting with the correct **flip** technique. One of the most important techniques on the flip we learned from watching world record holder and Olympic champion, Cesar Cielo. It has to do with his arm motion during the flip. Most swimmers will bend their arms and press down with their hands, as they bring their legs over the top of the water toward the wall. By the time the feet hit the wall, the arms are bent overhead. At this point, they can delay while they straighten their arms before they push off the wall (getting *stuck* on the wall). Or they can push off the wall and straighten their arms as they leave. With either choice, they will lose time from a delay or increasing the frontal drag while leaving the wall. Even the elite swimmers often make this mistake. A small bend in the elbows during the flip is acceptable, so long as the arms are straightened by the time the feet reach the wall.

Cielo would not bend his arms backwards during the flip, but preferred to press downward with his hands using straight arms, while his legs were carried over the water. With this technique, when his feet arrived on the wall, his arms were already in or near the streamline position. He would waste no time leaving the wall and would accelerate quickly off of it in the streamline position.

We teach Cielo's arm technique by using a snorkel, kicking into the wall with the hands at the swimmer's sides. They then do the flip turn into the wall, while leaving the arms in the water overhead, keeping them straight. By the time their feet reach the wall, the hands and arms are already in a *hyperstreamline* position.

Masters swimmer Kristina Cook practices the proper arm motion for the flip by kicking into the wall holding her arms at her sides. She will keep the arms in that same position as she makes the turn. They end up being straight over head, not bent.

When Masters swimmer Hank Wise's fins hit the wall, his arms are already in *hyperstreamline* position, ready to go.

Another law of physics comes into play on the flip into the wall. That is the Law of Conservation of Energy. According to that law, the energy in a rotating system, like a swimmer doing a flip turn, remains constant. The energy of a rotating system is determined by its mass, the angular velocity and the radius of the circle of rotation. If we were to change one of those three variables, one or both of the other two would have to change for the energy to remain constant. We can't change the mass of the swimmer during a flip turn, but if we shorten the radius of the turning swimmer (circle of rotation), that would mean that the angular velocity would have to go up. And it does.

A great example of the Law of Conservation of Energy is the figure skater that starts to twirl around on the ice at the end of his routine. The skater pushes with one foot on the ice to start the twirl. With the arms extended fully outward to the sides of the skater, the skater twirls around relatively slowly. When the skater draws the arms into the body tightly, the twirling speed goes up so high, one cannot even see the skater's face any longer. By shortening his radius, he increased his angular velocity. Since the relationship is exponential (to the square of the radius), the angular velocity of the skater goes up tremendously.

That same law applies to our swimmer's flip turns. When the swimmer tucks the knees in tighter to his chest, the feet will get to the wall more quickly. It requires more work for the swimmer to tuck in tighter, but every tenth of a second counts.

The initiation of the flip begins with a flexion of the hips. As the head drops down during the hip flexion, the hips continue moving forward. At some point in this motion, the knees start to flex and continue flexing as the legs come over the top until they are as tight as they can be, as the hips continue to flex. If the knees are not flexed all the way to a tight position, the angular velocity of the legs coming over the top will be slower. Getting the knees tucked in tight is the biggest challenge.

A good drill to use to teach swimmers to tuck their legs tight on the flip turn is the underwater turn. Have the swimmers dive down under water just outside the T as they approach the wall.

Then have them make the flip turn with their legs completely submerged. The drag in the water is so severe, they will learn to tuck their legs tightly to get them around to the wall.

This swimmer is doing an underwater flip turn, learning how to tuck the knees tightly on the flip turn.

Another common mistake seen on the freestyle flip turn is rotating the body on the way in to the wall, so that the feet get planted on the wall at an angle to one side or the other. The fastest way to get the feet on the wall is by going straight over the top. The feet should be planted on the wall with the toes pointed straight upwards. Often, one foot is slightly higher on the wall than the other, with the lower foot being on the side toward the direction of rotation. But they should not be angled. All of the rotation of the swimmer's body should happen as the swimmer is leaving the wall or kicking away from the wall. Rotating the body while maintaining a tight *hyperstreamline* will not slow the swimmer down during the underwater or push off the wall.

Masters swimmer Joe Miller over rotates his body on the flip and ends up with the feet angled to the left.

Olympic gold medalist Jimmy Feigen plants his feet on the wall pointing straight up with his arms straight over head.

The only exception to the rule of not rotating on the way in to the freestyle flip occurs with the individual medley (IM). The rules of the IM state that swimmers must push off of the wall on their stomachs in the freestyle flip turns of the IM. For that to happen, swimmers need to partially rotate on the way in to plant their feet on the wall at an angle. From there, they can continue their rotation as they extend off of the wall to be more on their stomachs as they leave the wall.

As the swimmers **approach** the wall in freestyle for the turn, we try to accomplish several things. We want them to hold their stroke rate constant, not slow it down. We also want them to accelerate toward the wall and do so by increasing their kicking speed. We'd like them to swim to the wall, not glide to the wall, carrying their momentum (Mass x Velocity) all the way through the turn. On the final stroke, we like to see the pulling hand near the shoulder when the head drops down, not well past the shoulder. We also want the final stroke to be a longer one, not a shortened one. By kicking harder and accelerating toward the wall, lengthening their last stroke, glancing up only far enough to look at the bottom of the cross on the wall, then tucking the head down quickly into the flip, swimmers can develop an excellent technique of approaching the wall for the flip turn.

Another common problem on the approach to the wall for the freestyle flip turn is overlooking the wall. That means that the swimmers lift their heads and look forward way more than is necessary to make the turn, causing a serious deceleration.

We practice the freestyle approach techniques for the turn by having the swimmers start toward the wall from about 8 meters out, keeping their heads down in the correct position. One they reach the T on the bottom of the pool, signaling that the wall is near, they are allowed to glance up and look no higher on the wall than the bottom of the cross at the end. We call that the *low-look* turn. Swimmers need to see the wall to get a correct reference point for the turn. If they try to make the turn by estimating the wall's location from the T on the bottom, they will often misjudge the distance to the wall. The feet will end up too high or low on the wall, or worse, they will miss the wall altogether. That mistake would cost them much more than lifting the head forward. Swimmers do not need to look straight forward at the wall. They just need a glimpse of it and can achieve that with a partial head lift.

Swimmer Owen Matteson takes a low look at the cross before initiating his flip turn.

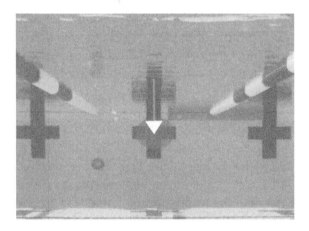

It is not necessary to look at the center of the cross or higher during the turn. The bottom of the black cross is as high as a swimmer should look in order not to over lift the head during the turn.

This is as high as Zane Grothe will lift his head going into his freestyle flip turn. He looks low on the wall for reference.

Swimmers should also avoid doing a double-arm pull on the approach to the wall. With that technique, they hold the lead arm out in front, waiting for the other arm to catch up. When both arms reach the front, they take a double arm pull to make the turn. By holding the lead arm in front and not continuing to pull, they lose valuable momentum going into the turn, gliding into the wall.

Age group swimmer Stone Miller does a double arm pull as he approaches the wall for his freestyle flip turn.

Once we correct most of the mistakes made during the first half of the turn, the approach and the flip, we put the two halves together and practice the entire turn. In our camps we love to create a little competition among the swimmers by pitting 2 or 3 swimmers of equal ability against each other. We start them 8 meters out and finish the race 8 meters out. The first swimmer back wins. Of course, we watch them carefully and if any swimmer makes a technical error, they are disqualified. With this competition, they not only learn to do the turns fast, they learn to do them correctly.

In summary, fast turns require much more work than slow turns. If a swimmer wants to win races, however, he or she needs to develop fast turns. Like everything else in swimming, doing great turns requires dedication to performing them well in practice—finessing the turns all of the time. We don't even like to see lazy turns done in warm up.

A swimmer needs to focus on the mistakes that he or she is making, correcting them one at a time, and work the turns all of the time in practice. Soon, the flip turns will be lightning fast.

Backstroke Turns

The mechanics of the backstroke flip turn are very similar to the freestyle flip turn. As swimmers approach the wall on their backs, they are allowed to roll over onto their stomachs for one freestyle stroke before making the turn. Therefore, swimmers must use the backstroke flags to judge the ideal time to make that rotation on to the stomach. The ideal time to make the rotation depends on the swimmer's speed, height and stroke rate. They should also be prepared and trained to turn to either direction, left or right, to avoid slowing the stroke rate, rotating too soon, or jamming the wall. Ideally, the stroke rate and speed should remain constant once a swimmer is inside the flags, and there should be very little glide into the wall before the turn.

The rotation of the swimmer onto the stomach should begin when the final backstroke pulling arm is in the early front-quadrant propulsion phase of the underwater pull. The swimmer should reach his or her stomach after the rotation simultaneously with the recovering arm striking the water. The backstroke pulling arm should now be in the back-quadrant propulsion phase.

As the swimmer rotates onto the stomach, the underwater pulling arm from the final backstroke pull should remain at the swimmer's side. The recovering arm then goes into an immediate freestyle pull after entering the water. Once the freestyle pulling arm completes its underwater, both arms will be at the swimmer's side when the flip is initiated. The timing of this motion differs from the freestyle flip turn, where we like to see the pulling hand closer to the shoulder when the flip is initiated. The motion of the swimmer to this point should be continuous with a steady kick. As in the freestyle flip, the swimmer should a avoid a double-arm pull into the wall.

It is very common to see swimmers rotate too soon and glide much too long into the wall. It is also common to see swimmers *over-look* the wall by lifting the head forward too far, increasing frontal drag. As with the freestyle flip turn, swimmers should look no higher than the bottom of the cross on the wall, using the *low-look* turn. The same principles of the flip turn should be used as in freestyle, knees tucked in tightly and arms held in a straightened position overhead (no bend in the elbows).

Since the swimmer remains on his or her back on the push off the wall, the feet should be planted evenly at the same height on the wall. With the arms straight over head in the *hyperstreamline,* the push off the wall should happen immediately after the swimmer plants the feet.

Since most swimmers will stay underwater longer than in freestyle, the trajectory off the wall should be angled downward slightly. Once the toes leave the wall, the swimmer should immediately begin a down kick. Gliding for any length of time will slow the swimmer's speed to 5 meters from the wall. The longer the glide, the slower the speed to 5 meters. The subsequent up kick should be a tight, fast kick, not a big, knee-bendy kick.

Dolphin kick on the swimmer's back is faster than kicking on the stomach, and backstroke is slower than freestyle. For those two reasons, we usually see at least one or two more dolphin kicks taken off the wall during the underwater phase compared to the freestyle turn. However, typically, swimmers take one or two less kicks on the backstroke turn than they do on the start. With the large vortex to push down against with the soles of the feet, backstrokers should really emphasize the force placed on the down kick with both the dolphin and the backstroke kicks.

The ideal and exact number of kicks depends on the swimmer's underwater dolphin kick speed on the back compared to the swimmer's backstroke speed. These times should be tested and compared for 25 meters. As with the backstroke start, the air should be kept in the swimmer's lungs until the breakout for the same reasons we discussed in Chapter 24. This can be achieved by using the swimmer's upper lip or by using a nose clip. The breakout on the turns should be done exactly as was described in Chapter 24.

Backstroke Finish

The fastest way to finish the backstroke race is by submarining into the wall, with the upper body completely submerged. This requires that at the right time, on the final backstroke taken, the swimmer extends or arches the lumbar spine more than usual and dives backward underwater. Since some part of the body must always be above the water in backstroke, the swimmer should simultaneously kick one foot upward to break the surface, as he or she dives downward underwater with the head and extended arm.

Elite backstroker Amy Bilquist submarines hard into the wall at the finish. As her head and shoulders submerge, she pushes her waist above water, followed by a strong up kick that breaks the surface.

The swimmer should NEVER try to look backward with the neck extended toward the wall. The finish is blind, so the head should remain in alignment with the upper body to cause the least amount of frontal drag. Once the head submerges into that position, the swimmer needs to kick really hard into the wall. Since the finish is blind, the swimmer needs to dorsiflex the wrist slightly so that the pads of the fingers will touch the wall first. With the wrist straight, a swimmer can injure the hand or fingers by jamming it directly into the wall.

Whenever two or more swimmers are finishing in a close race, it seems as if the swimmer that finishes HARD into the wall always wins, no matter how it looks from the deck. The most famous example of this is when Michael Phelps (USA) defeated Milorad Cavic (Serbia) in the 100-meter butterfly finals at the Olympic Games in 2008.

It is important for each swimmer to know exactly how many strokes after passing the backstroke flags to initiate the turn and the finish. That can be determined with enough practice at race speed. Gliding too long or jamming the turn or finish can lead to a close race lost.

Finish your backstroke races by submarining into the wall hard, touching with the pads of your fingers. Kick one of your feet up into the air and keep kicking fast all the way to the finish.

Chapter 26

Open Turns

The Spin Turn for Butterfly and Breaststroke

The Law of Conservation of Energy, another law in physics, comes into play on the open turns, as it does on flip turns. The concept is simple. Swimmers have only so much energy they can put into an open turn. Obviously, the degree of effort by the swimmers making the turn has a lot to do with the kinetic energy generated by the swimmers during the turn.

If swimmers are racing, and we assume that they try to get around on an open turn as fast as they possibly can, then, if we can shorten their turning radius, they will spin around on the turn faster. That is what this law of physics demands. It is the rationale for doing the *spin technique* for open turns.

In the past, many swimmers were taught to do open turns by touching the wall with both hands, then rotating the body by turning one shoulder toward the wall and the other shoulder back away from the wall. From that point, the swimmer was told to *elbow your brother and phone your mother*, by dropping one elbow under water, passing by the swimmer's side (elbowing the brother) and bringing the other arm bent over the top of the head, near the ear (phoning the mother). With that technique, the swimmer would turn more vertically in the water, with the head elevating well above the water.

With the vertical open turn technique, the upper body remains more erect in the water. The diameter of the turning swimmer is from the lowest point to the highest point, which is usually from the swimmer's feet to the top of the swimmer's head. The more elevated the head and the lower the feet, the longer the turning radius.

With the *spin* technique, the swimmer lowers the head and upper body above the water and elevates the feet under water during the turn by spinning more horizontally than vertically. In doing so, the swimmer's diameter gets compressed from both ends. The shorter the radius (diameter), the faster the angular velocity of the swimmer. Since the relationship between the two is based on the square of each (exponential), a small decrease in the diameter of the swimmer during the turn will lead to a significant increase in angular velocity, or shortening of the turn time.

The *spin turn* technique can be used with open turns for butterfly and breaststroke. For some reason, the elite butterfliers have adopted this technique faster than the elite breaststrokers, where we still see some swimmers using the older, more vertical open turn technique. We prefer that swimmers use the *spin turn* for both breaststroke and butterfly open turns.

With the vertical open turn, the head and shoulders elevate high above the water level.

Using a spin turn, Olympian Kelsi Dahlia keeps her left ear on the water and head close to the surface.

Using a vertical open turn, Masters swimmer Joe Miller tucks his knees and feet in tight. The feet are considerably lower in the water than his bum.

Using the spin turn, Kelsi's feet are just slightly lower in the water than her bum. Her head is considerably lower above the water than with the vertical turn.

At The Race Club, we find we can teach the fundamentals of the *spin turn* fairly easily to most swimmers. It is a concept that swimmers seem to grasp quickly.

We often start with a drill with the swimmers away from the wall. The swimmers lay out on their stomachs with the arms held in front of them. They drop their heads down into the water. On the coach's command, the swimmers tuck their knees up forward toward their chests and turn horizontally in the water as quickly as possible, taking a breath on the turn. We ask the swimmers to keep their ears on the surface of water on the side toward which they are turning. For that to happen, the head needs to turn back for the breath, as the swimmers rotate around.

Swimmers practicing the spin drill without using the wall. They spin around with one ear on the water, turning the head back for the breath.

After a few tries with this drill, the swimmers are ready to practice the *spin turn* on the wall, with either butterfly or breaststroke. When teaching swimmers to do the *spin turn* correctly, in addition to keeping the ear on the turning side on the water, we also find these key points helpful:

1. Release the non-dominant hand from the wall immediately, tucking the elbow under the water close to the swimmer's side on its path backwards. Refrain from bringing the non-dominant arm over the top of the water or from swinging it under water out too far to the side. Young swimmers tend to hold on to the wall with both hands.
2. Tuck the knees in and the lower legs in (flexion) as tight as possible, with the feet overlapping one another, during the spin around. That shortens the turning radius and reduces frontal drag of the legs under water.
3. Keep the shoulders square as the swimmer spins around, rather than rotating the shoulder backward on the turning side.
4. As the swimmers spin around, they should look backwards toward the wall or the gutter to get the breath, not to their side. One ear should remain on or in the water. The mouth should be elevated some to make sure that air is reached.
5. Plant the feet sideways on the wall, pointing toward the turning side, before pushing off the wall. Avoid trying to push off the wall on the stomach. The swimmer can get to his stomach quickly while pushing off the wall.
6. Release the dominant arm from the wall into a bent-elbow position, not a straight arm, moving over the top of water. There is no rationale for keeping the arm straight as it comes back around, which requires more work. By bending the elbow, the swimmer can get the arms back together into *hyperstreamline* faster.

Point 1. Kelsi releases her left hand immediately from the wall, tucking the left elbow underwater into her side on its way back in front.

Point 1. Kelsi tucks her left elbow under water, close to her side on its way back in front.

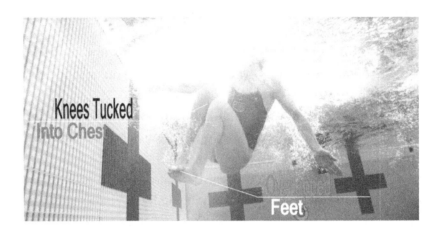

Point 2. Kelsi makes the tightest possible tuck with her legs, overlapping her feet to reduce drag on their way forward.

Point 3. With the vertical turn, one shoulder rotates backward and the other forward toward the wall. With the spin turn, the shoulders remain squared and lower.

Point 4. As she spins around on the turn, Kelsi looks back toward the wall and lifts her mouth for the breath.

Point 5. The feet should be planted sideways on the wall, not down. By the time his feet leave the wall, Masters swimmer Joe Miller will be rotated back more onto his stomach.

Point 6. When the lead arm recovers over the top of the water, the turning radius increases with the elbow now becoming the highest point. Tuck the lead arm under water and into the side of the swimmer.

In summary, with a little bit of practice, most of our Race Club swimmers do a really good *spin turn*. This is not a turn or technique that takes years of practice to do well. By paying attention to the key teaching points outlined above, nearly every swimmer can master the *spin turn* quickly.

Using the *spin turn* in butterfly and breaststroke races will help shave off valuable time and improve performances.

Chapter 27

Turns and Transitions

Learning the Crossover Transition for the Individual Medley

As far as we know, there are only four techniques used in the sport of swimming to make the transition between backstroke and breaststroke in the individual medley (IM): the **open turn,** the **reverse flip or somersault,** the **bucket turn** and the **crossover transition.** Of the four, the bucket turn is rarely used or seen today, as was taught decades ago.

There are three important considerations in selecting the best transition. The first is the time it takes to make the transition. The second is the amount of work required in doing the transition. The third relates to the aerobic system and considers the length of time the transition requires in between consecutive breaths. From those three standpoints, let's evaluate each technique.

The **open turn** is likely the slowest of the four transitions. It also does not take advantage of the law of inertia. By that, we mean that while doing backstroke, the swimmer's body and arm are travelling in one direction backward and downward. Then, when the hand hits the wall, the body essentially comes to a stop and has to reverse its direction, upwards and forward. That is not a mechanically efficient way to make a transition, so it takes more work and time to accomplish.

One advantage of the open turn is that it enables the swimmer to take the breath before the breaststroke pullout late, minimizing the time between that breath and the first one coming out of the pullout. We see the open turns still used by some swimmers in the longer 400 meter individual medley races, because of this one advantage.

Elite swimmer Josh Zuchowski demonstrates an open turn for the individual medley backstroke/breaststroke transition.

With the **reverse flip or somersault,** the swimmer touches the wall and continues in the same path, allowing the head to go underwater with the feet and legs coming directly over the top into a backwards somersault. While this technique is less hindered by the law of inertia than the open turn, and can be accomplished fairly quickly with a tight tuck, it has some drawbacks. First, it tends to be disorienting going into a backward somersault. The swimmer may have trouble knowing exactly where he or she is and have a problem getting the right trajectory off the wall for the breaststroke pullout. Second, there is a risk of taking water into the sinuses through the nose, since the head is going upside down in the water. That is an unpleasant experience, to say the least. The swimmer either has to apply some positive pressure to the nostrils during the transition, using the upper lip, or wear a nose clip. Finally, the final breath needs to be taken early in the process, which results in a longer period of time before the next breath is taken.

The reverse somersault transition is still used by some, but not by many because of the drawbacks. We don't recommend using this technique to any of our Race Club swimmers. Comparing it to the crossover transition, it doesn't measure up.

Josh demonstrates the reverse flip or somersault, where his head goes straight backwards and legs come over the top.

The **bucket or table** turn is an antiquated transition that has its history dating back to the days when backstrokers were required to touch the wall on all turns. It is seldom, if ever, used today. Some of the swimmers of that day, like Olympian John Naber (1976), adopted a different way of turning in backstroke by remaining more horizontal, lifting their legs out of the water to make the turn. The thought was that while the legs weigh more out of the water, they could be moved more quickly through the air than through the water.

A similar turn was then adopted for the individual medley, whereby, after touching the wall with the hand, the swimmer's legs are lifted above the water and rotated around to the side to reach the wall with the feet planted sideways. The swimmer then rotates back to his stomach during the push off the wall into the breaststroke pullout. The bucket turn for the individual medley is really a modified open turn, recovering the legs above, rather than below the water. It does have the same advantage as the open turn of getting the final breath very late in the process.

Josh attempts to do the bucket turn, by lifting his legs up and over the water to one side, while the head moves to the opposite side. This technique is slower and cumbersome.

The fourth technique is the **crossover** transition. In our opinion, it has three distinct advantages over the other three techniques. First, it is the only transition where the swimmer can see the wall before reaching it. With the other three techniques, swimmers are blind to the wall. Using them, swimmers have to wait until they actually touch the wall with the hand before reacting. With the crossover transition, by seeing the wall before reaching it, the swimmer can anticipate when the hand will touch the wall much more accurately. The swimmer can then react more quickly.

A second advantage of the crossover transition is that the swimmer is on his or her side and can hyper-extend the shoulder of the lead arm forward, sub-luxating it from the joint, to reach farther and touch the wall sooner. Swimmers have more ability to extend their arms farther toward the wall and reach the wall from their sides than they do from their backs.

A third advantage of the crossover transition is that it is likely the most efficient technique. It takes the most advantage of the law of inertia. The swimmer begins rotating the body toward one side or the other, and continues the rotation in the same direction, even though the legs are drawn above the water on the opposite side of the rotation.

With these three advantages, the crossover transition is not only the most efficient technique, it is also the fastest one. If done well, a swimmer that uses the crossover transition can gain a considerable margin on the swimmer using any of the other transition techniques.

One disadvantage of using the crossover turn is that the final breath is taken sooner than with the other three techniques. That means swimmers that use this technique must be old enough or aerobically fit enough to hold their breath for that additional time, all the way through the breaststroke pullout. The crossover transition requires more aerobic capacity of the swimmer than the other techniques.

Another disadvantage of using the crossover transition is that there is a higher risk of being disqualified. The swimmer must remain on his side, but short of vertical, until the hand touches the wall. Some swimmers will get over-anxious and start to rotate their bodies before the hand reaches the wall, leading to a disqualification. Also, if the feet are planted too vertically on the wall, swimmers can be disqualified on the push off the wall for not being on their stomachs soon enough.

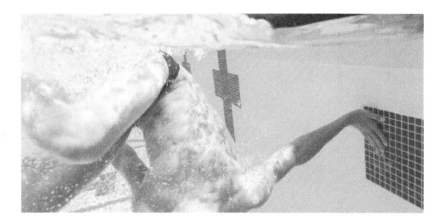

Rising star Samuel Quarles shows excellent technique in a crossover transition. He finesses the wall with his strong right hand and brings the legs over the water on his left side to the wall.

We are not certain which swimmer was the first to do a crossover transition in the individual medley in competition. Kristine Quance, one of the world's fastest individual medley swimmers of her day, was disqualified in the 1996 Olympic Trials in the 400-meter individual medley, using the crossover transition. It was a controversial call, but the technique was so new, not many of the officials had seen it used in competition before.

At The Race Club, we believe that the advantages of the crossover transition outweigh the risks and disadvantages, particularly with the shorter individual medley races—the 100 meter and 200 meter events. At the elite level, virtually every swimmer uses the crossover transition in those two events. In the 400-meter individual medley, we are seeing more swimmers use the crossover transition each year. There are still some that choose to do an open turn or transition in the longer IM, taking the oxygen as late as they can.

For any swimmer that comes to The Race Club that swims individual medley, we teach them how to do the crossover transition. It is a technique that is difficult to learn by watching elite swimmers use it. When the elite swimmers use the crossover transition, it happens so quickly that all one sees is a splash of water and it's over. To help swimmers learn this important technique, we have broken the crossover transition down into five relatively easy teaching steps. Here is how we do it:

Step 1

The swimmer swims backstroke away from the wall for 4-5 strokes, then rolls toward the side of the non-dominant hand, as if he were doing a backstroke flip turn in the middle of the pool. We want the swimmer to start by using the dominant arm on the wall. The turn is completed when the feet hit the water.

Sam swims backstroke toward the middle and makes a turn like a backstroke flip turn in the middle of the pool.

Step 2

The swimmer swims backstroke toward the wall from about 8 meters away. Once the swimmer passes the flags and approaches the wall, he or she begins to turn to the non-dominant side on to the stomach, similar to initiating a backstroke flip turn. Don't worry about touching the wall, yet. Instead of pushing off on the back, however, the swimmer should rotate the body during the flip to the non-dominant side and push off into a full and correct breaststroke pullout.

Sam approaches the wall in backstroke as if making a backstroke flip turn, then pushes off into a breaststroke pullout.

Step 3

Lying prone in the water, with his head toward the wall, the swimmer holds on to the wall with the dominant hand. The non-dominant hand is at the swimmer's side. To keep the legs floating, the swimmer can kick lightly. On the coach's command, the swimmer drops his head down into a flip turn, pushing off into a breaststroke pullout.

Sam begins with his right hand on the wall and his left hand at his side. He then drops down into a flip and pushes off into a full breaststroke pullout.

Step 4

The swimmer kicks backstroke toward the wall from about 5 meters away, with the dominant arm overhead and the non-dominant arm at his side. Once near the wall, the swimmer rolls onto his side, with the dominant arm on top. The biceps of the dominant arm should remain behind the swimmer's ear. Officials often look at the position of the biceps with the swimmer's ear for the legality of the turn. The swimmer then looks back and to the side under water to see the wall and continues kicking, holding his breath. Once the swimmer touches the wall with the dominant hand, he rotates over toward the stomach slightly and makes the transition into the breaststroke pullout.

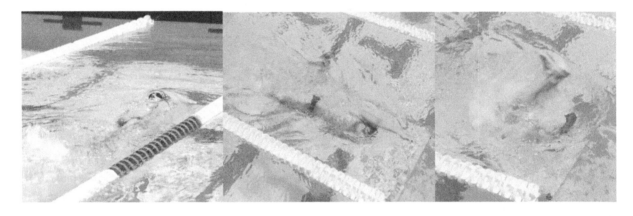

Above water shots of Sam kicking toward the wall, then rotating to his side, touching the wall and making the transition.

BICEP BEHIND EAR

Underwater view of Sam touching the wall after kicking in from his side. He keeps the biceps muscle of his right arm behind his ear. When he plants his feet on the wall they are pointing in the other direction for the push off the wall.

Step 5

The swimmer is now ready for the complete crossover transition. He swims backstroke into the wall from about 8 meters out. Once passed the flags, as he nears the wall, he rolls over onto the non-dominant side, holding the dominant hand above. He must keep the biceps of this arm behind the ear and avoid going onto the stomach. The swimmer must look underwater and see the wall before his hand reaches it. Once he touches the wall the swimmer must rotate toward the stomach slightly to make the transition. If the swimmer does not rotate some, it won't work out well.

The tucked legs come over the water in the transition on the opposite side that the swimmer is looking. The feet should end up pointing in the opposite direction of the side that the swimmer begins rotating. If the swimmer starts the transition by rotating to his left, the feet end up planted on the wall pointed to the right. In other words, the swimmer is facing in one direction on the way in and the other on the way out.

As the swimmer pushes off the wall on the transition, he must rotate toward the stomach so that by the time his feet leave the wall, he is mostly on his stomach, not his side.

On step 5, Sam does the entire backstroke to breaststroke crossover transition. He starts his last stroke far enough away to lengthen his arm and reach for the wall, kicking fiercely.

261

Sam completes the transition by bringing the legs over the other side, planting his feet pointing toward the farther lane line. After a strong push off the wall, he quickly rotates back to his stomach for the breaststroke pullout.

Here are the most common mistakes we find in teaching the crossover transition:

1. The swimmer turns to the dominant arm side and uses the non-dominant arm on the wall.
2. The swimmer fails to rotate to his side soon enough and jams the transition (the swimmer is better off being too long rather than too short with the crossover transition).
3. The swimmer starts to rotate too soon and glides too long into the wall.
4. The swimmer starts the rotation too soon after going onto his side, ending up on the stomach to make the turn.
5. The swimmer doesn't look at or see the wall to anticipate when it will be reached.
6. The swimmer touches the wall and fails to rotate some toward the stomach, trying to make the flip happen from his side.
7. The swimmer touches the wall but bends the lead arm, and the momentum brings him too close to the wall to make the transition.
8. The swimmer is long on the final stroke, but fails to kick hard into the wall to maintain his speed.
9. The swimmer rotates the body to the wrong side, ending up with the feet pointed in the same direction as the side of the initial rotation.
10. All of the common mistakes we find on breaststroke pullouts (Chapter 17), including pushing off too deep or too shallow.

Some coaches believe that the crossover transition should not be taught to young swimmers, as they have not yet developed the aerobic capacity to be able to complete the underwater pullout after the transition. While that may be true, there is another approach to this challenge.

In testing a few dozen athletes of all abilities, we have found that there is very little time difference to 8 meters from the wall, whether using the full breaststroke pullout or using a shortened version of the pullout with a strong dolphin kick before breakout. In fact, for most swimmers, it was faster to 8 meters using the single dolphin kick to breakout, omitting the pulldown and breaststroke kick, than by using the complete pullout.

That may not be true for all breaststrokers, but when a young swimmer does the crossover transition, what usually happens is that the full pullout becomes abbreviated, as the swimmer is anxious to take another breath. In some cases, the swimmer emerges from the breaststroke kick almost vertically to make that happen.

The point is that young swimmers may be better off learning to do the crossover transition for the individual medley, of which most of them are fully capable, which is measurably faster than the other three transition techniques. Then, if they shorten the pullout time by using a single dolphin kick to breakout, that will enable them to take the next breath sooner. The result may be a faster transition than by using an open turn or reverse somersault with a full pullout. Eventually, as their aerobic capacity develops, they can consider using a full breaststroke pullout with the crossover transition, if that technique is really faster.

At whatever age it is learned, the crossover transition takes a while to master. In fact, we do not recommend that any swimmer attempt the crossover transition in competition until he or she has practiced using it over 100 times. The crossover transition may require 500 to 1000 practices to become excellent at doing it. By that time, the swimmer can start to learn to become equally adept at it with either hand on the wall. Until then, a swimmer can learn to adjust the stroke rate as he or she approaches the wall to make the turn possible always with the dominant hand.

In summary, any swimmer can use the five easy steps above to learn the crossover transition, if he or she is planning on competing in the individual medley. Then, each swimmer should decide on using the full breaststroke pullout, or the abbreviated pullout with a single dolphin kick, depending on the age, aerobic capacity and which technique is fastest. With or without the full breaststroke pullout, the crossover transition is the way to go in the IM.

Chapter 28

The Five Disciplines of Swimming

For any swimmer, regardless of his or her age, who is interested in becoming the best swimmer that he or she can possibly become, there is much more to fast swimming than simply the quantity and quality of swimming workouts. **Swimming training** is one of the five essential disciplines that are required for a swimmer to reach his highest potential. The other four are **strength training, nutrition, recovery and mental training.**

The purpose of this book is not to focus on swimming conditioning, which, in our opinion, is valued at one half of the swimming training in the important equation to swim faster. The purpose is to focus on swimming technique, which is valued as the other half in the same equation. Although we are more than capable of writing about swimming conditioning, or developing the physiological capacity of the swimmer, that subject is well covered by others.

We would be remiss, however, if we did not mention again that there are five disciplines that are required to fully develop a swimmer's talent and reach his or her highest potential. While we may be experts in swimming training, we do not believe that swimmers need an expert in each of the five disciplines. An entire book could be written on each of these five disciplines and how they affect an athlete's performance, in any sport. However, swimmers do need a good solid program in each of these five disciplines. The following story describes how Gary Sr. first discovered the importance of including all five disciplines into a swimmer's training.

I first became aware of the profound impact that each of these five disciplines has on a swimmer's performance in the year 2000, while preparing 13 athletes for the Olympic Games of Sydney. That year, Mike Bottom, then Head Men's Sprint Coach at Cal Berkeley, hand-picked the 13 swimmers (12 men and 1 woman) to come to Phoenix, Arizona, to the Phoenix Swim Club and train for four months leading up to the USA Olympic Trials. Six of the athletes were from the United States, and the other seven were from other countries around the world.

That year, I was managing the programs and facilities at the Phoenix Swim Club, while practicing Ophthalmology. Mike decided that for the first time ever, we should provide expertise to our athletes in all five of the disciplines, not just swimming. Curiously, independently in California, Richard Quick, Head Women's Swimming Coach at Stanford University, was doing essentially the same thing with his group of women swimmers, which included Jenny Thompson and Dara Torres. In the past, other coaches had provided expertise to their swimmers in some of these five disciplines, but never, so far as we knew, in all five.

With the support of a Phoenix foundation, we brought in experts in strength training (Tim McClellan), nutrition (Dr. Doug Herthel), recovery (Joe Coe), and mental training (Dr. Rayma Ditson-Sommer). Each expert was extremely competent in his or her specific discipline. Two of them, Dr. Sommer and Dr. Herthel, were considered to be world-renowned in their specialty. Including the expenses for the swimming coaching, training facilities and accommodations, the cost per athlete for those four months to provide all of this expertise was about $25,000.

I had a vested interest in this experiment, as one of the swimmers that was selected to train was my son, Gary Jr. By June of 2000, after the USA Olympic Trials, it appeared that the experiment was working. Ten out of the thirteen swimmers qualified for their respective country's Olympic Team and would be competing in Sydney in about six weeks. All six Americans qualified for the Team. Only three swimmers failed to make their Olympic Team that year.

At the 2000 Summer Olympic Games in Sydney, the United States Olympic team earned 93 medals in all 31 Olympic sports it participated in. Of those 93 medals, 10 Olympic medals were won by our group of six swimmers and one pole vaulter. Nick Hysong, gold medalist in the pole vault, had trained at the Phoenix Swim Club (we set up a pole-vaulting pit on the property) and followed a similar program for the five disciplines.

11% of the total USA medals won in those Olympic Games came from our small group of six American athletes. That would not have happened were it not for bringing in expertise in all five disciplines. From that year forward, we have fully appreciated how important each of these five disciplines is in contributing to any athlete's success. Swimmers do not need to have a leading expert coach in all five disciplines, however, to benefit from them. They do need to have a well-designed program outlined for each discipline, if they are to swim up to their full potential.

At our Race Club camps, for four successive days, we use the first hour of each day to discuss one of the important five disciplines (we usually cover strength training and recovery on the same day). Since swimming conditioning is so variable, depending on age, ability, event and time availability, we provide just a sampling of a Race Club workout during the camp. The rest, besides the lectures on the important five disciplines, is focused on swimming technique.

Here is the current format for The Race Club technique camps:

Day 1

Morning (3 hrs)

- Welcome and introduction of staff and athletes
- Lecture on applying physics to swim faster
- Pool: Freestyle technique. Drills and fundamental techniques to reduce frontal drag
- Pool: Breathing techniques in freestyle with short lecture on physiology and energy systems

Afternoon (2 hrs)

- Dryland: Traditional stretches, core exercises and evaluation of swimming anatomy for all strokes
- Pool: Freestyle Technique: Drills and fundamental techniques to increase propulsion

Day 2

Morning (3 hrs)

- Lecture on nutrition and supplements
- Pool: Freestyle technique: Drills and fundamental techniques for sprint freestyle and freestyle flip turns
- Pool: Techniques to improve dolphin kicking

Afternoon (2 hrs)

- Dryland: Yoga session for swimmers
- Pool: Backstroke technique: Drills and fundamental techniques of backstroke

Day 3

Morning (3 hrs)

- Lecture on strength training and recovery
- Pool: Breaststroke technique: Drills and fundamental techniques of breaststroke
- Pool: Crossover transition for the IM or fundamentals of freestyle and backstroke starts

Afternoon (2 hrs)

- Pool: Continuation of the 10 points to a great start
- Pool: Race Club circuit training: Includes sprint swimming and strength training. MVP awarded to the best athlete on the circuit

Day 4

Morning (3 hrs)

- Lecture on the five steps of mental training
- Pool: Butterfly technique: Drills and fundamental techniques of butterfly
- Pool: Open spin turn techniques for butterfly and breaststroke

Afternoon (2 hrs)

- Pool: Review of drills and techniques of all four strokes covered in the camp
- Pool: Swimming races. Variable race distances of all strokes, depending on age and events
- Conclusion: Race Club cheer and prizes awarded.

The following is a brief summary of the lectures given at our camps on the five disciplines of swimming:

Swimming Training

Swimming training incorporates both conditioning and technique. The focus of our camps is on swimming technique. As one would expect, the lecture on the first day of camp is also on swimming technique, with explanations of how the three Newtonian Laws of Motion impact swimmers. Later, in the first session of the first day, we explain the rationale for different breathing patterns in each event, based on the physiology of using the various energy systems.

On the third day of our camps, we do a sample workout, called a Race Club *Circuit*, that incorporates both swim training and strength training into the same workout. It is a particularly beneficial way of training sprinters, though it can be adapted to any distance event.

Many of the swimmers who come to us for our camps or private instruction have good swimming programs at home. Some do not. For those swimmers who are lacking in swimming training, we have compiled a library filled with workout schedules for swimmers of various ages and abilities. We then customize the training for each swimmer who needs additional or different training through our online subscription service (Lane 4), whereby The Race Club coach becomes a primary or secondary coach, filling in the gaps that are present in training. We find the online coaching is an extremely effective way for swimmers who need to get extra coaching. For swimmers who come to our camps or for instruction, the online coaching helps to continue our coaching beyond the few days spent with us.

Dryland and Strength Training

Dryland exercises, stretching and appropriate strength training can benefit all swimmers from sprinters to distance swimmers. Having extraordinary flexibility is such a key component of fast swimming, and particularly, fast kicking, that stretching often needs to be incorporated into a swimmer's program. The ankles, hips, lower back and shoulders are the primary joints that require extra flexibility in swimming. Strength training and stretching can also help prevent injuries to swimmers. On the first afternoon of our Race Club camps, we do an hour of traditional stretching. On the second afternoon of our camps, we do an hour of yoga for swimming.

Being strong in the correct swimming motions is also vital to a swimmer's success. However, it is impossible to replicate the precise motions of a swimmer on land. That is not the intent of most strength trainers. They try to improve the swimmer's coordination, ballistic movements, balance and strength in muscles with similar, but not exact, replications of swimming movements. Swimming requires a lot more coordination and ballistic type movements than one might think from watching fast swimmers.

Because of the extraordinary sensitivity of frontal drag forces to the shape, girth or size of a swimmer, strength trainers in the sport of swimming need to be a little careful. It is the one sport where an athlete can potentially gain paradoxical strength, where he gets demonstrably bigger and stronger, yet swims slower. Or, at least, he may not swim faster. For that reason, many strength trainers develop programs that focus on the key muscles used for swimming, so-called _swim specific strength_, and not develop some of the muscles that will get in the way, causing additional drag.

Professional tennis players are a good example of developing sport specific strength. The serving arm is much bigger, stronger and more developed than the non-serving arm. Since the non-serving arm is not really used that much in tennis, if it were as big as the other arm, it would be just much more weight for the tennis player to run around the court with.

At the elite level, there is a common physical appearance of swimmers. They have very strong and broad shoulders and upper backs, from developing the muscles surrounding the scapula and the latissimus dorsi muscle. From front to back they are extremely thin, with not hugely developed pectoralis muscles, which helps keep their drag coefficient lower. Women's bodies are even more compressed in the chest and abdomen by wearing tight fitting competition suits. Their core muscles are extremely strong, as are all of their leg muscles. The arms are also strong, but more so in the triceps area than the biceps muscle. The forearms are usually not huge.

We are not certain a swimmer can ever develop too much core strength. The core muscles, including the abdominals and all of the back muscles controlling the spinal position, are working virtually all of the time while swimming. In addition, some of the most important motions in swimming, such as fast body rotation, aggressive turns and starts, require extraordinary core strength.

The leg strength required for the kicking motions is also somewhat unique. While the muscles involved in freestyle, backstroke, dolphin and breaststroke kick can all be strengthened and improved by strength training, there is really no substitute for kicking in the pool. Much is required of the legs in swimming fast, so much is demanded in their conditioning.

There is not one strength training program that is ideal for all swimmers. Dryland and strength training, as in swim training, needs to be customized to the age, ability and needs of the swimmer. For some swimmers, lack of flexibility is the primary problem. For others, it may be the lack of key strength. To this end, it is important to know each swimmer's strengths and weaknesses before designing a dryland and strength program.

Throughout a season, most strength trainers will vary the program, either weekly or monthly, to increase the benefit to the swimmers, and perhaps, to prevent boredom. For example, in a given week, one workout may focus on upper body, the second on legs and third on core. It is most common to do three strength training sessions per week. However, if there is a great need for increasing flexibility, some stretches should be done on a daily basis. Typically, depending on the age of the swimmer, the dryland and strength programs will last from 30 minutes to 1.5 hours.

To develop a great strength and dryland program for swimmers, it is not essential to have expensive equipment. Some of the best programs we have seen developed use body weight, medicine balls, boxing gloves and mitts, TRX devices, pull up bars and climbing ropes. What is required is the swimmer's attitude of commitment and intensity to the dryland and strength training program. With the right design and implementation, a consistent dryland and strength program will help make every swimmer faster.

Nutrition

This is the most controversial of all of the five disciplines. Everyone agrees that nutrition is important for athletes. They just can't agree on what to feed them. Of the three basic food substances, fat, carbohydrate and protein, everyone agrees that there are good fats and bad fats, good protein and bad protein, good carbs and bad carbs. They just can't agree on which are the good ones and the bad ones. There is a simple reason for that. The nutritional needs and the body's responses are different for every athlete.

There is a company, called Day Two, that uses technology developed in Israel to evaluate the nutritional response of each person to one parameter being tested, blood sugar. The effect it has on a person's blood sugar level is just one of many parameters used to evaluate the quality of nutrition, but it is an important one. Elevated blood sugar triggers the release of insulin, which sets off an entire cascade of other reactions in the human body, some causing inflammation. We know that having frequent spikes in blood sugar is not healthy for our bodies. Over time, it can lead to type II diabetes and other illnesses.

It turns out that the intestinal flora of the small and large intestine, called the *microbiome*, is largely influential in determining the amount of elevation of the blood sugar resulting from eating. There are trillions of bacteria living in our guts, keeping us alive. We depend on them for the digestion and absorption of our food, and they depend on us to keep feeding them. Obviously, foods that contain more sugars or carbohydrates will cause more elevation of blood sugar than foods that do not. Not everyone responds equally in blood sugar elevation to the exact same ingested food, and that has to do with the variety of microorganisms living in each human gut.

Surprisingly, each person's microbiome doesn't change drastically throughout life. But one person's microbiome can be drastically different from another person's microbiome.

Day Two determines the person's microbiome, then measures how the most populated 100 bacteria in the microbiome process virtually all of the most common foods that we eat, and how each food affects the blood sugar levels. They then rank each type of food on a scale from 1-10, on the basis of each person's microbiome and the impact that they have from eating that food on the blood sugar level. Here is what Gary Sr. found after taking the Day Two test with his wife.

My wife, Mary, and I are almost the exact same age, but were raised in different parts of the country. After taking the tests, we discovered that our microbiomes are quite different and so is our body's blood sugar response to the many of the same foods. This makes eating at home a bit more challenging, but at least we now know what foods are better for each of us.

We are not advocating that everyone has their microbiome determined by Day Two. The point in all of this is to say that we cannot define the ideal foods for all athletes, when the needs, metabolic rates, microbiomes, allergic responses and other responses to diet are all different. We believe that someday soon, we will be able to customize nutrition for athletes in the same fashion that we customize swimming and strength training.

In the meantime, rather than recommending a specific diet for each swimmer, it is much easier for us to advise swimmers on what to avoid doing with respect to nutrition, to help them perform better. Here is our favorite list of things to avoid:

1. **Never eat at fast food restaurants.** The food at these restaurants may be served quickly, but aside from that, there is not much good about it. It is largely full of sugar, preservatives, and unhealthy fats that will soon take their toll on your body. While some fast food restaurants now offer 'healthy' alternatives, it is arguable how healthy they really are.

2. **Avoid processed sugars as much as possible.** The American diet is laden with processed sugars. Now that our fast-food chains are expanding around the globe, so is the diet of many other countries. Try to minimize the sugar in the diet. Start by eliminating all soft drinks and drink purified water. Pure, fresh water is the best drink on the planet.

3. **Avoid processed and preserved foods as much as possible.** Just about every food that comes in a bag or a can has been processed or preserved to help keep it from spoiling. Although the chemicals used to process or preserve foods have been deemed *safe* for human consumption by the FDA, that does not mean that they are healthy. It may just mean that our bodies tolerate them better than other chemicals. Avoid them as much as possible.

4. **If there is a familial tendency toward allergies or auto-immune diseases, avoid eating the glutelins (gluten), and possibly lectins and genetically modified foods.** Although controversial, it is becoming clearer that certain individuals do not respond well to certain types of proteins in the diet. In fact, some of these proteins may lead to a *leaky gut* syndrome and ultimately cause auto-immune disease. The effect these proteins may have on athletic performances is also highly variable. The variable responses may also have to do with an individual's microbiome. If you do not respond well to them, avoid them.

5. **Avoid any foods before competition that you have never tried and proven that work well before.** We are all creatures of habit. Through our competitive careers, sooner or later, we figure out what foods we perform the best using. Stick with those. Your body is telling you something really important when you swim well after a certain meal. It likes that food. Never try a new food substance or type of meal before any important competition. It is just a bad time to experiment with nutrition.

Besides the three basic food substances—fats, carbs and protein—vitamins, minerals and other micronutrients are also essential to the human diet. In general, fresh, organic and whole foods will provide more of those important nutrients than other sources of food.

Another controversial topic in nutrition is the use of supplements. Unfortunately, the food supplement industry has been a highly unregulated and uncontrolled industry. To this day, an athlete taking supplements cannot be 100% certain as to what he or she is ingesting. Since the United States Antidoping Administration (USADA) and the World Antidoping Administration (WADA) have compiled a list of banned substances that are known to enhance athletic performances, there is risk of inadvertently ingesting a banned substance by using supplements. There have been many cases of that happening.

In spite of that, most of the elite athletes (not just swimmers) take supplements to help them perform better. Do they work? Apparently, they think so.

We will share one anecdotal story from one of our Race Club swimmers that we find interesting with respect to taking supplements. In 2015, we had the opportunity to work with an elite Masters swimmer, Siphiwe Baleka. Siphiwe is an African-American swimmer, who at around 45 years of age, decided to make a comeback in the sport of swimming. He hadn't competed in over 20 years. He had swum at Yale University as an undergraduate, and was an accomplished freestyler and breaststroker. His goal was to win the Masters World Championships in 2017 in at least one event and improve his times from twenty years earlier. To say that he was determined would be a vast understatement.

In the few days we shared with Siphiwe in Florida, we quickly learned that he knew a lot more about nutrition than we did. He ate only the very best foods available—whole foods, fresh, organic, grass-fed meat, using the best source of fats, proteins and carbohydrates he could find. He also took supplements. When we asked him why, here is what he said.

For six consecutive months, before he began taking supplements, he sent a blood sample to a laboratory in Houston, Texas, that tested for over 100 different blood parameters. That is far more than would usually be screened for in all of the typical physician-ordered routine blood work. The test included the quantities of trace minerals, such as zinc, selenium, iodine and other substances, that while vital to human function, are not usually tested for.

What he discovered is that even with the best diet he could manage, he was still getting only between 80% and 85% of the *ideal* total nutrients for his body. What he used to determine the *ideal* total nutrients for athletes was based on some military research he had found. Was that accurate information? Who knows the truth? The blood tests were likely accurate.

Each month, the missing nutrients were different. In other words, he couldn't be sure what was exactly in the food he was eating. He began using what he considered to be a good and reliable source of supplements, containing vitamins, minerals, *good* complex carbohydrates, non-animal protein and *healthy* fat, as well as antioxidants. Of course, we use the words *good* and *healthy,* fully understanding their controversial status.

For six consecutive months, after starting supplements, he sent his blood to the same laboratory in Houston. The results showed each month that he was getting 99% to 100% of the 100 parameters being tested. Siphiwe did not know how much a deficiency of 15% to 20% of what was considered the *ideal* amount of the specific parameters being tested would hurt him. He just didn't want to find out the hard way. He figured that he needed all of the help he could get, so he took supplements.

Long before we met Siphiwe, all of our Race Club swimmers that were training with us for the 2000, 2004 and 2008 Olympic Games took supplements. None of them were forced to take them. They took them voluntarily (although they weren't paying for them). Did they perform better by taking them? We will never know, but they also didn't want to take that chance.

All of the supplements that they took came from one very high-quality control company, called Platinum Performance. They were not miracle drugs. Like Siphiwe's supplements, they were designed to help the swimmers recover faster. Subjectively, they believed that they worked. Over 200 drug tests were performed by the anti-doping agencies on all of our athletes over those three Olympic Games without having one positive test for performance enhancing drugs. That gave us confidence in using their products.

For the fastest post-workout or meet recovery, we now recommend Vitargo (complex carbohydrate, mixed with Platinum Power (protein). Both come in powder form, mixed together with 24 ounces of purified water, and are taken within 15 minutes after practice. Before workout or during competition, we recommend using the Platinum Bars (Flaxseed Oil) as the best source for your energy.

Perhaps the most notable improvement in our athletes' recovery is from a supplement that we discovered more recently, called Mito Q. It is Coenzyme Q10, which is a commonly used antioxidant, but it is positively charged. With the positive charge, it has an affinity for the negatively charged muscle mitochondria, where the ATP is produced. It seems to have more benefit than using the normal Coenzyme Q10. Many of our athletes have reported feeling a faster and improved recovery using this supplement.

To summarize our recommendations for nutrition, take our advice and avoid the five things listed above. Eat as well as you can, whatever that means, but mostly whole foods that help you perform better. If you decide to take supplements (after reaching puberty), make sure you get them from a reliable, quality control company. Check them out. Don't take their word for it. Don't think that there is a magic pill out there that will suddenly turn you into Michael Phelps or Katie Ledecky. There isn't one.

Recovery

Of the five important disciplines, recovery may be the most neglected one. Swimmers train very hard, and, in the process, their muscles need time to recover or heal. The faster and better that a swimmer recovers after a hard practice, the sooner he or she will be able to train at an intense level again. Not every practice can and should be an intense practice. Some workouts are *recovery* practices, where little exertion is required. Some days are better spent without practicing at all. However, the intense, exertional, high quality practices help make swimmers faster. Usually, the more of those that a swimmer can have in a season, the better.

Every athlete recovers at a different rate, some of which is determined by the swimmer's own physiology and metabolism. However, there are other important factors that influence an athlete's recovery rate. These are the five most important outside influencers in the swimmer's recovery rate:

1. **Sleep.** Sleep may be the most important factor in assisting recovery rate. During Stage IV and Rapid Eye Movement (REM) sleep stages, the two deepest stages in the sleeping cycle, the human pituitary gland secretes the highest amount of human growth hormone (HGH). HGH has a profound impact on the body's ability to heal, or specifically, to rebuild the skeletal collagen fibrils in the muscle.

2. **Nutrition.** The body cannot repair itself without having the proper substrate or building blocks to use, which comes largely from our nutrition. With better nutrition, the swimmer's recovery rate will be faster than with poor nutrition. Appropriate supplements may help the recovery process, also, by providing missing protein, vitamins, minerals or other micronutrients that the body requires. They may also help protect the muscles cells or organelles from oxidative stress during recovery.

3. **Stress.** The amount of stress in a swimmer's life influences the body's ability to recover. Reducing outside stress in an athlete's life is not always easy to do. The lifestyle of training and competing induces enough stress by itself. When additional stressors are added to that, physiological changes begin to take place which can adversely affect the immune system and the recovery rates. Keeping outside stress to a minimum level is important for any serious athlete in training.

4. **Compression or Massage Therapy.** The amount of blood flow and manipulation of the muscle can influence its rate of recovery. Massage therapy is an effective way of reducing muscle spasms (cramps or knots) in fatigued muscles and improving the blood flow to the affected muscles. If massage is not an option, then compression sleeves and devices have also been shown to increase blood flow to the recovering muscle and increase venous return, flushing lactate out of the fatigued muscle.

5. **Professional treatment.** In the intense training environment of today's high-level swimmers, injuries are not uncommon, particularly in the shoulder joint. In one study, the incidence of shoulder injuries among collegiate women swimmers in the USA was over 50%. Most of these are *overuse* injuries from training. If an injury extends beyond the normal soreness and fatigue of the muscles and joints experienced through hard training, it is advisable to seek professional treatment. Professionals that may be qualified to provide such treatments to athletes include physicians, chiropractors and physical therapists, or a combination of them. Alternative sources of treatments, such as acupuncture, may also be helpful. For any persisting pain or soreness from training, seeking professionals that specialize in sports-related injuries is usually advisable.

There are many other modalities of treatment that are being used for improving rates of recovery. Examples include the use of cold-water immersion, cryotherapy, hyperbaric oxygen chamber therapy, trans-epidermal electrical nerve stimulation (TENS), whole-body vibration and magnetic field therapy. Success rates reported in using these modalities are mostly subjective, but they are included for completeness.

In summary, in the effort to reach a swimmer's full potential, the recovery plan is as important as the training plan. Swimmers working at intense levels of training require more sleep, better and more nutrition, less stress and any other assistance possible to aid in their recoveries when compared to non-athletes.

Mental Training

The control that the human mind has over the physical performance of a swimmer's body in competition and training is astonishing. The brain has the power to *unleash* the human body to reach athletic performances well beyond what may seem to be its limit. Of course, there are physical and physiological limitations to what any swimmer can achieve at any given time. The key to great athletic performance, however, is to not allow the mind to impose more limitations on the swimmer's performance than are already there. That problem occurs often in competition.

The question is, *how do we enable the mind to unleash the body?* Some swimmers seem to be born with incredible mental toughness and strength, the so-called *killer instinct*. Others do not seem to have as much of that mental toughness. Regardless, here are five mental training techniques that we have found to improve a swimmer's mental toughness:

1. **Goal Setting.** At The Race Club, we like to define three sets of goals with respect to swimming. What is the swimmer going to accomplish today or this week in practice? What are the specific targeted goal times for this season and when and where are they to be achieved? What is the long-term goal and vision of the swimmer? For the seasonal goals, we ask each swimmer to write down his or her goal times for each event next to the personal best times he or she has already achieved. Once we approve the goal times, we then ask the swimmer to transpose the times onto a large poster board to put up on the bedroom wall. It is very important that the goal times be written down and they be seen often throughout the season. There is a much higher likelihood of achieving the goal times when they are specific, written down and visible, as opposed to just thought about occasionally.

2. **Visualization.** Nearly every elite swimmer we have known visualizes his or her races in some fashion before competing. Swimmers who see themselves vividly in their minds swimming a perfect race have a much better chance of swimming that race well than swimmers who do not visualize themselves doing so. In preparing our Olympians for the biggest competition of their lives, we directed the group of swimmers to lie down on towels in the shaded grass under the coconut palm trees of Founder's Park in Islamorada. Then, for 15 minutes three times each week before practices, we asked them to vividly visualize their races with their eyes closed, down to the smallest details. These visualization sessions became a routine part of their training throughout the entire season,

not just at the very end. During the final week before competition, our athletes visualized their races daily, and began to visualize more details of the pool and environment they would be competing in. The positive impact these sessions had on their ultimate success cannot be overstated. Without working up a sweat, elevating their heart rate, getting fatigued or exhausted, these swimmers improved their performances by lying under a palm tree for 15 minutes three times each week. That is a worthwhile exercise.

3. **Confidence Building.** There are many ways that swimmers can build confidence. By competition day, swimmers must have confidence. They must believe in themselves and have no doubt about their ability to achieve their goal times. Three of the most effective ways for swimmers to build confidence leading up to the championship meet are the following:

   a. **Swim fast in practices**. Swimming fast in practices does not guarantee that swimmers will swim fast on race day, but it helps. If swimmers occasionally achieve times in practices that are commensurate with their goal times, then it gives them great confidence in being able to achieve those times.

   b. **Swim fast in test meets.** Practice meets are really important to prepare swimmers for the Championship competition. Swimmers will always race better when they practice racing. Test meets are a different kind of preparation for swimmers than training, and they are essential. As with swimming fast in practices, swimming fast in these preparation meets leading up to the major competition doesn't guarantee that swimmers will swim great at the Championship. Good performances in these meets, swum under less than ideal conditions, only help to build a swimmer's confidence. When swimmers do not swim fast in these test meets, they also need to be able to learn from their mistakes, but not let the slower times bother them.

   c. **Look in the mirror.** When it comes down to believing in someone, it really doesn't matter too much what the coach or the parents think. It really only matters what swimmers think of themselves. One way for swimmers to start believing in themselves is by looking directly into the mirror, smiling and reminding themselves of how good they are. The smile is an important part of that process. Swimmers telling themselves that they have the ability to do something special is always a good thing. Smiling at yourself in the mirror and telling yourself how good you really are is a nice way to start each day.

4. **Focus.** To be at their very best on race day, swimmers cannot get distracted for too long, either during the season or at the Championship meet. There are always unexpected events that occur during any given season: sickness, pool closures, injuries, family emergencies, just to name a few. Losing a few days of regularly scheduled practices will likely not ruin a season. Any prolonged loss of consistency in training will affect any swimmer's ability to compete well. Focus also pertains to a swimmer's ability to not get distracted at Championship meets, to remain in the mental *zone*. At Championship meets,

there is a lot of excitement, noise and other distractions. Swimmers must have the ability to not allow any of that to bother them and stay focused on their swims.

5. **Anchoring.** The final step in the five-step mental training process is called *anchoring*. It is something that swimmers do or say just before stepping on to the starting block, or even while on the block, to solidify the moment. The *anchor* is like the light switch that turns on the light, or the curtain rise that begins the play. It is a crucial part of the mental preparation. It lets swimmers know that they are ready to go. The *anchor* can be anything from a subtle whisper of something important to oneself, to a few boxing jabs in the air, to a dynamic arm swing stretch, like Phelps did, to whatever works. It must happen to reach the final moment of preparation. Every swimmer should plan on doing something to anchor them in the final moment before the race.

Wherever swimmers may fall on the *killer instinct* scale, following these five steps will help strengthen their minds and bring out the best possible outcome at the Championship meet.

In summary, we have presented an overview of the five important disciplines needed to reach a swimmer's full potential and how we approach them at The Race Club. We feel that they are so important in the development of swimmers that we dedicate an hour each morning of our camp sessions to help them understand them. For many of the swimmers that we coach on-line, we help design a customized program for some or all of these five disciplines.

To become the best swimmer possible, make certain that you have a plan for each of these five important disciplines.

Chapter 29

Life is Worth Swimming

"I built my talents on the shoulders of someone else's talent. I believe greatness is an evolutionary process that changes and evolves era to era."- Michael Jordan

Since the beginning of time, mankind has had a fascination with water. Besides depending on water for life itself, people love to be near the water, or in the water. Perhaps it is the feeling of being weightless, or the sensuous feeling that the water creates as it caresses our bodies as we swim through it. Perhaps it is because water cushions us, rather than pounds our bodies against the concrete or asphalt as we run over it. Whatever the reason, millions of people worldwide are drawn to be in the water each year, trying to figure out how to turn a body that evolved on land into one that functions well in the pool, lake or ocean. Not only are people drawn to water, they seem to want to stay there. Swimming is one of the few competitive sports in the world with a 100-and-over age group.

People are also fascinated with speed. There is something very instinctive and tempting within the human body, mind and spirit to want to get from here to there faster than anyone, whether it is in a car, on a boat, riding a bicycle, on foot or in the water. In the Olympic Games of Ancient Greece, the athletes that were the strongest and fastest in competition were idolized and rewarded for life. The Olympians still are today, though not to the same extent.

We are not certain when the first official swimming competitions began, but certainly the inclusion of swimming in the first Modern Olympic Games in Athens in 1896 marked the beginning of a global recognition of swimming as a competitive sport. It wasn't until the 1908 Olympic Games in London that the first 100-meter freestyle was contested. An American, Charles Daniels, won the race in 1:05.6. Fourteen years later, in 1922, American Johnny Weissmuller, broke one minute for the first time, setting the world record in the 100-meter freestyle with a time of 58.6. It took 54 more years for the first swimmer to break 50 seconds, when American Jim Montgomery won the gold medal in the Olympic Games of Montreal in 1976, posting a time of 49.9. Excluding the two years of using the polyurethane racing suits (2008 and 2009), which are now illegal, it took over forty more years for a swimmer to break 47 seconds. In 2019, Caeleb Dressel swam a time of 46.9 at the World Championships, a drop of 3 seconds from 1976. It could take 50 more years for a swimmer to go one second faster and break 46 seconds. We shall see.

There has been a remarkable progression of swimming speed in just over 100 years. If Caeleb Dressel and Charles Daniels were in the same 50-meter pool today, simultaneously racing a 100-meter freestyle, when Caeleb touched the wall at the finish, Charles would not even be half way back on the second 50 meters. That is remarkable improvement. The question is *how much faster can a human being swim?*

The limit of speed of humans swimming comes back to physics, to what is called the *terminal velocity.* If someone were to jump out of an airplane without a parachute, the person would accelerate toward the ground because of the gravitational force acting on the person's body.

Their velocity will continue to increase as they fall until they reach a point where their body's drag force (from the air) equals the gravitational force (somewhere around 120 mph). From that point on, their speed will remain constant all the way to the ground.

If we were to put a parachute on that person, the drag coefficient increases tremendously, so that the drag force will equal the gravitational force at a much slower speed. The terminal velocity is more like 12 mph, a 90% reduction in speed. That makes it a lot safer to land with a parachute.

There is also a *terminal velocity* for swimmers. Based on the similar drag coefficients of a human swimmer, and the exponential relationship between speed and drag force, there is a point at which the propulsion will not be capable of exceeding the frontal drag force. At his peak velocity, Caeleb Dressel is probably getting close to the maximum terminal velocity of the human being.

The closer we get to whatever the limit of human speed is in the water, the harder it becomes to reach it. There is a limit to the propulsion a human being can generate, and there is a limit to how much a human can reduce frontal drag. For those reasons, the future improvements in human swimming performance will come in tenths of seconds or even hundredths of seconds, not seconds. In fact, in the shorter swimming races, we are already there.

As coaches, we will always seek ways of increasing a swimmer's propulsion, without contributing excessively to the drag coefficient. We will always seek ways of training a swimmer better, so that he or she can increase propulsion and sustain it longer. However, in this era of winning or losing races by hundredths of seconds, the biggest game-changer may be in finding ways of reducing frontal drag. Part of that will come from wearing a better suit or racing cap, but most of the improvement will come in the form of better swimming technique. In other words, as swimmers become faster at any age, technique becomes even more important. For our ability to improve swimming technique, we will have to turn to science and technology to help us. Here are Gary Sr.'s thoughts about Doc Counsilman, considered the father of science in swimming.

As a collegiate coach at Indiana University, Doc would sit on the pale green bench attached to the walls inside Royer Pool, with a stopwatch in one hand, watching over the team working out. Often, he was surrounded by scientists or other coaches that had come from around the world to learn from him.

Doc was brilliant. His PhD was in physiology, yet he read incessantly about all of the sciences that contributed to swimming, including physics, psychology and kinesiology. His appetite to learn was voracious. In addition to his vast scientific knowledge, he was also a keen observer, loved opera and had a great sense of humor. He authored the very first scientific book on swimming, The Science of Swimming, which included photos of many great swimmers of that era, such as Mark Spitz, Charlie Hickcox, Don McKenzie and other I.U. swimmers (including me.). It is still being used by coaches as a resource. Today, Doc is considered the father of science in swimming.

Doc was beloved and respected by swimming coaches all over the world. While he understood science, he was also a skeptical scientist. He trusted his experience and instincts far more than he trusted scientific studies, particularly those that came from the non-coaching, so-called swimming experts.

Almost every Sunday during the season, Doc would assemble his swimmers in his small office and load the projector with his 16 mm black and white film, sharing the slow-motion, underwater movies that he had taken with his high-speed Bolex camera. He studied every underwater movement of the swimmers—the arms, hands, legs, feet and body—trying to understand what motions enabled them to swim so fast. There were times when he would have his swimmers wear small waterproof lights on their hands. He would turn out all of the lights inside the natatorium. With his SCUBA gear on, he would lie motionless on the bottom of the diving well, filming the swimmers as they swam across the pool above him. All of this effort was to learn how the hands of the elite swimmers moved in the water.

Even without having the technology we have today, Doc discovered much about the importance of propulsion and lift. He even speculated for the first time about the Bernoulli effect in swimming, generating lift. What was not appreciated as much then was the impact of frontal drag force in the sport of swimming. Although we have advanced in our knowledge in the fifty years since Doc's contributions, we have not progressed as much as we could have. Technology such as the Velocity Meter, Pressure Meter and Propulsion/Drag Meter have recently helped tremendously to understand some of the details of swimming propulsion and of passive frontal drag.

Measuring the active drag force acting on a swimmer (drag forces while a swimmer is swimming) remains challenging, even today. The technology is available to be able to measure active drag forces on a swimmer, but it is expensive. It requires the use of computational software, similar to finite element analysis, and precise animation to replicate the swimmer's body and motions. Engineers at Johns Hopkins University have already developed a system to do that, but it has not been widely used. Hopefully, we will see this technology used in swimming more in the future.

Finally, we must say that not all swimmers care about swimming fast. Here is a story that Gary Sr. often remembers whenever he gets overzealous in his attempts to improve swimmers.

I recall one day watching a lap swimmer at Founder's Park pool in Islamorada struggle swimming freestyle up and down the 50-meter pool, with his head completely out of the water. After each 50-meter swim, he would take a minute to rest before slogging his way through the water for another one. It made me tired watching him. Ultimately, I couldn't help myself. I went over to the end of his lane and waited for him to finish another lap.

"Do you mind if I offer you some advice?" I asked. I didn't even know his name.

"Sure", he responded.

"If you put your head down into the water in freestyle, it becomes much easier to swim", I explained.

"Why would I want to do that?" he asked.

"Well", I answered, "I just thought you might want to swim a little more efficiently. A little faster."

"Actually", he said, "I am trying to get a good workout. I'm trying to make it harder, not easier."

From that day on, I stopped offering unsolicited advice. While I enjoy helping swimmers get faster, that is not always the goal of the swimmer.

There are far more swimmers in the world that just love to swim for health and exercise than there are swimmers that are trying to win races. In fact, we have become two of them. Three times each week, we swim for about 45 minutes because we love doing it. It makes us feel better. Don't get us wrong. We still love to swim fast, occasionally, so we also try to use good technique. Swimming is a healthy sport. It is like getting a workout and massage at the same time. By swimming, however, we also become better coaches. We can be our own guinea pigs by testing our swimming ideas, new equipment or devices on ourselves first. We always test and measure before recommending.

Whether you are out to win swimming races, improve your times and efficiency, or, like us, just swim for the love of it and for the workout, keep swimming. Unless you are trying to make it harder for yourself, we hope that some of the intricacies of swimming, starting and turning techniques that we have discussed in this book will make you more knowledgeable, faster and even more passionate about swimming than you already are. We hope that you will come to realize that our Race Club motto is really true: *life is worth swimming*.

About the Authors

Gary Hall Sr. has been involved in swimming for nearly his entire life. He rose to prominence quickly as a young competitive swimmer in Southern California, breaking 22 National Records by the age of ten. By 16, he qualified for his first of three Olympic Games of 1968, 1972 and 1976, where he earned three individual medals and was part of the gold medal winning medley relay team in 1972. He was twice voted as the Men's World Swimmer of the Year in 1969 and 1970. From 1969-1973 he attended Indiana University, swimming for legendary coach, James 'Doc' Counsilman. While there, he won seven individual NCAA titles and helped Indiana University win four consecutive team championships. Among his many honors, his greatest occurred during the 1976 Olympic Games, where he was selected by the Team Captains of all sports to carry the United States Flag, leading Team USA into the Opening Ceremony. He was the first American swimmer in history to receive that honor. Michael Phelps received the same honor in 2016.

After completing his swimming career, Gary finished medical school at University of Cincinnati. During medical school, he supported his family by coaching swimming at the well-known Cincinnati Marlins. After completing his Residency in Ophthalmology at Indiana University Medical Center, he practiced in Phoenix, Arizona until 2006. During his 24 years as an Ophthalmologist, Gary built a large practice, pioneered surgical procedures and performed clinical research. On the side, he managed the very successful Phoenix Swim Club and competed in triathlons and Masters swimming.

From 1996 to 2004, Gary proudly watched his son, Gary Jr., surpass his swimming accomplishments by winning ten Olympic medals in three Olympic Games. To this day, Gary Sr and Gary Jr are the only father and son in sports history to each compete in three Olympic Games.

In 2003, Gary Jr. co-founded The Race Club in Islamorada, Florida, as a training program for aspiring Olympic swimmers. Gary Sr. joined his son in this endeavor in 2006, moving to Florida from Arizona.

After he retired from competitive swimming in 2008, Gary Jr. began to focus on finding the cure for Type I Diabetes, with which he was diagnosed in 1999. He has become one of the world's leading advocates for diabetic patients.

Gary Sr. and his wife, Mary, transitioned The Race Club from a training program into a teaching program, which it has been ever since.

Today, The Race Club coaches improve swimmers' technique in Islamorada, Florida and Coronado, California. Gary Sr.'s second son, Richard, joined The Race Club in 2010, becoming the video production manager. Richard's Race Club educational videos are widely acclaimed by swimmers and coaches worldwide, with over 15 million *Youtube* views. Thousands of swimmers, coaches and triathletes all over the world subscribe to The Race Club instructional videos at www.theraceclub.com.

Head coach, Devin Murphy, joined The Race Club organization in June, 2016. Devin competed as a young swimmer in Ohio, before attending Wheeling Jesuit University in West Virginia. He graduated with a degree in Theology and Religious Studies, serving as swimming Team Captain twice. Each year in college he was honored as an All-Conference swimmer. After graduation, Devin began his coaching career as assistant at Saint Leo University before taking on the Head Coach position at Malone University. He helped both schools to reach a national top 10 ranking. Devin also developed a vast experience in Tampa with USA Swimming Club coaching.

With an intense interest in swimming technique, Devin's contributions to understanding and applying the technology used at The Race Club have been extraordinary. Among The Race Club members, including swimmers and parents, Devin has earned a wide reputation for his excellence and results. To this day, Devin remains a devout swimming coach and Ohio State fan.

Coach Gary Hall Sr.

Coach Devin Murphy

Video Producer Richard Hall

Gary Sr. enjoying a swim in Islamorada 2020

Made in United States
North Haven, CT
01 December 2024

61152303R00154